K. D. LANG

k.d. lang

ALL YOU GET IS ME

VICTORIA STARR

Random House of Canada
Toronto

Canadian Cataloguing in Publication Data

Starr, Victoria
k.d. lang: All you get is me

ISBN 0-394-22369-1

1. lang, k.d., 1961-   2. Country musicians -
Biography. I. Title.

ML420.L196S73 1994   782.42164'2'092   C94-930488-3

1 3 5 7 9 10 8 6 4 2

This book is dedicated to Linda Villarosa, without whose love, encouragement, and support it would have never happened.

To my parents, who have always stood by me, even when they had their doubts.

And in memory of Jay Scott, who died of AIDS-related complications on July 30, 1993.

CONTENTS

CONTENTS

WARMEST thanks and big, wet kisses to Rosa Ainley, Caroline Azar, Jaqueline Benyes, James Bernard, Amy Bertch, Cindy Bloomberg, Daniel Brooks, Joe Clark, KT Danger, Tanya Dewhurst (and Hannah), Denise Donlon, Rachel Felder, Jennifer Flemming, Richard Flohil, Jim Fouratt, Noelle Hanrahan, Richard Houghton, Alan Hustak, Janis Ian, Nancy Kariel, Larry Kjearsgaard, Pam Koslyn, Liam Lacey, Connie Lofton, Lance Loud, Bob Oermann, Sue Patel, Allan Pepper, Rachel Pepper,

Gretchen Philips, Retha Powers, Toshi Reagon, Susie Reed, Renee Russak, Catherine Saalfield, and Lisa, Barb & Betty Ann in Nashville—all of whom helped keep me moving on this project.

For professional guidance, support, and much hand-holding, I'd like to thank my agents, Barbara Lowenstein and Madeleine Morel, along with Rhonda, Norman, Bobby, and Greg at the office; my editor at St. Martin's Press, Jim Fitzgerald, along wth Evie Greenbaum, Jaye Zimet, John Murphy, and Bonnie Lee; my editor and publicist at Random House Canada, Doug Pepper and Sheila Kay; and Richard Wheaton, my editor at HarperCollins in England.

Extra special thanks and much respect to Polly Thistlethwaite, Lucinda Zoe, and the Lesbian Herstory Archives. Congrats on the new brownstone.

I would also like to acknowledge all of the journalists who have charted k.d.'s course over the years, exploring the music, the artist, and the larger cultural landscape in which she thrives. In particular, I'd like to thank Rosa Ainley, Kevin Allman, Jeff Bateman, Michael Bates, Leslie Bennetts, Laurie Brown, Sarah Cooper, Michael Corcoran, Richard Cromelin, Bob Curtright, Alex Demyanenko, Steve Dougherty, Donna Freedman, Gillian Gaar, Don Gilmore, Holly Gleason, Peter Goddard, John Griffin, Edna Gunderson, Jimmy Guterman, Peter Gzowski, Nancy Hamm, Neil Hickey, David Hiltbrand, Geoffrey Himes, Tanya Indiana, Bill Jarnigan, Dave Jennings, Burt Kearns, Lisa Keen, Larry Kelp, Junu Bryan Kim, Larry Kloss, Linda Kohanov, Ann Kolson, Nick Krewen, Charla Krupp, Jerry Lazar, Brendan Lemon, Dan Levitin, William Lieth, Craig MacInnis, John Mackie, Michael McCall, Kristine McKenna, Marlene Mehlhaff, Paula Monarez, Steve Morse, Kathy Mulady, Terry David Mulligan, James Muretich, Melinda Newman, Ralph Novak, Tom Philip, Kevin Prokosh, Greg Quill, Stephen Rae, Sheila Rogers, Sean Ross, Robert Sandall, Jay Scott, Giles Smith, Liz Smith, Mat Snow, Michael Specter, David Staples, Perry Stern, James Strecker, Dana Thomas, Mim Udovitch, Gerry Woods, and David Zimmerman.

IT was a crisp, overcast January morning in Brooklyn's Prospect Park, but the day was neither cold nor dreary. How could it be, when only twenty-four hours earlier, Bill Clinton had been inaugurated as the 42nd president of the United States? As the cheery strains of "Miss Chatelaine" wafted through the trees from the nearby ice-skating rink, many residents of this mostly working class neighborhood felt optimistic that, after twelve long years, the shift in the nation's power

structure meant that the notion of "a kinder and gentler nation" was still a possibility. There was no denying it: change was in the air.

A few days earlier, down in Washington, D.C., the presidential inauguration had brought with it a massive wave of parties, several of which k.d. attended. She flew in on the eve of Clinton's Big Day to be a guest of honor at the Animals Ball, a $250-a-plate benefit dinner for the People for Ethical Treatment of Animals (PETA), pausing at the airport to distribute protest stickers to fur-wearing travelers. Later that night, it was off to a cocktail party honoring openly gay political consultant David Mixner.

The gatherings were just a taste of what was to come the following night, including two unprecedented inaugural parties: the MTV Ball, saluting the young and restless who'd helped "get out the vote" among the college-age crowd, and the Triangle Ball, a celebration of what some were confidently calling "The New Gay Power." k.d. attended both, the latter of which contained an added element of historic charm for the capacity crowd of over 2,000 gay people and their friends who packed the National Press Club. Not only was this the first lesbian and gay inaugural ball, but the euphoria at the party was so palpable people were coming out of the closet even as it unfolded. Most notable was rock artist Melissa Etheridge, whose proclamation of lesbian pride was preceded by her acknowledgment that k.d. had paved the way.

The extraordinary moment began when k.d.'s PETA pal Cassandra "Elvira" Peterson stepped up to the podium and said, "You know, I'm not a lesbian . . ." There was a brief, awkward pause before she continued, ". . . but I could certainly be talked into being one tonight." Cheers filled the room. Then suddenly, on the giant TV monitors scattered throughout the hall, the back of a head cut in front of the camera. Someone had grabbed Elvira and was burying their face in her cleavage. As the head slowly turned to face the camera, the audience screamed wildly with recognition.

Calm, cool, and extremely sexy with her tailored suit and tousled hair, k.d. lang leaned over the railing to gaze proudly at the crowd below. "You know," she said, addressing her fans, "the best thing I ever did was to come out." Again, the audience roared with applause. Then she stepped aside to reveal Melissa Etheridge standing close behind her. "My sister k.d. lang has been such an inspiration," said Etheridge. "She did the greatest thing I've ever seen this year. I'm very proud to say I've been a lesbian all my life." With that, she too was grabbed by k.d. The crowd went berserk.

■

There was a time in k.d.'s life when all the odds seemed stacked against her. In 1990, with four albums to show for having endured a tumultuous six years in country music, the young Canadian artist found herself in a swirl of controversy that climaxed with an international call from the North American Cattlemen's Association to boycott her music. It was yet another hurdle in a career that had been plagued with obstacles, not the least of which was her tenuous relationship with Nashville. Exhausted, fed up, and unable to get her music played on the radio, it was then that she made a career decision that would alter the course of her life forever. She announced she was leaving country music. For two years the former workaholic took a break from the recording industry to reconsider her life.

In the spring of 1992 k.d. reemerged, and unveiled *Ingénue,* a dark, brooding album that redefined the singer and found a whole new audience, many of whom had never even heard of her before. Almost overnight she became a household word, not only in Canada, but in the United States, England, and much of Europe. Then, on the eve of an international tour that would eventually draw in excess of 300,000 fans to 94 shows in 6 countries, she went a step further: she announced to the world that she was a lesbian.

Today k.d. lang is recognized as one of the world's finest female vocalists, a young and vibrant artist possessing the best voice of her generation. And if her staggering voice isn't enough, k.d.'s "coming-out" makes her the first openly lesbian pop icon in the history of the entertainment industry. She is the first of what many think will be a wave of entertainers, politicians, and other well-known public figures who dare to stand and declare their gay pride, marking a turning point in the struggle for gay rights.

But she's an inspiration not only to the gay community: an enigma and an iconoclast, she's a fashion rebel who wears men's clothes and little or no makeup—a self-proclaimed feminist whose appeal to modern women is summed up when she says, "I'm offering women something that they don't have a lot of: a strong example." Her look, her mere existence, challenges long-standing conventions about music and image, fashion and sexuality, and offers a new definition of what it means to be a woman in the nineties.

At the same time she eschews the role of political crusader, preferring to charm young men and old ladies, children, animals, and fellow artists ranging from Willie Nelson to Madonna in a way that has enabled her to build a strong career over the past decade. The country music industry may have shunned her, her songs were rarely heard on the radio, and none of her first four albums yielded hit singles. Yet her record sales have been steady, her concert tours successful, and her press coverage extremely supportive of both her image and her craft. In short, she has beat the system, bringing joy to millions of people as she battled the odds, retaining her strength, her focus, and a commitment to herself in a way that few artists do.

■

As 1993 drew to a close and the Clinton clan settled into the White House, it became apparent that k.d.'s ascending star was dragging the lesbian and gay rights movement with it, and that her one simple but courageous act—coming out—may have been the key to unlocking the closet door for the entire pop music industry. Her honesty had a domino effect, and within a year David Geffen, Elton John, Janis Ian, and Melissa Etheridge joined several other lesser-known celebrities to go on record as being gay. In case there was any confusion, Boy George chimed in, too, while newcomers RuPaul and Me'Shell NdegéOcello proved that even up-and-coming artists could finally get major-label record deals while being open about their sexual orientation. Not that others hadn't tried before. Alix Dobkin, Holly Near, Stephen Grossman, Sylvester, Phranc, Two Nice Girls, and a host of others were well known among gay music fans. But none had achieved much in the way of mass-market success. Now it seemed that the right personality with just the right talent had come along at precisely the right time and, suddenly, everything was changing.

Naturally, k.d.'s courage didn't come without its typical flourish of lang outrageousness, and in the summer of 1993, she posed for a cover of *Vanity Fair* that would outshine a nude and pregnant Demi Moore as the magazine's top-selling issue. Wearing a man's pin-striped suit vest and pants, with a white work shirt and tie, k.d. appeared reclining in a barber chair, her cheeks and neck covered with shaving cream, smiling dreamily while a scantily clad Cindy Crawford leaned close to give her a shave. It was a drag scene, a gender bender, set to a Norman Rockwell theme, and it was k.d.'s own wild fantasies that had inspired it. Moreover, it made headlines and nightly news several days before the magazine had even hit the stands.

With that, "lesbian chic" arrived squarely in the public eye, and while many hotly debated the pros and cons of the media's sudden interest in women-loving women, nobody could disagree that k.d. was the first lesbian many North Americans had ever knowingly embraced. Just ask the tall, attractive, boyish-looking woman who was stopped in an airport by two young boys who mistook her for k.d. The joke is that this woman looked nothing like k.d., although it was a welcome compliment. But as she herself noted, years ago kids like these would have likely snickered as they tried to decide whether the person strolling confidently before them was male or female. In 1993, they not only recognized that this was a woman; in an oh-so-subtle way, they recognized her as a certain *kind* of woman.

■

It's hard to imagine what k.d. could do to top the events of the early nineties. Yet it's equally hard to imagine anyone tiring of her talent or her spirit. "I'm just getting started," she says assuredly. "Everyone keeps talking about 'the change, the change.' Well my God, I hope I never stop changing, and that I never stop searching. I have a long career ahead of me, and I could never see myself doing the same thing for sixty-five years." Neither could anyone else, since every time she turns around she sheds another skin. And each time, out comes something magnificent.

In 1990, k.d. was voted Artist of the Decade by the Canadian music industry, an honor she shares with fellow Canadians Bryan Adams and Rush, and from the previous decade, Gordon Lightfoot and Anne Murray. Introducing k.d. at the awards ceremony, Canadian novelist Margaret Atwood said, "Every once in a while, someone comes along who refuses to be stuffed into the accepted pigeonhole, who defies the limits of category, and who takes a popular form and stretches it beyond what was thought possible, making it bigger in the process. Usually, you can't get away with this unless you are very, very good. k.d. lang is very, very good."

k.d.'s response was typical and straightforward. After joking that on the way to the ceremonies a flight attendant had mistaken her for Bryan Adams, she said, "I'm overwhelmed. It's been a wonderful seven years, and I'm very, very proud to be Canadian."

There's no telling where k.d. lang would be today, or for that matter, if she would exist at all had she not sprung from the soil of Alberta, in western Canada, where the people are known for their iron wills and rugged individualism. She claims compatriot Joni Mitchell as one of her favorite songwriters, Mitchell's black crows and wheat moons reflecting a shared, heartfelt vision of the Canadian prairies. Country "Snowbird" Anne Murray was a big influence. And k.d.'s a Leonard Cohen fan.

The importance of such a rich cultural history has never been lost on k.d., and despite all the money, fame, and glory her superstardom has ushered her way, she has remained unwaveringly true to her roots. She will never forget that she was once a geeky prairie kid roaming wild in Consort, Alberta. Nor will she ever, even for a moment, pretend to be someone she's not.

1

"There's been some turbulence between my roots and me, but what I loved about it I still love about it. I like the geography, the wind, the openness...."

BARRELING east across Alberta, through one-stop towns like Coronation, Throne, and Veteran, Consort takes you by surprise. Approaching on Highway 12, you hit a curve at the top of a small hill

just short of the Saskatchewan border. Suddenly, across the gently sloping valley, Consort appears. An unassuming town boasting a current population of 679 (a few heads more than when Kathy Lang lived there), it's the type of rural environment where kids are hard pressed to find trouble. "It was the kind of place where you knew everyone from the day you were born until the day you could get yourself out of there," k.d. would later recall. It's also the kind of place that stays in people's blood long after the farm-fresh rosiness has faded from their cheeks.

While a sudden truce between warring Indian tribes is said to have inspired the town's name, farming and cattle ranching dictate modern culture in the area, grain elevators dotting the horizon as proud announcements for the Alberta Wheat Pool. Consort is a three-elevator town, and as Albertan novelist Robert Kroetsch writes, "We have ways, on the prairies, of measuring status." The elevators dominate the valley, butting up against the creek and the railroad tracks designed to carry the grain away. On the hill beyond, blue-and-black oil pumps steadily bob their heads under the constant flame of a burn-off stack. It's Alberta's other resource—the northern version of Texas Tea.

Several years ago, a visitor cresting the hill that leads to Consort would have been greeted by a sign proclaiming it the "Home of k.d. lang." The sign was taken down after the town's most famous daughter raised a beef with local cattlemen. But that story comes later.

■

If the Albertan farmer has suffered in recent years, it's not apparent in Consort. The empty lunch tables at the Consort Dining Lounge would seem to reflect bad times, but on closer inspection, CJ's Cafe, the town's *other* diner, is doing a brisk business. In fact, the thoroughly modern split-level homes and carefully manicured lawns that lie adjacent to Consort's main strip indicate that at least a few farmers and ranchers have learned the art of "economies of scale," the mantra of the agriculture industry.

A few blocks up the street, past the Consort Hotel, the grocery store, and the IDA Drug Mart, sits a series of white buildings that house the Consort school system. Grade school, junior high, and high school all lay claim to part of the property, with a municipal library tacked on for good measure. Inside the front door, on the wall next to the principal's office, senior class graduation photos mark the passing of time. Kathy Dawn Lang smiles assuredly from the photo of the class of '79.

Behind the school lies the Community Sports Ground, and next to it the Sports Complex and public pool, three of the most important gathering spots in Consort.

With that you've reached the edge of town.

■

Kathryn Dawn Lang was born in Edmonton, Alberta, on November 2, 1961—a date known as "Langmas" to die-hard k.d. fans. She was the fourth and last child of Adam Frederick Lang and his wife Audrey, who met and married shortly after Fred returned from the service following World War II. Her brother John was eleven when Kathy was born, her sisters Jo Ann and Keltie were six and three. Like most North Americans, it's a family of mixed blood, combining Icelandic, Dutch, Irish,

Scottish, English, and German Jewish ancestry. Kathy has also said that she is part Sioux, an assertion that makes her father chuckle. "Not Sioux—Cree," he grins. "An old uncle of mine once did our family tree and came to the conclusion that one of my grandmothers was part Cree. But I wouldn't put it down as a verified fact. It's true that I'm often mistaken for Cree, but we just kind of took his word for it and never really looked into it any further."

In 1962, when Kathy was six months old, the family moved to Consort and her dad opened the IDA, where he apparently also had the short-lived idea of selling Consort postcards. "The Langs have always been entrepreneurs," she quipped to a journalist who followed her home one year. While Fred was setting up shop, Audrey Lang took a job teaching second grade, registered the family at the local Protestant church, and settled her kids into a standard routine of sports, music, and wholesome country living. It was a way of life she knew well. After all, she too had grown up in Alberta, in a town not far from Consort.

■

As the youngest child, it didn't take long for Kathy to assert her personality. Her mom says she was happiest when she was the center of attention and that she was a performer from the very beginning. According to her sister Keltie, she was a tomboy, a show-off and a pest, while her father remembers her as "a real bomb," an attribute he adored. "She was always very strong-willed, and she always knew exactly what she wanted, even as a kid," he recalls.

Like many tomboys, Kathy was a daddy's girl. She and her father would spend hours horseback riding together, or tearing across the countryside on Fred's racing Skidoo, often at speeds of up to 85 miles an hour. He called his fearless daughter his "boy-girl"—as opposed to his John, who he called his "girl-boy" because of his sensitive nature and tendency to be his mother's son. When Kathy was nine, he gave her a 50cc motorbike, on which she would scoot around town imitating Starsky and Hutch and other TV action figures.

Guns were a major hobby of Fred's, and he claims that his daughter learned to shoot by practicing in the pharmacy. "She had her own .12-gauge shotgun, and we'd practice target shooting in the drugstore," he told *Montreal Gazette* journalist Alan Hustak. "We'd lay at the front door and shoot through the doorway, through to the dispensary at the back." Browsing through the IDA today, it's hard to imagine a ten-year-old girl, belly-down, blasting cans from across the aisles. "I think they actually did it in the basement," says a neighbor, adding that perhaps the story has been exaggerated slightly.

When Kathy was old enough, her father took her on shoots throughout western Canada. "She was a tremendous athlete, and she would always win something at those events," he recalls. "There wasn't a shoot we went to that she didn't come home with some sort of prize or award." He pauses, then carefully adds, "We never shot anything that was alive. We weren't hunters."

Music was also a big part of the Lang family tradition. Neither parent partook in any formal singing or playing, but both enjoyed listening to music, especially Broadway show tunes, and movie sound-tracks like *Dr. Zhivago.* Audrey particularly loved Julie Andrews, and Kathy's first hero became Maria from *The Sound of Music,* whom she loved not only for her singing, but because of Maria's wholesomeness and her happy-go-lucky attitude.

Not long after moving to Consort, Audrey Lang took a small nest egg she had saved and bought the family a secondhand piano. Then she found a piano teacher, a nun named Sister Xavier who was among the last remaining Daughters of Wisdom, a religious order that had come to the area in 1911. The only glitch was that Sister Xavier lived at the Theresetta Convent in Castor, 52 miles west of Consort. So each week, Audrey loaded the kids into the car, and off they went.

When she was seven, Kathy joined her brother and sisters at the piano. She enjoyed the trips to Castor and was intrigued by the fantasy world of the convent, or what she imagined it to be. But she wasn't particularly happy with the discipline her lessons required. Never-theless, the music classes, combined with the time she spent waiting for her brother to finish his lessons, helped her develop a good ear, and soon Sister Xavier had Kathy singing. Amazed by a voice that the nun remembered as having moved her to tears, it wasn't long before she asked Kathy to sing in a local talent contest. "Could I?" the child responded eagerly. It was the first of many contests Kathy would com-pete in over the next few years.

The Theresetta Convent was closed in 1989, and shortly there-after Sister Xavier passed on. But before she died, she and three other nuns went to see her former pupil perform at a concert in Red Deer.

"Is that Sister Xavier?" k.d. asked when she spotted the women in the audience. As the nun sat blushing, k.d. pulled her suit jacket over her head, feigning embarrassment.

■

At the age of ten, bored with the rigors of weekly music lessons, Kathy struck out on her own, picking up her brother's guitar and learning a few basic chords. Her goal was simple: to become famous. She had already developed an inkling of her own talent, and had made her first stab at stardom a year earlier, when she wrote a poem and sent it to her idol, Anne Murray, with a note attached that read, "You have my permission to use these lyrics." Murray never responded, and barely even remembered the incident when she met k.d. years later. "She says I never wrote back," said the Snowbird, embarrassed.

As her musical tastes expanded, Kathy began digging into Keltie's rock'n'roll records, discovering artists like Creedence Clearwater Revival, Eric Clapton, Joe Cocker, and the Allman Brothers. Few of these bands ever passed through Consort, so the girls would rely on Keltie's copies of *Rolling Stone* to keep them apprised of what was going on beyond the prairie, living vicariously through the photos and stories in the magazine as they dreamed of traveling the world. As the years passed, Joni Mitchell, Kate Bush, and Rickie Lee Jones were added to the record pile, along with a smattering of jazz. The only music she never, ever liked was country music.

When she was twelve Kathy got a Yamaha guitar and, like many aspiring youngsters, spent hours imitating her favorite artists. Yet unlike most kids, who hide away in their bedrooms to perform in front of the mirror, she sought out audiences wherever she could find them. At thirteen she wrote her first complete song, "Hoping My Dreams Will Come True," and performed it for her classmates every chance she got, informing everyone that she intended to be famous someday— not an unusual fantasy for kids who gravitate toward music as a way of escaping the boredom of small-town life.

Aside from being a rock star, Kathy's other ambition was to be a roller derby queen. She developed her technique by watching the roller derby on television on Saturday mornings, then practicing with Keltie in their basement, or again, in the pharmacy. It was one of her favorite shows, second only to the "Beverly Hillbillies." "There was a time when I was headed straight for the Canadian Thunderbirds," she once told Jay Leno, grinning. "Amazons on wheels. Very exciting."

What really stood out for those who knew her was Kathy's incredible athletic ability. At 14 she was recruited to join the high school volleyball team, a badge of honor in a town where volleyball is the number one sport. "She was a coach's dream, in a way," recalls her former coach and ninth-grade teacher, Larry Kjearsgaard. She was very competitive, and very strong, and although she wasn't overly tall— usually a prerequisite for the sport—she worked very hard, and was one of the first kids in town to go to a volleyball camp in Edmonton to improve her skills.

In fact, if asked to predict what Kathy Lang would become when she grew up, most who knew her would have imagined her as a well-known sports figure, if she were to have any fame at all. After all, Consort was full of musical kids engaged in endless jam sessions, and although it was clear to anyone who heard her that Kathy had an outstanding voice, a career in music wasn't the kind of thing most people thought of as attainable. Yet Kathy was certain of her destiny, and even took to signing her name with a star next to it—a quirk which struck her teachers at the time. And once, after Keltie had gone off to college, her younger sister sent her a package with some "Charlie's Angels" bubble-gum cards and a handwritten letter. "Keep this," it said on the bottom of the note. "The signature will be worth something one day."

There are dozens of myths and legends about k.d. being an outrageous oddball at school, and one that even says she tried out for the boys' basketball team—and made it. But they are, by and large, exaggeration. "People always latch on to these stories about how eccentric she was as a kid," says Kjearsgaard incredulously. "But really, she didn't stand out like that." In class she was an average student, smart, but not overly zealous, happy to settle for a B or C in most subjects. One subject she made an extra effort in was writing class, but even then, the results were mixed. "I remember her being somewhat creative, but not . . . how can I put it?" says Kjearsgaard, choosing his words carefully. "I'm speaking as a language arts teacher, and not as a critic, but it was almost like she was trying too hard. Her poetry was very immature in terms of the things she was putting into it. But she was making the effort, and as a teacher, you like to see that." Talented or not, she enjoyed writing, and served as part of her yearbook staff for several years. As a senior, she became the editor, and folded several of her poems and musings into the book for the Class of '79.

■

The time-honored North American teenage ritual of spending vast amounts of free time cruising around in old sports cars and getting drunk never really attracted Kathy. Aside from an occasional jaunt to the drive-in movie theater in Coronation, her sports commitments were all-consuming. Volleyball ran for twelve weeks each spring and fall, with the team leaving town after school on Fridays to spend almost every weekend at tournaments. When volleyball wasn't in season, she played basketball and badminton, and in her senior year excelled in track-and-field, placing third in the province in the javelin-throw. Her performance at that level was the eighth best in Canada—remarkable considering Consort didn't have a real track-and-field coach. Her excellence at the sport was borne mostly of raw strength and natural talent, leading some to speculate that with proper guidance, she could have made a name for herself at the Olympic level.

Kathy also became the first student at Consort High School, boy or girl, to win the Athlete of the Year award in tenth, eleventh, *and* twelfth grades. She thrived on physical activity, and in the summers, when school sports were in recess, she sought out odd jobs that would allow her to remain fit and in motion. One summer she drove a three-ton grain truck, rising at six in the morning to make pickups for the elevators, and spending the days driving through the wheatfields with her radio blasting. Another year she and a couple of friends worked at the local pool. Finally, just before she went off to college, she got a small singing gig at Willy Wong's, a little Chinese restaurant and local watering hole on the Trans-Canada Highway, just across the border in Swift Current, Saskatchewan.

A popular girl who always seemed to have a lot of friends, Kathy was never far from most of the school's extracurricular activities, whether it was taking photos for the yearbook, or planning the school dances. "She was very outgoing," says Kjearsgaard, "and friends with everyone. Usually in junior high you have a very boy-girl dynamic going on. Go into any grade-nine class, and you'll see the girls on one side and the boys on the other. But Kathy always had lots of friends, both boys and girls." She didn't date boys, but neither did a lot of high school girls—especially girls as busy as she was. Instead she developed crushes on female teachers, again not unusual for a girl her age.

As it turns out, Kathy realized she was gay by the time she was in her teens, and it was an inclination that seemed quite natural to her. Even when she was very young, she knew there was little that appealed to her about the way women were *supposed* to behave. Remembering an incident from when she was only five and playing Batman and Robin, she explains that even then she refused to be typecast. "There was this point in the play where we were going home to our spouses," she recalls. "I was playing with two little boys, and they said they were going home to their wives. I said I was going home to my wife, too. They said, 'You can't have a wife.' I said, 'Yes I can.' "

As a teenager, Kathy found it depressing that the women she knew always ended up marrying somebody from their class, staying in Consort and having babies. Her instinct told her there had to be a better way, and whenever an intelligent, strong woman came to town who looked independent and who had traveled or gone to study at the university, Kathy was moved to get to know her. She also grew more and more committed to her music, convinced it would be her ticket to a more exciting life.

Whether it was a wedding, a community social, or a rural talent contest, Kathy jumped at every chance to sing in front of an audience, and was rarely seen without her guitar. One of her first paid gigs was a fund-raiser for the Consort Kinsmen Club, where she got paid $25 for a three-song set. But far more memorable were the impromptu performances she gave for her captive teammates as they traveled on the bus to sporting events. "To this day, I think that the most enduring memory I have are those trips," says Kjearsgaard. "Linda Ronstadt's [version of] 'That'll Be the Day' was the song that Kathy used to always belt out. I would usually be driving the bus, and I could hear her singing in the back and feel the power in her voice. It still sends shivers down my spine to think about it."

Perhaps the most notorious story etched in the folklore of k.d.'s childhood was when she competed in the Coronation Music Festival. The volleyball team was on their way back from one of their weekend tournaments, and as they neared Coronation, Kathy strode to the front of the bus and told Kjearsgaard, "Oh, I forgot to tell you. I'm entered in this festival." She asked him to please pull over and drop her off, hoping to bypass the school policy that all children riding on the bus had to be returned home on the bus. To appease her, Kjearsgaard pulled into a gas station and phoned Kathy's mom, who agreed to drive in and pick her up.

"She was wearing this god-awful yellow track suit," recalls Kjearsgaard. "A 'banana suit,' as they called them, with her volleyball uniform underneath. She hopped off the bus with her guitar, and ended up winning." To Kjearsgaard and her teammates, the sight of a teenage jock with a guitar might not have seemed so unusual. But at an age when most kids would cringe at the thought of standing out like that, Kathy's single-minded concern for her music should have been a clear indication of things to come.

■

With such a seemingly normal life, it's curious that Kathy Lang possessed such an insuppressible urge to break out. Nobody—not friends, teachers, or family, can explain where she got such an indefatigable will, or what gave her the confidence and incredible self-esteem to stay so clearly focused on her goals. She was not seen as a prodigy or treated in an exceptional way. On the other hand, she was never bullied or browbeaten into conforming to other people's standards of how a young girl should act, nor was she expected to do more than she was capable of. Instead, her parents encouraged her to be herself and to explore her possibilities—an approach to child-rearing that seemed to give her the security to take risks.

Kathy's relationship with her mother, which has always been very strong, contributed heavily to her sense of self-worth. Soft-spoken and refined, Audrey Lang hardly seems an obvious source of Kathy's outgoing personality, except in that she allowed and encouraged her daughter's natural exuberance. Being overbearing was not her style, and according to Kathy's dad, who says that his daughter could sing like Anne Murray from the time she was five years old, it was her mom who gently motivated Kathy to express herself through music.

Fred Lang, who looks to be a good forty years older than Kathy, again had the even hand of a more mature parent. His quick wit explains where k.d. might have gotten her keen sense of humor, and when asked where his daughter got her wild streak, he says he reckons it's just something that runs in the family. "We were all fairly outgoing," he says. "Particularly my side of the family."

According to Kathy, her family was always very liberal, possibly even "slightly oddball" by Consort standards. Yet in a town of 679 people, it's almost more difficult to *not* stand out. In a community where everyone knows each other for most of their lives, even the true eccentrics are just local personalities, whether it's the kid in the track suit toting around her guitar, or the guy who drives his tractor to school, or the guy who gets drunk every Saturday night on aquavit. All in all, the Langs were a pretty normal family, with Dad arriving home for dinner every night at six o'clock, and the kids doing household chores on the weekends. Still, the Lang children thrived on some unusual diversions, and as they moved through childhood and on to more serious passions, the parents remained unwaveringly supportive. The oldest child, John, was a left-handed genius, the top of his class in high school and, interestingly enough, a child prodigy on the piano. When he got older and went off to college, he discovered eastern religions, found a guru, and decided he wanted to go to India. His father bought him the plane ticket.

Although he was already living away from home by the time she was in her teens, John's involvement with the late sixties counterculture had a strong impact on Kathy, who stored the ideas away until she was old enough to explore them further. It was John, for example, who first introduced her to the concept of vegetarianism, which she embraced as part of her own lifestyle as soon as she left home. Jo Ann, too, had her own interactions with her little sister, although it was Keltie who Kathy spent the most time with and whom she missed the most when the older sibling went off to law school.

■

Until Kathy was twelve, she had what seemed to be a perfect childhood, and as far as she was concerned, her family was happy. But whether she was too young to sense any trouble, or simply refused to see it, a rift was developing between her parents, and one morning her father got up and left, never to return. He left everything, including the store, and Audrey took on the burden of trying to manage two jobs, teaching in the day and going down to run the store in the evenings. This meant that Kathy, too, had to take on extra responsibilities, whether it was working in the drugstore or getting home on time so her mother wouldn't worry. Suddenly, her happy-go-lucky childhood came to a screeching halt as she struggled to find the maturity to deal with her new family situation.

It would be years before Kathy would see her father again, and his disappearance would affect her in ways that would be profound and long-lasting. Yet apart from this loss, she was content growing up in Consort, even if it took leaving it behind before she could truly appreciate it. Church suppers, bake sales, and roaming around the countryside—it was a small-town life that remains a big part of who Kathy Lang has become.

As with many of the great narrative songwriters that have come from Canada—Gordon Lightfoot, Bruce Cockburn, Joni Mitchell, Murray McLauchlan, and in his own way, even Stompin' Tom Connors—k.d.'s art also reveals her uniquely Canadian perspective on the world. It's derived of a culture hovering carefully between Europe and the United States, peopled with highly literate land-lovers who, by and large, embrace a "live and let live" philosophy toward life. Add to that the particulars of living in the Canadian West, where wide-open spaces and long, dark winters offer plenty of time for introspection, and it isn't hard to see how Kathy Lang gets her inspiration.

The End of
Our Beginning

This is it . . .
The End Of Our Beginning.
They tell us we've just begun to learn.
But we've learned more than we're admitting
And taught as much in return.

Love and friendship you've taught to me.
Some demands but staying free.
With no doubt we have changed,
But my friends, we have gained
So rapidly.

And the clock marks
Just another minute.
Haste in time and we're caught in it.
A span of time can kill a feeling,
But ours will grow we're now revealing.

Now a chance to find the dreams,
Breaking out of dependent seams.
In some way glad we're gone
But still holding on
To memories. . . .

So this is it . . .
The End Of Our Beginning.

—Kathy Lang, 1979 yearbook

2

"My life choice had been made for me. There was no need for school, no need for marriage. Everything was just getting through. It was just an exercise."

IN the fall of 1979, Kathy Dawn Lang set off for Red Deer College, which had a strong music program and a famous volleyball team. The school was only a two-hour drive from Consort, making it a logical

choice for many teens who wanted to go away to school but who found the larger universities in Edmonton or Calgary intimidating.

Almost as soon as she arrived in Red Deer, Kathy was dealt a devastating blow: she didn't make the volleyball team. Legend attributes her failure to the fact that she was too much of a show-off, implying that although Red Deer's coach could see she had talent, he didn't like her attitude. But Larry Kjearsgaard, who worked closely with Kathy to prepare her for collegiate sports, remembers the story differently: "I know that coach fairly well, and let's just say that I don't appreciate his recruiting methods," he says, shaking his head.

Kathy was one of Kjearsgaard's first to show promise in volleyball beyond the high school level, and as such, he made every effort to see that she continued. He went out of his way to tell the Red Deer coach about her, and when it was time, off she went with a letter of recommendation and an invitation to try out for the college team. But Kathy had also enrolled herself in a full load of classes, one of which presented a slight scheduling problem.

"Practices were five days a week, and one of her music classes—

I believe it was a voice class—overlapped with practice on one of those days," says Kjearsgaard, recounting the story Kathy told him. "So she asked permission to miss half of practice this one day a week, and the coach basically told her no, she would have to choose." In retrospect, the idea makes him snicker. "I guess she made the right choice," he laughs.

At this point Audrey Lang began to worry. She didn't mind that her daughter wanted to become a famous singer, but she wasn't convinced that a sustainable career could come of it. It had been okay when volleyball was on the agenda, since sports offered tangible results and were highly regarded in Alberta, a land where hockey legend Wayne Gretsky is considered second only to God. But when Audrey realized that her daughter was spending 100 percent of her time on music, she began to gently suggest other options, asking Kathy if she might not consider studying to be a policewoman or a phys-ed teacher. Her hope was that her daughter would find some sort of vocation to fall back on. But Kathy wasn't interested in anything of the sort.

■

It didn't take long to adjust to life in Red Deer, and soon Kathy got involved with a group of local bohemians. Some of them were fellow music and art students, while others were young people who lived and worked in Red Deer. But all of them had two things in common: they each considered themselves artists of one sort or another, and they all *loved* to party.

One of her new friends was Richard Houghton, a twenty-something journalist who wrote for the *Red Deer Advocate*. Another was a guy named Gary Elgar, known to his friends as Drifter. In Houghton's eyes, it was Drifter who was at the center of this ragtag crew, and who held the key to a very special bond between four individuals, among them: himself, Drifter, Kathy, and a guy named Kelly Clarke. "There's just no way to describe this man without making it sound cliché," says Houghton wistfully. "But Drifter had an influence on people that made you feel free. Free to do what you wanted. Free to go home or not go home. Free to get in the car and go for a five-hour drive in the country. Free to sit down and sing like banshees."

Drifter became Kathy's soul mate, playing a role in her life that was so profound it almost defies description. The two were the best of friends, and although he was seven or eight years older than she, they developed an intense relationship. "It was like we were the same

14

person in different bodies, we were that close," she said later. "Our relationship was very spiritual."

Houghton met Drifter when the two of them auditioned for a local theater production of *Jesus Christ Superstar*. Drifter had come to Alberta from Ontario to work on the oil rigs—in "the oil patch," as the locals call it. But as another college friend pointed out, "Drifter wasn't really the kind of guy to be a 'rig-pig.' He was more the sensitive type." Instead, he too enrolled in the music program at Red Deer College, and there he met Kathy.

Houghton remembers clearly the first time Kathy Lang drove by his apartment in her little black Toyota. He was moving, and Drifter and a couple of other friends were helping him pack up his furniture. Kathy roared up to say hello to Drifter, and Houghton was immediately transfixed. "Just to look at her," he recalls, "it was obvious that she wasn't your run-of-the-mill woman that you'd see in Red Deer, Alberta. She had fairly short, close-cropped black hair, and she tended to wear a lot of black or dark clothes. And she had this little black Toyota, which she drove really hard and fast." Coming from a family of race-car enthusiasts, he liked her style right away.

At that point Kathy and Drifter were living the lives of starving artists. They would do odd jobs from time to time, but never enough to put more than a couple of coins in their pockets—especially Drifter, who was the quintessential beatnik. "Drifter didn't care much about money," says Houghton. "He was always broke. When I was hanging out with him and Kathy, I was the one who was gainfully employed, so I was the one who would buy the beer, or fill the car with gas so that we could go for a drive." It never bothered him, though, since he felt that what he got from their friendship was worth a lot more, including an entertaining respite from the tedium of the *Advocate* newsroom.

Drifter's and Kathy's shoddy employment records didn't mean they were lazy. It's just that they had more important things to do, like making art. Drifter had very few possessions, one of which was an Akai reel-to-reel tape recorder that he carried with him everywhere he went, gathering sound effects and bits of conversation. He would also entice his friends to make music for the tapes, organizing jam sessions on the school racquetball courts in the middle of the night. They would sing and play with the echo of the courts, and everyone was encouraged to participate, whether it was reciting avant-garde poetry, singing, or just banging on a borrowed kitchen utensil. "Drifter's philosophy was that if you were making art—which his tapes were—then whatever you did, if it was honest, it was acceptable," explains Houghton. "He wasn't judgmental, and that gave you a lot of freedom. If you couldn't play the guitar, it didn't matter. You just picked it up anyway."

Needless to say, Drifter's approach to music had an amazing impact on Kathy, whose creative energy was ready to explode, and soon she was creating things with Drifter that she had never dreamed of. One time, for example, they were visiting friends who had a lot of nice crystal, when suddenly the urge hit them. They took all the crystal out of the cupboard and placed it carefully on the dining room table. They filled the glasses with water, altering the levels to get different sounds. Finally, they began composing, tapping the glasses with sticks. "It was all recorded on the reel-to-reel," says Houghton, "and I wish I had that recording. It was just so beautiful, like something you'd hear from the best avant-garde artists—Philip Glass, or whoever."

Drifter and Kathy were so amazingly compatible when it came to music that Houghton always thought they'd eventually become a professional team. "They had a very good dynamic going when it was just the two of them working together," he recalls. "Kathy had just enough desire to be organized—not to be commercial, necessarily, but to have a form and structure, something that people would agree was a song. And Drifter had this incredible ability to make her feel free enough to try different things. Put them together and the cliché is Lennon and McCartney, but it was kind of like that. Together they were more than the sum of their parts."

On all of these projects Kathy would contribute her share of singing, but there was no special importance placed on it. Rather than being *the vocalist,* she was an artist working with other artists, learning to collaborate and share ideas. Singing was not the domain of any one person. Still, it was hard to ignore the fact that Kathy had real talent. "There was never any question that her voice was an amazing instrument," Houghton says assuredly, recalling that her voice at the time was fairly untrained, and a little raw. "It had this tremendous quality of being unspoiled, unvarnished—like the wind or the sky, almost remarkable in its unremarkability," he says poetically.

Sometimes Kathy would sing songs that Drifter had written. Other times, she would ad lib, improvising melodies to fit the guitar chords. She would sing simple lyrics, often just words for the sake of words, like "evening." Or "watermelon." Then they'd grab the reel-to-reel and dub the songs onto cassettes, which Houghton would carry around in his car. The tapes made Drifter proud, and he would use them to remind everyone that they didn't need the music industry to have music to listen to. "That was one of the things that was so neat," Houghton smiles. "We'd go on road trips, out driving around, and we'd be listening to *us*. Not John Cougar Mellencamp, or something like that. Just us, the people that we loved, singing our hearts out."

Many of the tapes Drifter made were later scooped up by Kathy, to serve as reminders of her college days and, presumably, to prevent any bootlegs from appearing once she had become famous. Thinking about them over a decade later, Houghton rises and paces the room, as he tries to find words to explain their significance. "There were miles and miles of tape there that were practically unlistenable," he says. "But there were some spots that were real genius. I would just really love to hear them again."

■

Back at school, Kathy was disappointed to find that her classes weren't adding up to much in the way of inspiration. Aside from helping her to better understand the technical aspects of her craft, like the fact that vocally, she was a mezzo-soprano and not a contralto as she'd thought—a discovery that led her to eventually increase her range by almost an octave—she wasn't really interested in the formal structure of what was being taught. She yearned for more freedom to explore her creative impulses, but that was something that seemed impossible within the confines of Red Deer College.

In fact, according to Houghton, Kathy and Drifter both experienced "serious conflict" in the music department, as they rebelled against even the most basic tenets of the field. He illustrates the point by recounting the time one of Drifter's instructors asked the students to each name some kind of musical instrument. "Drifter's musical instrument—the answer he gave—was 'a fingernail on hair,' " he says, howling with laughter.

It was finally somewhere in his second year that the people at Red Deer College politely asked Drifter to go away and to not come back. For Drifter, the feeling was mutual. "The school had really just been a place for them to go," Houghton explains. "There were musical instruments there, and studios to play in, and racquetball courts and such, but after a year or two, the school had served its purpose." It wasn't long after that Kathy, too, dropped out, complaining that the

17

school suppressed her creativity. It was time for her and Drifter to move on to bigger things.

■

By 1981, Kathy Lang had become a real slacker, accomplishing very little other than a couple of gigs here and there, and working from time to time as a record-store clerk or mechanic's assistant. Mainly she hung out, drinking beer, and going on road trips with Drifter, Houghton, and whoever else was around.

Most of Kathy's closest friends were guys, but her relationships with them were platonic. Although she was very masculine-looking, her charm and charisma, along with her natural beauty, appealed to both men and women, and Houghton admits that both he and Drifter were probably attracted to her on some level. But that's not the kind of friendship they had. "We all loved each other," he explains, "and that was the neat thing about the dynamic. We didn't have to fuck each other." This amazed Houghton, who finds it rare for men and women to have such close, intimate bonds without sexual politics interfering.

Kathy also had a circle of women friends that remained fairly separate from the guys. In retrospect, Houghton figures that they were probably other lesbian friends and lovers, but at the time nobody really paid much attention. What he did notice, though, was the network of people she seemed to know whenever they went on one of their road trips. This might not have surprised other gay people, since lesbians and gay men have always known how to seek each other out, even in the most remote places—a survival mechanism jokingly known as "gaydar." But Houghton was duly impressed.

"Kathy and I would be driving around out in the 'east country,' " he recalls, referring to the prairies east of Red Deer. "We'd stop some- where, and she'd take me into some house, and there would be friends of hers—gay friends." He also remembers a trip he, Drifter, and Kathy took to Toronto one Christmas break. Kathy had never been that far east before; nonetheless, she once again knew women with whom she intended to spend a few days. "That made a big impression on me," Houghton says, amazed. "This was not just some neophyte prairie girl. She had friends, she had a network, and she was okay."

It was on this particular trip to Toronto that Drifter dropped a bomb on his two friends, announcing suddenly that he was going to stay in the East with his family for a while. Kathy and Houghton were shocked—this was not part of their plan. Sadly, the pair returned to Red Deer without their spiritual guide, and as her mom remembers it, Kathy had a difficult time adjusting to her best friend's absence. "She used to bring him home weekends, or when they had days off, and I'd have music all weekend," she remembers fondly. "When he went back to Ontario, I could see she really, really missed him. She almost grieved to have him back."

With Drifter gone, Kathy decided it was time for her to buckle down with her music. She declared that she was through working in dead-end jobs—that she was an artist and a musician, and to do anything else was simply a waste of her time. She had business cards printed up that read *Kathy Lang, Vocalist,* then turned to her newspaper friend and asked him to manage her. He refused, terrified by the prospect.

"I guess she thought I had the gift of gab," Houghton figures, "but I knew I didn't have what it took to help her, and I told her I thought she needed a real manager." The truth was that Houghton, like others before him, was skeptical of Kathy's ability to survive solely on her music, but he kept his skepticism to himself and wished her luck as she set off in search of stardom in the nearest big city.

■

By the time Kathy moved to Edmonton, a two-hour drive north of Red Deer, she had already been spending a lot of her time there, attracted by both a large and thriving music scene and a more visible gay community. She had established a network of friends, some of them other lesbians, and she soon moved in with a woman named Verna, who was a couple of years older than Kathy and who, in many ways, looked after her while she continued to struggle as an artist. According to Vikki Pym, a friend who spent a lot of time at Kathy's house, it was Verna who really helped Kathy along, feeding her, clothing her, and otherwise giving her whatever she needed to get through the dry spells. "Verna was her backbone," says Pym. "She really took care of Kathy." It was Verna more than anyone else who believed in the enormity of Kathy's talent, and encouraged her to stick with her music even when others were rolling their eyes.

To Verna's friends, Kathy was the resident artist and all-around eccentric—almost deliberately so. Not only did she make music, but she painted as well, and Pym recalls Verna's basementful of big bizarre paintings that Kathy had done. "She was really inclined artistically," says Pym, "and I guess because she was so young, it was almost like she overdid it. She was the 'artiste,' you know, and she didn't work. She just hung out, ate vegetarian food, and cut her own hair. We're talking a real beatnik type."

Kathy loved putting on shows whenever friends were around, going out of her way to entertain whatever guests dropped by. Whether it was to get attention, or simply to hone her craft, to Pym and others, she was just some crazy young girl with a guitar. "She'd just bang on that thing, making funny noises, and trying to be really alternative," laughs Pym. "And we'd all be like, 'Wow. Okay. That's Kathy. Whatever.' She was on her own trip."

Even though Kathy had years of experience under her belt, her avant-garde approach to music gave Pym the impression that she didn't even know how to play this instrument she carried around with her everywhere she went. But Kathy didn't care whether her friends understood what she was doing or not. Nor did she worry herself with more mundane matters like paying the rent or finding a real job. She just did her thing as Drifter had taught her, letting luck, coincidence, and some sort of higher power guide her course.

"She was really a star in her own mind, even from the beginning," Pym stresses. "She really believed in herself, even if the rest of us were like, 'Oh yeah, sure Kathy.' And it's funny to look back on it, because we all knew she had a good voice, but we never thought she'd be famous. Honest to God, *I* never thought it."

Lin Elder, an Edmonton-based singer and songwriter, was another who was skeptical of Kathy Lang's talent in the beginning. The two first met when Elder was performing in Wainwright, a small town in central Alberta, not far from Consort. In the audience was a group of women who, during a break in the set, invited Elder over for a drink. Kathy was among them, and when it came to introductions, her friends let it be known that she was also a singer. To be polite, Elder asked her if she wanted to come onstage and do a song, an offer Kathy declined. "She said, 'No thanks,' and I thought, well, okay, maybe she can't sing," Elder chuckles. It wasn't until a few years later that k.d. lang's name began appearing all over town, and Elder put two and two together. "When I realized it was the same girl," she marvels, "I just about shit."

Given k.d.'s penchant for grabbing the spotlight, it's ironic she didn't jump at Elder's invitation to get up onstage. But as the two later became friends, Elder noticed that Kathy's relationship to her art was something very deep and spiritual, and that at times, she was nearly possessed by this thing that rose up from her soul. "It was quite bizarre," she says in bewilderment. "We'd just be sitting in the living room talking, and suddenly, *kapow,* she would burst into song, like out of nowhere. Just this voice that would come out at you, but only for about a minute, and then it would go away. And I'd think, 'God, that was weird.' "

Elder could never figure out exactly what it was that caused these sudden outbursts, but she admits that it put her on edge. "I assumed she was looking for something, although I don't know what," she explains. "It just made me feel kind of uncomfortable, but maybe it's because I'm a singer, and I'm shy that way. Maybe she was trying to make me burst out too. I don't know."

■

To most of her friends in Edmonton, Kathy was just someone else to hang out with. Alan Hustak, who would later interview Kathy, remembers seeing her often at a local gay disco called Flashback, one of the very first gay bars in Edmonton. This was before gay discos were in vogue and before the gay scene in Edmonton had really taken off, and according to Hustak, respectable people were not to be seen entering such clubs. Nevertheless, Kathy was there, and usually with a rather motley-looking crew of friends. "She used to always be really spaced out," he says of what he assumed was the result of some heavy partying. As Pym concedes, it was a special time in their lives. "It was a time where we had all just come out, and it was really overwhelming," she recalls, marveling at the exuberance with which they threw themselves into the wild side of life. "We just wanted to have fun. Nightclubs were really important, and it was all this sort of free-love thing. It was like 'anything goes.' Everything just seemed like a big playground."

■

During her first year in Edmonton, Kathy returned to Red Deer often to visit Houghton, Clarke, and a few other friends who were still there. She would drive down for the weekend in her newly acquired vintage car—a 1964 Mercury Meteor, robin's-egg blue, with a slanted rear window that rolled up and down—occasionally ending up at a party hosted by one or another of Houghton's newspaper friends. Most of these people were fairly uptight and inhibited compared to Kathy's crowd, and they would always be surprised when this scruffy-looking crew would wander in, sit down in the middle of the floor, and begin to strum their guitars. Nevertheless, when Kathy opened her mouth, people stopped what they were doing. "When Kathy would start to sing," Houghton reports, "everything would go quiet, and everyone would turn and listen. When she stopped, the party would start up again."

It was at one such party, in January, 1982, that Kathy stumbled upon an opportunity that would permanently change her life. Attending the party was a Red Deer drama professor by the name of Doug Newall, who was working on a play called *Country Chorale* in conjunction with Edmonton's Theater Network. The piece, a musical written by Raymond Storey and John Roby, was set in the 1950s, the story of a young woman who listens to the radio and dreams of becoming her favorite singer. Newall knew that the play's artistic director, Stephen Heatley, was having a tough time finding someone to play the singer in the piece, and when he heard Kathy's voice, he immediately asked her if she'd be interested in the part.

The play was to open in Edmonton in February, and with only one month to go, Heatley was desperate. When Newall phoned him to say that he had found a woman who could sing, he called Kathy in for an audition, explaining that there was no money in the project, and that she would have to go to Red Deer for the rehearsals. Without even asking what the play was about, she agreed, thrilled to have a legitimate project that gave her the chance to sing.

At this point, however, Kathy's acting skills were untried at best. She had dabbled in performance art, like the time she built a sculpture of a 36-foot man out of helium-filled balloons, or the day she took part in a twelve-hour "real time" reenactment of Barney Clark's famous heart transplant, complete with a heart fashioned from pickled beets. But for Kathy these projects had not been acting as much as self-exploration, and an opportunity to learn spontaneity, concentration, and how to interact with other artists in a collaborative process.

Whether or not she could conform to the rules and requirements of a fairly traditional theater production was another question entirely. So was the issue of whether she would be right for the character Heatley had in mind for her. On first meeting, Raymond Storey was skeptical that, at five feet nine, Kathy even had the grace for the part. "Kathryn Lang was not a particularly elegant and delicate performer," he recalled in an interview after the show was over. "The role required someone who could project sensuality, and that didn't come naturally to her. Besides, she was very tall and very adolescent. But she projected such a strong stage presence that we gave her the part."

Then there was the struggle over the music. Kathy's character was to sing several very important numbers in *Country Chorale,* and it was country music, which she didn't really care for. In addition, she wanted to change the keys of all the songs. "Everything was too high for her," Heatley laughs, adding that John Roby, the musical director, wasn't interested in what Kathy had to complain about. "Everything's always too high for an actor until you get into a performance, and then everything's suddenly too low. Artists often get performance energy that makes everything much easier, so John wouldn't change anything, and Kathy was pissed off." Eventually, Kathy realized that she was dealing with professionals and she submitted, agreeing to sing the songs in the keys in which they'd been written. And although it took her a while to click into the rhythm of what was going on around her once the performance started, she blossomed.

The play's design featured a "chorale" of singers and musicians, among whom Kathy was the main vocalist. When they weren't singing, these artists were required to stand silent in the "chorale," as if they were voyeurs watching the central drama unfold. This worked fine for Kathy when she was singing, but when it came time to stand still, she had a lot of trouble figuring out how she was supposed to behave. "I remember her saying something like, 'What do we do while we're standing there?' " says Heatley. "And the question, basically, was 'What do I do with my hands?' "

Storey tried to help Kathy by engaging her in a discussion of who her character might be, telling her that in his mind, she was Patsy Cline. "Who's Patsy Cline?" she asked. After explaining who Cline was, Storey showed Kathy one of the country singer's album covers, which pictured her standing sideways, hands on her hips, gazing out at the audience. It was a stunning, intense image, and Storey suggested that Kathy try the pose. When she did, the results were riveting.

"Sometimes you give a performer one thing that becomes the key that unlocks the door," says Heatley, "For Kathy it was this Patsy Cline stance. Once she had that, she had a sense of the character." There's a videotape of *Country Chorale* that shows Kathy in action, dressed in a tacky brown dress and giant blue button earrings that would shock anyone who came to know k.d. lang in later years. But even then her dark, rich voice was unmistakable.

It's no surprise that someone Kathy's age had never heard of Patsy Cline. At the time country music had yet to experience widespread popularity in North America, and for a young kid growing up with rock'n'roll and alternative music, there was no reason for her to have come upon Cline, save for an occassional K-Tel ad on TV. Yet once she perfected her Patsy Cline imitation for *Country Chorale*, she often stole the show, inspiring many to ask, "Who was that girl with the blue earrings?"

More astounding was the way Kathy took to Patsy Cline. She began to collect all of the singer's old records, many of which came as gifts from family and friends. Then something really strange happened: she began recalling dreams she'd had as a child, dreams of fiery plane crashes, and when she discovered that Cline had died in a plane crash, Kathy, who was already predisposed to the more spiritual aspects of life, she became convinced that there was a link between their souls.

She began telling people that she was the reincarnation of Patsy Cline, and, according to her friends, the more she talked about it, the more she believed it. And the more she believed it, the more she was able to find proof that it was true, going so far as to claim that Patsy herself had been psychic. "Somehow I've inherited her emotions, her soul," she told a journalist a year later. "I know that sounds weird, but I do believe it. I have a recurring dream about a plane crash, and others where I actually have conversations with her." Needless to say, Kathy's friends were a little surprised at her new persona, but most were careful not to be too critical.

"I wouldn't pass judgment on her relationship to Patsy Cline," says Richard Houghton slowly. "Frankly, that whole thing served her purposes really well, and *Country Chorale* really helped get her going." This is not to say that he thinks Kathy made up the Patsy Cline story either, because in his mind, nothing regarding his friend was quite so simple. Nor was he about to question Kathy's unique sense of her own spirituality.

■

Despite Kathy's overwhelming success in *Country Chorale*, when it came time for Heatley to pare down the cast to take the show on the road, Kathy Lang was one of the actors who were cut. In hindsight it was one of the many strange coincidences that began to mark her career.

"It's my biggest regret, if I were to have one," says Heatley wistfully. "After the play ran in Edmonton, we were remounting it the next year for a national tour, and we had to cut the company from eight people, down to six." He had really wanted Kathy to remain in the cast, but in order to keep her she had to be able to play an additional part, doubling for the role of a shy and rather ditzy young girl. Heatley worked hard with Kathy to teach her the part, but it was to no avail. "It was a scene for an actor," he explains, "and she just couldn't do it. She tried, but it was a part that she just wasn't cut out for." To make a long story short, *Country Chorale* went off to tour Canada, and Kathy went off to become a star.

3

"To dance is human, to polka is divine."

KATHY Dawn Lang found the man who would help make her a star in a classified ad in the local newspaper. His name was Larry Wanagas, owner of Homestead Recorders, a small recording studio on Edmonton's west side. It was November 1982—just days after Kathy's twenty-first birthday—when she walked into his studio to audi-

tion for Dance Party, a western-swing band that was looking for a female lead singer.

Up until now, her one paid singing gig in Edmonton had been opening for a local artist by the name of Holly Wright at Alberta's Provincial Archives Museum—a gig Kathy supposedly got following an impromptu audition in a hotel parking lot. That and her stint in *Country Chorale* were the only real music-related jobs on her resumé. Still, she was determined to find work as an artist.

The members of Dance Party were amazed by Kathy's vocal abilities, and Kathy immediately got the job. But her time with the band was short-lived; Dance Party split up after just one show. Not one to miss an opportunity, Wanagas thought Kathy would be great doing voice-overs and radio commercials for some of the clients that comprised his studio's bread-and-butter accounts, and quickly got her a job singing a jingle in an ad for a local waterbed store. Soon her voice was heard on the radio all across Alberta. Yet Wanagas could sense that Kathy was destined for things far greater than radio spots, and after a couple of chats over coffee that spring, the two agreed he would become her manager.

Wanagas was already managing a couple of other local Edmonton bands, and had a lot of contacts in the local music scene. One particularly close friend was Geoff Lambert, the guy in charge of booking acts at a popular nightclub called the Sidetrack Cafe. Wanagas told Lambert all about Kathy, and asked him to give her a chance at the club, assuring his friend he wouldn't be sorry. Lambert agreed, and booked her as the opening act for an evening of two sets by Leo Kottke. But when the time came and she walked onstage and sat down with her guitar, he began to have his doubts.

"She was so scared," he whispers, grinning at the memory of that evening. "She was just *so scared.*" It was her first time onstage in front of such a big crowd, and Lambert recalls that she was extremely timid. She didn't have an amp, and, because she was used to playing in front of a much smaller crowd, didn't know how to make good use of the mikes. Instead she just sang quietly, and gently strummed her guitar.

The audience responded the way an audience usually responds to a warm-up act—they didn't pay any attention. "The conversation level went right back up after the first couple of chords, when they realized she was a nobody," says Lambert matter-of-factly. "And that made it worse. When a person is up there as an opening act, it's just brutal. It's like being a comic and nobody's laughing at your jokes." As Lambert recalls, Kathy had a such a hard time that she didn't even do the second set.

Ordinarily, Lambert's memory of such a performance would have been swept away with the empty beer bottles at the end of the night. But Kathy didn't just give up and disappear, and the next time he heard her perform, he was shocked by how much it contrasted with that first painful night at the Sidetrack. What changed was everything. Wanagas hadn't been the least bit phased by the way Kathy bombed her first time out. He had worked with enough young musicians to know that it would take some time for her to warm up to the idea of being on a real stage. And while she could sometimes seem quite shy and withdrawn, he knew there was another side to her. In the studio she was a ham, goofing off and dreaming up all sorts of silly antics. In fact, it was almost as though she was developing two distinct personalities: one that loved clowning around and being the center of attention, and the other that was far more aloof and self-contained. Wanagas was enamored of the wild side he saw in his new artist and would

28

brag about it to his friends, certain that with a little encouragement, the show-off in her could flourish onstage. He also knew that her singing was good, but that she needed musical support, so he immediately set to work helping her pull together a band.

Wanagas's ultimate goal was to mold Kathy's obvious ambition and her apparently limitless energy into an act that could be placed in the local clubs. At first she expressed interest in becoming a jazz singer, a reasonable choice given the depth and range of her voice and her attraction to improvisation. But she and Wanagas both knew that, beyond the world of Holiday Inn lounges, there wasn't much work available for unknown female jazz vocalists. So he suggested that she try her hand at something a little more marketable, figuring that if she wanted to be a jazz singer, she first had to build herself a platform that would gain her some notoriety. Otherwise, they were all going to starve.

Two types of music that were popular at the time and easy to book in local bars were country and the blues. Neither seemed much of a stretch from the folk music she was playing, and in fact, Kathy already had a fair amount of blues material in her repertoire. But as she had recently discovered with *Country Chorale,* country music could be a lot more fun. So she and Wanagas selected a few songs, hired a handful of local musicians, and began booking gigs in some of the bars around Edmonton. And for no real reason, other than she liked the way it looked on paper, Kathy Dawn changed her name to k.d. lang, written entirely in lowercase letters in honor of a favorite poet, e.e. cummings.

■

There was no shortage of good musicians in Edmonton, and although k.d.'s first band was unimpressive, within a month or two and a few personnel changes, she and Wanagas had settled on a pretty strong lineup. Soon posters were going up on telephone poles announcing "The K. D. Lang Band," featuring Stu McDougall, Dave Bjarnson, Farley Scott, and Gord Matthews. For people familiar with the local music scene, these four guys were all fairly well-known, and each had their own significant following. They played well together, and by November, k.d. lang was ready to return to the Sidetrack Cafe.

Despite warnings from his pal Larry, Geoff Lambert was unprepared for what he witnessed as k.d. mounted the stage that second time. Not only was she immensely more confident than before, but she had completely transformed her persona and now bore an eerie, intangible resemblance to the woman who stared out from a picture frame on top of the piano. In short, k.d. lang had re-created Patsy Cline in her own image.

Her costumes were a hodgepodge of country kitsch: long, full skirts, torn stockings, and blouses with rhinestone buttons—all items dug from the bins of a few secondhand clothing stores. She had taken to wearing a pair of lensless, wing-shaped glasses, and a pair of battered cowboy boots cropped just above the ankles. She told people that the boots had been a gift from a Ukrainian farmer, a suggestion that makes Vikki Pym laugh. "We all shopped at Salvation Army," she says, "and it was always a contest to see who could get the coolest boots."

What k.d. couldn't find, she made, astonishing her friends with her expanding creativity. Pym was particularly shocked to see that even some toys she had given Kathy for her birthday wound up as part of an outfit. "When it came to giving Kathy birthday gifts, you had to find something really different—you couldn't bring her something normal, you know," she explains. "So one year I gave her this big bag of little plastic cowboys and Indians. She was really into stuff like that, just things to entertain her mind, and we played with them for hours. Later on, when she was getting famous, I saw her in this video, and I noticed that she had sewn all these cowboys and Indians to her skirt!" She was also still giving herself spiky, homemade hair cuts, which, along with her size, made her look a bit like a cowboy in drag.

More amazing than her costume was the character Kathy became when she put it on. She strutted effortlessly around the stage, singing Robert Gordon's "The Way I Walk," or did crazy things like twirling a plastic globe then choking herself as she coughed out the final verse of Patsy Cline's "Stop the World." A weather-beaten rocking horse hung from the wall behind her during every show, and when it was time, she would pluck off its tail and toss it on her head like a wig for a campy rendition of "These Boots Are Made for Walking." Throughout the show she encouraged the audience, who she referred to as "Bobs and Bettys," to have a "wing-ding daddy-o of a good time" as she led them through the Mashed Potato and other assorted dances. Invariably, she'd do a kind of bird-dive curtsy at the end of every show, a move reminiscent of Minnie Pearl. But for k.d., this last act had another, deeper meaning: it symbolized Patsy Cline falling out of an airplane.

With these antics alone, she began to fill the clubs. "Some of the stuff she'd do would be just outrageous," says Lambert, his eyes big with excitement. "Like she'd have disco go-go dancers on the stage with her, a couple of girls just dressed up and dancing. And she had a refrigerator box she used to bring out, with the insides painted white, and a painted window with a flower sticking through it. She used to do that old Kingston Trio song about playing solitaire, and this was the house she was sitting in as she sang it. She'd bring the box out, open it up, and just sit inside of it."

Between sets Kathy would sit quietly in a corner by herself, which, to those who only knew k.d. lang the performer, made her act seem all the more astounding. "She'd be up there ranting and raving," recalls Lambert, "and then you'd go backstage to say hi or to see how things were going, and the person you'd talk to would be real quiet."

■

Nearly everyone who knew Kathy Lang was surprised by the emergence of k.d. Even Wanagas, who had watched her cutting up in the studio, was shocked by how she was able to meld all of her wacky ideas into such a coherent presentation. But more surprising to those who had worked and hung out with Kathy was her newfound obsession with country music.

She would spend years trying to explain to the world why country music made sense to a wild young beatnik like herself. But much of the theorizing came after the fact. In the beginning, not even *she* knew exactly where the project was going. "There's a long-term concept around k.d. lang, but I can't tell you exactly how it goes because it's very difficult to put concepts into words," she told Liam Lacey, a reporter for Canada's *Globe and Mail* who spent a lot of time with Kathy in those early years. What she claims to have loved most was that her new routine was such a departure from the avant-garde performances that she had previously been involved with. She was growing bored with the performance art scene, and its emphasis on being "alternative," which she says was all too often little more than a competition to be the weirdest. Country music, in contrast, came with a structure and tradition that gave her something to work for—maybe even something to conquer. In the end it just seemed to her like a natural progression into something new and different.

Her friends, of course, thought she was either crazy, or very, very smart. k.d. lang certainly wasn't the Kathy they knew, but then again, the Kathy they knew was capable of just about anything when it came to art. Most saw k.d. lang as just another Kathy Lang creation. "I think it was just a matter of circumstance," says Vikki Pym, who watched Kathy move through this genesis. "I remember her seeing that ad in the newspaper for a band that needed a lead singer, and it was a country band, so she went with it. Whatever came up, Kathy would take it. She knew it was like, 'fake it 'til you make it,' and since she wasn't working, she took whatever she could."

Ultimately, she just wanted to sing, and country music seemed as good a style as any to showcase her talent. Even now, there aren't many musical genres where a voice like hers can be put to good use, and she understood that if she was going to get anywhere, she needed music that would highlight her voice. Her dream was to follow in the footsteps of Ella Fitzgerald or Peggy Lee, artists whose vocal talents she has admired and emulated over the years. But since contemporary pop music wasn't moving in that direction, country music seemed to be one of the few places where she could really let go.

Besides, she adored the country gear and paraphernalia that went with the territory, and began to collect it hand over fist. In her living room stood a lamp featuring a glowing motif of cowboys riding the range. A cowboy hat hung on the wall. A tattered square-dance flag decorated the hood of her car, and on her shelves sat miniature farm scenes she created with plastic cows and pigs. None of these things were hard to come by in Alberta—Canadian cowboy country—where the Calgary Stampede, a world-renowned rodeo, is still one of the most important cultural events in the region. For all intents and purposes, Kathy became a caricature of the quintessential farm girl, even though she had never actually lived on a farm.

■

It may have been jarring to see a woman k.d.'s size moving around onstage the way she did, but that was part of the fun of it. "I like to be a cow sometimes," she once said. "I like to be very ungraceful because I think people have just about had it up to here with trying to be perfect." The other thing the k.d. character did was to put some distance between the artist and her audience. It's a technique that many performers use to enable them to feel less inhibited onstage, while at the same time protecting themselves from becoming too exposed and vulnerable. For Kathy Lang, k.d. became an alter ego able to deal with the spotlight in a way that was difficult for her to do on her own.

As for her fashion statement, she had all sorts of explanations for why her look didn't jibe with the more traditional female country songbirds. She claimed that her getups were meant to help people let go of their inhibitions, so they could enjoy the sentimentality of her crooning without feeling like total suckers. She was convinced that by making herself look stupid, people would loosen up and enjoy themselves. The same was true of the toys and props she used on stage, which she hoped would encourage people to overcome their paranoia and prejudice of corny tearjerkers.

Clearly k.d. was designing her show with an alternative-music crowd in mind, figuring that the humor of the country bumpkin would make the music easier to swallow. It worked, and in the beginning, most of her fans were other young hipsters—people who loved just about anything that had an edge to it. Yet somehow, she also had the notion that k.d. lang could appeal to more traditional country fans. "I enjoy having that double edge in everything I do," she explained. "It's like a ladder, where some people can reach the top: the real bizarros. And the very straight people can catch on to the bottom rung and just cry into their beer."

Whether this approach would really work when she moved beyond the supportive arms of Edmonton's music community remained to be seen. Even in Edmonton, she began to attract people who had heard about her tremendous talent and dynamic stage presence, but who had a hard time reconciling her voice with her look. Lin Elder, who had been hanging out with Kathy, remembers that her mother attended one of these early shows and found it disconcerting. "My mom knew who k.d. was, because she used to call the house, and because she was getting really well-known around town," Elder recalls. "But she had never actually seen her. After the show she kept saying 'Why does she look like such a boy?' I don't think she really understood where k.d. was going with it, but despite all of that, she loved her singing."

Even k.d. herself didn't necessarily know where she was going with her new character. In hindsight it seems obvious that part of the reason she dressed the way she did was because she just never could have pulled off a more traditionally feminine look. She had *always* looked like a boy, and no amount of big hair and makeup would ever change that. Yet, for all the theorizing about what her fashion presentation meant, Liam Lacey suspects that it wasn't nearly as calculated as she made it seem. Instead, he pictures a young artist cutting off the top of her boots, putting on her work socks, looking in the mirror and laughing, "What am I getting into here?"

"As far as it seemed nutball, with the sawed-off boots and the glasses with no glass, there were things that connected," he explains. "The glasses, she said, were sort of an homage to her mum, and the boots were something a Ukrainian farmer had given her. Then she decided to cut them down, and it was just sort of finding out what it meant to put these things together. I think with pop stars this is fairly common. I mean, why did David Bowie wear dresses onstage and shave his eyebrows? I'm sure he couldn't tell you. He probably just thought, 'This is interesting, it's fun, and it might work.' That's often what it comes down to."

The glasses may have been an homage to her mom, but it doesn't mean her mother wasn't shocked to see her daughter looking like she did onstage. "I'm sure that my mother would have preferred me to look more like Anne Murray," k.d. confesses. "But I'm also sure that now, she is very proud to have someone who is willing to take chances, willing to be different, and who has enough self-confidence to do that." And her mother admits that, although she wasn't exactly crazy about Kathy's new look, she forgot about the clothes once Kathy started to sing.

■

Almost immediately on the heels of her extended appearance at the Sidetrack Cafe, k.d. lang made her Canadian television debut on "Sun Country," a national country-music show hosted by the popular Canadian singer Ian Tyson. Next came her first print media interview, a small piece in the weekly regional magazine *Alberta Report*.

"Sun Country" gave k.d. her first taste of what the country-music industry might expect from her. Word of mouth about her singing had already traveled around enough of western Canada that the program's producers were practically obligated to have her on the show. But they weren't at all pleased with her look. "First my boots were condemned," she told journalist Tom Philip in *Alberta Report*. "Then they came at me with a curling iron, saying they wanted to take the 'edge' off my hair." For the first, and probably last, time, k.d. agreed to allow "the industry" to tone down her look in an attempt to make her more palatable to the country-music audience. It would become an ongoing battle throughout her career.

Philip, delighted by her oddball behavior, gave her an easier time during the photo shoot for the piece he was writing. "I remember going over to her house with my little 35mm camera," he laughs. "She posed with all sorts of strange objects—bicycle wheels, bridal veils. She had a real sense for the camera, even then. She really knew how to have her picture taken." She also must have believed that if she could just continue to do it her way, being a star was going to be a lot of fun. Little did she know what she would be up against.

■

With the phenomenal reception k.d. was receiving on the club circuit, Larry Wanagas wasted no time in getting Kathy and her band into the studio to produce something that could get them on the radio. In December they released their first single, "Friday Dance Promenade," pressed on white vinyl and backed with a cover version of the Roches' "Damned Ol' Dog." The little seven-inch was a hit, and has since become a collector's item.

Kathy loved showing off her first record, and immediately made a trip to Red Deer to take some copies to her friends. She also hand-delivered a copy to Red Deer's local radio station, hoping to get it on the air. But the radio station, CRKD, didn't give a hoot about some little farm kid named k.d. lang. "They just looked at the record and said, 'Sorry, we can't play it. It's not on our playlist,' " recalls Houghton. "That's the way it is in small towns. If you're from there, you ain't anybody until you go and prove it somewhere else. Of course, five years later they were all dying to play her record."

Back in Edmonton, the crowds kept coming, and eventually k.d. decided to give her band a real name, christening them "the reclines" in homage to her idol. Soon k.d. lang and the reclines were getting booked in Calgary, Red Deer, and small clubs all over Alberta, and within three months they had made an unprecedented splash through-out the province. Nearly every show drew a sell-out crowd, and after a few more gigs at the Sidetrack Cafe—each one earning her $500 more than the previous show—they had outgrown the venue.

Amazingly enough, it was around this time that Kathy's friend Drifter decided to return to Alberta, determined that he, too, could have a career in music. As Houghton recalls, Drifter had just finished a program in music electronics at a school in Toronto, and was probably hoping to hook up with Kathy to continue their lives where they had left off. She would be the voice, he would be the electronic wizard, and together they would be quite a team. Unfortunately, things didn't work out that way.

Drifter returned to Alberta just as the winter of '83 was drawing to a close, and immediately went to visit Kathy in Edmonton. But by then her music had become all-consuming and her hectic schedule left little time for running around with friends. Some people found themselves a little disgruntled that she was no longer hanging out on the scene, but it was a choice she had to make if she was going to succeed. "Three years ago my immediate priority was where I was going to find a chunk of hash to get me through the day," she remarked of her time spent as the-girl-about-town. "But I stopped when I realized it was draining my energy."

Houghton understood that Kathy's priority was her career, although he too longed for more carefree days. And although Drifter never said as much, Houghton's sure he must have been quite disappointed to find that so much had changed in his absence. "That period that we all spent together in Red Deer was like a magical window in time," he says longingly. "But it may just be that by the time Drifter returned, that window had slammed shut." Eventually, Drifter bid Kathy farewell and headed down to Red Deer to look for the rest of his old friends.

Houghton was out of the country when Drifter arrived back in Red Deer, but Kelly Clarke was there, still working on the oil rigs and still hosting his famous wild parties. Clarke lived in a place called the Bargain Barn, a rambling, run-down flat above a former used-furniture store. The place was too crude to even call an apartment, but it was a perfect gathering spot for Clarke and his friends, situated right around the corner from the biggest, roughest bar in town. Frequently, after the bar closed, everyone would go over to the Bargain Barn to continue the party. On April 6, 1984, one such evening resulted in tragedy.

"I'd been to lots of those parties, and they could really get rough, but Kelly could usually handle it," says Houghton. "Kelly was a pretty rough guy himself, and as long as he was around things were okay." But on this particular night, Kelly went to bed before the party was over, leaving his guests to fend for themselves in the living room. Shortly thereafter, a fight broke out following a disagreement over a song that was playing on the stereo. "One of the girls put on a record,"

Houghton explains, "and one of guys said, 'We don't want to hear that shit,' so Drifter kind of stood in between them and said something like, 'C'mon, let her play the record. It'll be over in a minute, and then you can play something else.' But this guy was totally cranked up on whatever he had ingested, and probably wasn't in his right mind. So he hauled off and slugged Drifter, very hard."

The first blow crushed Drifter's temple, which may have killed him instantly. But in case that wasn't enough, once Drifter had fallen to the ground, the guy put the boots to him, stepping on his throat and crunching his esophagus. "It happened just like that—snap, in five seconds," says Houghton, blinking back the tears. "It was just boom, boom, boom, and the guy went out the front door. The rest of the people carried Drifter down the hall, and laid him in front of Kelly's front door. And Kelly, who was in bed with a girl, gets up, opens the door, and there was his best friend. Dead."

k.d. and the reclines were performing at a small tourist lodge in Jasper the weekend Drifter was killed, and the next day, someone managed to track her down and give her the news just moments before she was to go onstage. She was stunned, but rather than call off the gig, she went in and sang her guts out. After her performance, she left the hotel and spent the rest of the night walking through the mountains alone.

It terrified her mother to later discover that her daughter had been out in the wilderness all night, given the threat of bears and other dangers of hiking in the mountains at night. Yet she understood her daughter enough to know that Kathy had to deal with Drifter's death in her own way. "It was really strange, because she called me the next day, and it was almost like Kathy was consoling me," Audrey Lang recalled. "She said, 'Mom, you're a Christian. You know that Drifter's all right now. It's the other fellow we have to pray for.' "

The tragedy of Drifter's death stunned everyone who knew him, in part because he had been such a gentle, nonviolent soul. But Kathy was particularly shaken. In the weeks following his murder, she was plagued with dreams of her lost friend, and told Tom Philip that once, in the middle of the night, she woke to find him there with her. Ultimately, she came to terms with his departure from her life, and took solace in her belief that fate had its reasons. She also confided to Houghton that she believed Drifter knew it was his time to go. "She said that when he said goodbye to her that day he saw her in Edmonton, *that it was goodbye,*" he recalls.

As the months passed, Kathy grieved quietly, keeping her feelings mostly to herself. She built a shrine of candles, photos, and a few of Drifter's possessions—an altar in homage to her lost soul mate, and Lin Elder remembers that she would sometimes sit for hours and lose herself in it, completely transfixed. But she never really talked about Drifter once he was gone. To the material world, it was as though she had closed a chapter in her life, letting go in order to accept what was her destiny. But in her heart she kept Drifter alive and with her.

"I observed how Drifter's death affected Kathy in her professional life," says Houghton, "and it was profound. It was as if nothing worse could happen to her." Houghton knew that k.d. had rarely been intimidated by the music business, or by anyone. She had never had any problems coming to terms with what she needed to do to make it as a singer. Yet Drifter's death seemed to cast a mystic light over k.d.'s career, as if to say that there would be no more sacrifice. "After this happened," he continues, "it was as though the tough choices were made, and the business would not intimidate. Johnny Carson, David Letterman, it didn't matter. They're just folks, and they're not any different than the guy who pours the coffee at the cafe in Consort. And if somebody in her band needed to get replaced, well, they got replaced, because there was only one reason for doing this, and that was to be a success."

Houghton was right—it was at precisely this point in Kathy's life that her musical career began to soar, and she was convinced it was thanks to Drifter. "It was almost like there was a price to be paid, and Drifter paid that price for her," Houghton says quietly. "As soon as he got killed, her career just went off like a rocket, and all of a sudden, she could do no wrong." It was as if Drifter had paid the gods.

Almost immediately after Drifter's death, k.d. lang and the reclines went into the studio to record their first album, an 8-track recording made with $2,000 Kathy borrowed from her mom, plus labor and some expenses that Wanagas took care of. Rather than sitting down and writing songs, the band, which had been playing together only a few months, simply laid down their best tracks, taking time off from the studio only to watch the Edmonton Oilers stomp their way to the Stanley Cup—an event k.d. claims was a source of inspiration. In June they opened for the internationally known band Rank and File. Then, with one day left before the all-important Edmonton Folk Festival, where the reclines had landed a choice Friday-evening spot on the lineup, they finished their final mixes and released *a truly western experience.*

■

It was a warm Friday evening on August 10, 1984, and the air tingled with the kind of lazy anticipation that comes with the start of a late-summer weekend. Over in Gallagher Park, the opening night of the fifth annual Edmonton Folk Festival was well under way, winding through a lineup that included Dick Damron, Dr. John, Sylvia Tyson and the Great Speckled Bird Band, and k.d. lang and the reclines.

The Edmonton Folk Festival is a major event in the Canadian music scene, not only because of the wealth of talent it brings to Alberta, but because of the various talent scouts who descend on the event in hopes of discovering some great new act. Scattered among the 4,000-odd people attending on this particular night were many from the music business: record label executives, booking agents, and other industry riffraff—among them a guy named Richard Flohil, a publicist and concert promoter from Toronto.

Flohil had been warned by a friend in the business to keep an ear out for k.d. lang, but he hadn't paid much attention. "This guy Peter North had told me about k.d. lang, and he kept telling me that I ought to bring her to Toronto," he recalls. "And I said, 'Yeah, yeah, yeah,' and did absolutely nothing, because I hadn't seen her, and you can't sell a pig in a poke."

What happened that night was another in a long list of happy coincidences that have graced k.d.'s career, as months of hard work dovetailed with divine providence to open yet another door on the road to impending fame. The band that was due to follow the reclines got lost on the way to the festival, and k.d. suddenly found herself with forty minutes, instead of twenty, to get the crowd up and dancing. As was her style, she rose to the occasion.

"She roared around the stage like a riderless motorcycle," wrote an *Edmonton Sun* critic the day following her high-energy performance. Other newspapers took note as well. But it wasn't just k.d.'s stage antics that captured the crowd's attention. To make sure nobody missed her voice through all the high-handed aerobics, she ended the set with an a cappella rendition of "Amazing Grace." It brought the crowd to its feet, and k.d. received the first standing ovation of her career. She responded by returning to the stage for a chilling version of Patsy Cline's immortal "I Fall to Pieces."

Flohil was floored by k.d.'s ability to impress so many people, including other artists like Sylvia Tyson, and industry players like Bernie Finkelstein, who manages Bruce Cockburn. To most of these people, k.d. was a completely unknown act. And yet they were blown away. Before he left the park that night, Flohil had a chat with Larry Wanagas, and he returned to Toronto with a phone number and a mission, heading straight to Derek Andrews, the manager of a local Toronto blues bar called Albert's Hall. "I came back to Toronto on Monday, and Tuesday I went around to see Derek," he recalls. "I said, 'Derek, I've got this incredible act. It ain't blues, but it really rocks out.' He said, 'Are you talking about k.d. lang?' and I said 'How do you know?' He said, 'Well, I've already had three people from Sylvia Tyson's band in here telling me how they just got blown off the stage by her.' "

With that, it was a done deal. k.d. lang and the reclines were booked into Albert's Hall for the end of October. Larry Wanagas agreed to pay Flohil $200, plus a 5% commission from what the band made at the door, along with his expenses. In return, Flohil would act as promoter, publicist, and whatever else it took to fill the club for the five-night run. It was to be k.d. lang's East Coast debut.

4

"**I** have this crazy idea that this whole thing with k.d. is actually going to work!" wrote Richard Flohil to Larry Wanagas on October 14, 1984. Looking back ten years later, it's probably the greatest understatement of Flohil's long career. But at the time it was nothing but a hunch. The street buzz around k.d. was building, and after playing together for only nine months, she and the reclines had garnered an enormous amount of attention. Reviews of their live shows and their debut album

flowed in from western Canada almost daily, not a single one with anything negative to say. Flohil used the momentum to work his Rolodex for all it was worth.

Toronto was an important next step for k.d., as it is for any Canadian artist in search of national or international fame. In a sense it's like Los Angeles and New York rolled into one, with Nashville, Chicago, and perhaps even Atlanta thrown in for good measure. Some Canadians resent that fact, but it's a fact nonetheless: nearly all the record labels have offices in Toronto, and it's also media central. "When Toronto is in love with somebody, Toronto does it big time," says Richard Houghton, shaking his head. "Once Toronto says you're a star, then everyplace in Canada falls all over themselves, too. You have to. It's the rules. If Toronto says you are, then you are."

There were those who thought that now was the time for k.d. to dump Larry Wanagas, trading up for a manager who had experience as a major league player. As one industry executive put it, "Larry Wanagas probably didn't even know the area code for Toronto before he took on this project." In other words, he had no contacts to speak of. Yet what Wanagas didn't know he was determined to learn, and with the help of enthusiastic supporters like Richard Flohil he dug in, laying the groundwork for what he hoped would launch Canada's next musical superstar.

For her part, k.d. concentrated on the one thing that mattered most: perfecting her performance. Singing became all she did, day in and day out; everything else was left to her manager. She never cared much for the business side of things, and had no interest in dealing with anything beyond her show and what was going on with the band. If Wanagas said to be somewhere at a certain time, she made sure that she was there, and that the band was there, too. Beyond that, it was up to him to make all of the arrangements.

■

k.d.'s debut album, *a truly western experience,* surpassed everyone's expectations, selling out its initial 1,000 copies in a month. By mid-October a second pressing of 1,000 copies was being distributed from the trunks of the band members' cars and in mom-and-pop record stores that catered to the alternative music crowd. Wanagas eventually pressed 5,000 copies, many of which found their way to critics' turntables around the country. (Sire Records later rereleased the album on CD.)

The album's cover was typically goofy and attention-grabbing, a simple cut'n'paste job done by k.d. in the same do-it-yourself style that comprised the look of her show. On the front cover she balanced a picture of herself atop a cardboard fence leading to a barn. Peeking out from the second-floor barn window was a black-and-white photo of Patsy Cline. On the back of the jacket was the inscription, *"and the wind drifts through my soul, say hi to Patsy for me."*

Many of the record's raves came from people who'd seen k.d. lang and the reclines live, and who were happy to find the album as full of surprises as the artist herself. One reviewer found the twenty-six minutes of music "intriguing . . . eclectic and determinedly eccentric," calling the album "hokey and homespun, but always downright fun." Most of the songs were original tunes that ran the gamut from blues and western swing to rockabilly. At the end was a song that Drifter had written—a strange piece called "Hooked On Junk," that is completely out of place on the album, but which found a life of its own on college and alternative radio, including the seminal late-night Canadian program "Brave New Waves." Another cut, a k.d. favorite called "Pine and Stew," caught the attention of Peter Gzowski, the host and producer of a daily CBC radio program called "Morningside," and a man whose popularity inspires one Canadian journalist to refer to him as "Mr. Canada." Gzowski was fascinated by k.d., and played "Pine and Stew" often on his show, calling it the quintessential Canadian country song. He particularly liked the line "Do you think I'm mental . . ."—a phrase he was sure no American would ever utter.

k.d. lang was perfect for the CBC, which has always been biased toward homegrown Canadian talent. And because of the network's scope—a rough equivalent to National Public Radio in the States, but far more popular, it reaches one in ten Canadian households—and Gzowski's own huge following, being featured on "Morningside" gave her music an early boost. This, combined with her performance at the Edmonton Folk Festival and her appearance on "Sun Country," also helped land her a grant from VideoFact, a development offshoot of MuchMusic, Canada's music television network. MuchMusic loved k.d. lang and the reclines, and had already been airing home videos of the band shot during live performances. Now it was time for something a little more professional.

■

Riding high on so much publicity, Flohil pulled out all the stops for k.d.'s Toronto appearance. "I pulled a lot of favors for this one," he recalls. "I'd been a publicist in town for a long, long time, and I hadn't lied too much to too many people. So for this one I went out on a limb."

What he told people, simply, was that they had to see this woman. He described her outfits as coming "from the bottom of the Salvation Army box," and he stressed the energy and zaniness of her live shows. What he did *not* tell people was that she could sing. "In hindsight, I like to say that I did that on purpose," he confesses, "but I really didn't. It's just that you can't really tell people somebody's a great singer— it's just not credible. You can say she dresses weird, that she looks funny, or that she does a show that will knock you on your ass. But you can't say, 'She's got an amazing voice,' because people will just say, 'Oh yeah, we've heard that before.' " Yet he *knew* a voice like k.d.'s was rare, and he gambled that it would be hard to miss, even through her zany high jinx and offbeat looks.

Flohil called everybody who was anybody, including record com-

panies and all forms of print and electronic media. It wasn't the kind
of rallying that was usually done for an artist who'd never set foot in
Toronto, but the media hype from out West was so strong that a
number of journalists promised to attend the show sight unseen.
Knowing he'd have to deliver more than just a good performance,
il alerted Wanagas to the possibility of some interviews, asking him
to prepare Kathy for a potential media onslaught. "She should try to
be nice and articulate, but kooky as well," he wrote to the Edmonton
office.

Ultimately, Wanagas and Flohil were hoping to generate interest
among some of Toronto's record labels. With *a truly western experience* doing so well, they imagined a deal with a major company like
Warner Brothers or BMG. If that didn't happen, then at least they
would have greased the wheels for k.d.'s next recording effort. It was
a long shot, but in the end many companies did send representatives
to the initial round of shows—shows that proved k.d. and her band
had grown far beyond the quality of their initial recording.

■

k.d.'s Toronto debut made her a national celebrity, marking another
turning point in her career. The scene was the Brunswick House, a
timeworn tavern at the corner of Brunswick Street and Bloor, just
north of Toronto's Chinatown. Most days, the street-level bar, with its
high ceilings and beer-stained floors, is a haven for rowdy frat boys
and guys shooting pool. Upstairs, in a small narrow room, with a
smattering of tables and a tiny wooden stage, is Albert's Hall, a cozy
nook that holds about 150 people. It wasn't the kind of place that
normally attracted the "Queen Street West" crowd—the punks,
scenesters, musicians, and tastemakers who kept close tabs on the
underground art circuit. Yet these were the people who had heard of
k.d. lang, and when the time came many of them trotted over to Albert's
Hall, gambling on the chance they might be amused. Few went away
disappointed.

The first thing that caught most people's attention was how un-
restrained k.d. was. Unable to confine her energy to the stage, she took
over the entire venue, dancing on the tables, and running circles
around the crowd. Add to that her warped western wear, her Nancy
Sinatra imitation, and her ability to spray sweat on everyone within
ten feet of the stage, and soon she was yanking even the most jaded
Torontonians into the fray.

Liam Lacey was one of the many journalists who'd been tipped off by reports from the West of this wacky, crazy kid who thought she was the reincarnation of Patsy Cline. But looking back on that first Albert's Hall gig, what Lacey recalls most was k.d.'s voice. "I remember her singing '(Write Me) In Care of the Blues,' " he says, humming a few bars until the title comes to him. "I was standing there watching her work up to this one crucial point in the song, and I remember the flash I had at the time, for some reason, was of Janis Joplin. I don't know why, but the way she hit this note, it was sort of like watching someone leap from one apartment building to another—you know, like you see in the movies. You'd just think, 'She's not going to go for this.' And when she did, you could feel the hackles rise, and the hairs go up on the back of your neck. When she hit this note, it was so explosive, I felt tears come to my eyes."

Lacey remembers very few artists in his career who've elicited such a dramatic response, and the next night he dragged his wife to the show. She, in turn, told Stephen Stohn, one of the partners at the entertainment law firm where she was working at the time. It wasn't the first time Stohn, who was soon to become k.d.'s lawyer, had been urged to check out this new sensation. By midweek the reviews of k.d.'s Albert's Hall shows were so strong, lines were forming to get into the club. By Saturday, the lines stretched around the block three hours before show time. The buzz was turning into a roar.

■

A mild, even-keel kind of guy, Stephen Stohn has done quite well for himself as an entertainment lawyer. He's represented many artists over the years, among them Alannah Myles and the Cowboy Junkies. His office, perched atop the Dominion Bank Tower in Toronto's financial district, takes in a wide view of the city's landscape, embodying the kind of comfort that only comes with making lots of money. Yet, for all he's seen and done, his eyes still twinkle when he remembers the fateful chain of events that brought him in contact with k.d. lang, and moreover, how he almost missed her altogether.

"Her first performance was on a Monday night," Stohn recalls, "and the next morning, a friend of mine gave me a call and said, 'Stephen, if you never see another act, you've got to catch this woman country singer.' And I sort of said, 'Okay, it sounds great.' But I wasn't a country music fan, so I didn't do anything.

"Then on Thursday, another old friend who was then a VJ at

MuchMusic called me up and said, 'Stephen, if you never see another act, you have to go over to the Brunswick House and catch this country singer.' So I said, 'Fine. Wonderful.' But I never made it over to the Brunswick House.

"Then on Saturday, Liam Lacey's wife Nancy called at 8:30 *from* the Brunswick House and said, 'Stephen, your house is four doors away from here. If you and your wife aren't over here in five minutes, Liam and I are coming over to break your legs.' So I dutifully trotted over, went upstairs, and there she was, singing the blues."

What Stohn remembers best is a song called "Johnny Get Angry," an old rock'n'roll number that has become a staple of her live show. Although the song is not included on any of her albums, few who've seen it forget k.d.'s performance of this ironic tale of macho men and battered wives in which she taunts, "Johnny get angry, Johnny get mad/ Give me the biggest lecture I've ever had/I want a brave man/I want a cave man . . ." As she sings, she reels behind feigned punches, dramatically tossing her body about the stage. Mid-song she screams, falls flat on her back, and stops—often for sixty seconds or more, while the audience holds their breath in shock—before she finally belts out the final phrases of the song.

"She was throwing herself around and coming within inches of kicking the people at the tables," says Stohn. "It was just the most incredible experience I've ever had, and nothing like what I was expecting."

The following Monday, Stohn was on the horn to the record companies, describing k.d. to his colleagues in almost embarrassingly cliché terms. "I used an expression I'd never used before and have never used since," he recalls. "I said, 'I have seen the future of music, and her name is k.d. lang.' " All this before he'd even met k.d. or Larry Wanagas, yet instinct told him to get moving on the project right away. Sure enough, about two weeks later, Stohn got a call from Larry. "I'd be delighted to represent k.d.," he told Wanagas. In fact, "I've been out there beating the drums already."

■

In the wake of k.d.'s Toronto debut, the triumvirate of Wanagas, Flohil and Stohn worked day and night to keep their artist in the spotlight. Flohil was assigned the task of keeping the media mill churning at the national level, acting as a part-time booking agent on the side. Stohn's job was to focus on getting a record deal. But finding a label that was willing to sign k.d. lang and the reclines would prove far more difficult than Stohn had first imagined, and soon he was hearing the refrain from nearly every A&R scout he spoke to: "We saw her and she's amazing, but we can't do anything with her." The problem was that nobody knew exactly what to call k.d.'s particular brand of music, or how to define her audience, and in a business where audiences are referred to as "markets," and music is gauged by "units sold," this confusion scared them. Nobody disputed that k.d. had a voice that could thaw ice. But they all expressed concern that her music was too country for the pop/rock crowd, and way too weird for legitimate country fans.

Then there was the economic structure of the Canadian music industry, where most labels function merely as subsidiaries of a larger international corporation. "Basically you're talking about Canadian A&R people with multinational record companies," explains Richard Flohil, "who only have a certain amount of power as to what they can do. Yes, they can sign an act for Canada, but unless they can find a believer in the American organization, that's all it is, a Canadian signing." In other words, there's a big difference between an artist who captures a small percentage of the Canadian market and one who captures a small percentage of the American market, and nobody was interested in signing k.d. without marketing commitments from their American counterparts.

Liam Lacey sadly agrees. "If an artist seems intelligent and eccentric, that'll hook the critics," he explains. But the record companies have a different perspective. "What they tend to look for is the kind of corporate rock that can make money on American radio—bands like Loverboy or Bryan Adams. There generally isn't much interest in eccentricity, and with k.d. lang they just didn't see the commercial potential."

There are occasional exceptions to this way of thinking, and they often come in the form of an adventurous A&R person who loves music enough to see beyond the bottom line. David Bendith was one such person. In 1984 he was the new kid in the Toronto office of CBS records, hired specifically to pump some new blood into a roster of artists that included Platinum Blonde and Loverboy. His job was to try new things, discover some new artists and take some risks. Or at least that's what he'd been told.

Bendith had missed k.d.'s Albert's Hall appearance, but received a demo tape of the show from Stohn. A guy who appreciates the little pleasures of life, the CBS executive was immediately intrigued by the names: k.d.'s lowercase lettering, and even the name Larry Wanagas, who sometimes went by Lars. "You don't meet that many Lars Wanagases in the world," he chuckles. "And his company was called Bumstead Records." It's a testimony to the importance of good packaging, but it was the contents of the package that really got him going. From the moment he popped the tape into his stereo, he was riveted but what he described as "this voice from hell." He knew he had to see k.d. right away.

Flohil, meanwhile, was manipulating another bit of good timing. Liam Lacey, who had interviewed k.d. during her first visit to Toronto, was itching to do a "road piece" for the *Globe and Mail,* tagging along with a band on tour and writing about the experience. He didn't really care which band. He just wanted to get a feel for life on the road, which for Canadian artists can sometimes mean up to two days of driving between each low-paying gig. When Flohil heard that Lacey was looking for a band to hook up with, he invited him to join the reclines for an early spring tour, alerting Wanagas to "make room in the van."

■

By the beginning of 1985, Larry Wanagas had invested an estimated $20,000 in his new artist, including his fees as producer on *a truly western experience.* It wasn't an unreasonable sum, considering k.d. was now earning up to $4,000 a week in performance fees—double what she had been making less than a year before. Still, a few more things had to happen, and a cross-Canada concert tour was one of them.

Before Kathy took her band on the road she made a couple of personnel changes, ruffling a few feathers in the process. According to Kathy, Stewart McDougall had to be replaced because he wasn't interested in doing a lot of touring, and Farley Scott because he didn't like playing anything other than straight country music. "In those days the reclines had changing membership according to who she fired," Lacey explains wryly, adding that regardless of what others thought, it was all part of a necessary process. "They were in a situation where the band had been assembled around her fairly quickly, but her reputation was growing so fast that the caliber of musicianship wasn't always keeping up. So she had to keep trading up for better players."

Richard Houghton agrees that Kathy was never one to be satisfied until she got it right. "There's no fat on any of her tours and there's not a lot of screwing around," he says. "Sometimes it takes my breath away the way she's able to move people in and out of her band, and a lot of people might be a little judgmental of that. But those boys knew what their relationship was with her: she was the boss, and they were only around to serve her purpose. They had a good ride, they were well-paid, and some of them went on to other big things. That's how the business works."

In early April, the reclines set out for the wild Canadian yonder, piling into their rented blue Econoline van just in time to watch the prairie thaw as they crossed vast stretches of rural highway. Joining k.d. in the crowded cab were tour manager Neil MacGonigill and veteran band members Gordie Matthews and Dave Bjarnson. Keyboardist Ted Borowiecki and bass player Dennis Marcenko (affectionately nicknamed "Ted Beer and Whiskey" and "Dennis More Drink-O" in honor of traditional rock'n'roll road culture), the two newest members of the reclines, also shared the single mattress in the middle of the van floor. The reclines' sound-and-lighting team drove ahead in a second vehicle—a 22-foot, five-ton truck full of stage equipment. The truck rental and tech salaries weighed in at $1,100/week, which, along with salaries of $300 per week for each band member and $400 per week for MacGonigill brought the estimated cost of the tour to a total of $24,000. Hotels and some meals would be paid by the clubs, along with the band's performance fees.

The band and crew got along well, passing their days listening to Brenda Lee, jazz, and yoga instructional tapes on their Walkmans, eating Indian food, and spending far less time cutting up than one might expect. Spinal Tap they were not, and as Lacey soon found, the reclines were a group of fairly introverted people who spent a lot of time with their instruments. "When we're on the road, we're on the road," k.d. says of her strict work ethic. "Other bands may finish a show and screw their brains out. But when I finish my gig, I sit around, talk to the boys, and go to sleep." Keeping up her strength was important to her, and so was the discipline it required.

Although k.d. was the only woman in the group, Lacey noticed that she fit right in. "She grew up a rural tomboy," he explains, "and she was used to hanging out with guys like this. Her friends were not light and sensitive people." He also found her to be incredibly down-to-earth, an endearing quality he felt was in keeping with her roots. But whether her roots would endear her to the types of crowds she would encounter in the small beer halls of the Canadian outback would remain to be seen. Up to now, k.d.'s success had been the kind that comes with playing lots of gigs on home turf. She had made a big splash in urban areas like Vancouver, where difference is heralded as refreshing. But to take on barloads of farmers and ranchers would put her talent to the test.

The tour kicked off in Saskatoon, Saskatchewan, at a place called the Western Development Museum, and the show was an absolute hit. But as the van rolled farther into the heartland, k.d. soon discovered that not everyone fell in line behind her unique brand of music—at least not at first. Lacey remembers one particularly difficult evening in a place called Kenora, a small town near on the Ontario-Manitoba border. There was only one bar in Kenora, catering to a population that is half native and half weekend jet-setters from Winnipeg. It was the Grill Room, in the Hotel Kenricia, and when rock bands came to town it was transformed into Chez Le Rat.

Enter the reclines. It was a tough crowd, and by the end of the first set there was scattered booing, taunts, and even some name calling. Lacey remembers the scene vividly. "It was one of those dark, bowling-alley-type bars, and the local crowd was there. They were kind of waiting to rock out and it was like 'Who's this chick who looks like a guy?' Even the bar owner seemed incredulous, like 'What on earth is she all about?' There was just this whole antagonism built into what was going on."

After the band's first set, they slunk back to the dressing room, stunned and depressed. When it was time to mount the stage for round two, they dug in their heels, and decided to stick close to their more traditional rock and blues numbers. "The experience was like watching a boxer trapped in a corner, being progressively pummeled into sub-mission," Lacey remarked. It was not a pleasant experience for anyone involved. But in the end, k.d. handled it well, determined to put on a great show and get the public to react to her. After all, these were her people—the same type of folks she and her band had spent their whole lives growing up with.

k.d.'s outlandish approach to her music wasn't something the average rural Canadian easily understood. There were always a few in every audience who responded to her sheer and obvious talent, but a far greater number didn't know what to make of her. Sure, her voice was a marvelous instrument—anyone could see that. But she was different, and unlike the big cities, where her eccentricity was embraced as something exciting and new, the smaller communities often found it alienating.

The band worked exceptionally hard on tour, usually performing three 40-minute sets each night, with 20-minute breaks in between. In the morning they would rise and move on to the next town, performing five or six nights a week, depending on the distance between gigs. They also hawked albums and T-shirts for $10 apiece, which sometimes sold well, but at other times were seen as a joke. At Chez Le Rat, for example, the sole sale was to a guy who purchased a record, only to turn and face his friends as he broke it over his knee. "He paid ten dollars for a record to show how much he hated it," Lacey winces.

Despite a few uncomfortable moments, k.d.'s first national tour gave her a much better understanding of both her audience and her abilities as a performer. In general she remained philosophical about the disappointments that came her way, and did what she could to remain spiritually centered. Being an athlete had given her the ability to understand that she wasn't going to win the prize every time out, and from what Lacey could tell, she worked hard at keeping her emotions on a pretty even keel, primarily by running, eating well, and getting plenty of sleep.

It was also on this tour that k.d. slowly began to realize that she actually enjoyed the challenge of performing for a wide range of people, some of whom might not be initially inclined to like her. "To me, winning over an audience is almost better than playing to fans," she acknowledged a short time later. "It's good that people don't accept me easily. It gives me something to work for." It was something Lacey noticed as well, pointing out that she didn't really hide the fact that she had a certain amount of aggression when it came to her audiences. "One time when we were talking she said she really enjoyed 'conquering' them," he recalls. "And then she said, 'No, I don't want to use that word. What I mean is that I really enjoy *convincing* an audience...'" But Lacey couldn't help but laugh and think, "Maybe she really *does* mean conquering."

■

Lacey's time on the road with k.d. and the reclines resulted in a two-page spread in the *Globe and Mail*'s entertainment section, giving the band a true stamp of authenticity. With it, k.d. lang was well and truly launched, and by the time the tour wound its way back to Toronto for another round of shows at Albert's Hall, the lineups started on

K . D . L A N G

Monday night. This time all the major record companies were there, including a gang from CBS, who David Bendith had dragged along to check out his new discovery.

The band was relieved to be back in the city playing for a crowd that loved them, and Bendith remembers their performance being even better than he had hoped. "At that point, her show was a little bit more of a shtick," he explains. "She wore this dress with fringes on it, her hair was really short and she had these glasses on. She looked like an alien, and she was doing really weird things like getting down on her knees and banging her hands on the ground. But when she wasn't doing that, she was singing."

Bendith wasn't at all worried about how to market k.d. He loved her rockabilly influences, and was convinced that the success of bands like the Stray Cats, Rank and File, and Jason and the Scorchers proved the commercial viability of her act. The trouble was, Bendith's A&R boss wasn't impressed with k.d. Distressed, Bendith went directly to the president of the company, threatening to quit if he couldn't sign the reclines. He was told he could go ahead, but not until he could get his American counterparts involved. Bendith just thought, "Oh, shit." He knew he didn't have much time, since by now several other record companies were having a change of heart and beginning to court k.d., including both Virgin and Island Records. Several smaller Canadian labels had even made offers already. Yet amid all the excitement, the one major label that showed absolutely no interest in k.d. was Warner Brothers—ironic since that's where k.d. would eventually end up.

■

Bob Roper, Warner's A&R man, knew of k.d. long before the other bigwigs in Toronto, and while he thought she was unique, he saw no place for her on the Warner Brothers roster. He first heard her music when Larry Wanagas sent him the band's first single, which Roper admits he found quite remarkable. Still, he too was concerned that such an artist could never be marketed in a way that would make it worth his company's investment, so he sent word back to Wanagas saying thanks but no thanks, encouraging him to keep in touch on how k.d.'s career developed.

The next time Roper heard k.d. it was nearly a year later and she was well on her way to stardom. He caught up with her at a performance in Vancouver, and this time he could barely believe what he was seeing and hearing. "I sat there with my mouth open," he says. "It was an absolutely packed house, and people were up on chairs screaming. She rolled around on the floor, and really played it up— kind of half theater and half singing. It was really stunning." But again, he couldn't see the commercial potential for her. "I guess I didn't have the vision to think of what I could do with this," he confesses in retrospect. "I was afraid, like a lot of A&R people at the time, of signing an act, spending six figures making a record, and then going to my parent company in America and them saying, 'What the hell is this?' "

By now it was clear that any hope k.d. had of landing a major record deal would require doing a show in New York that would win the hearts of the American record labels. The question became, "How do we get into the Bottom Line?"

■

The Bottom Line is a 400-seat nightclub in the heart of New York's Greenwich Village. It serves drinks and light meals, has a superior sound system and not a single bad seat in the house—all of which make it the ideal place for record company executives to hear new bands in what's known in industry parlance as a "showcase." "The story of the Bottom Line is wonderfully designed," Richard Flohil recalls of the way they went about landing the gig.

Unfortunately, nobody working with k.d. had any real contacts at the Bottom Line. Flohil had placed several calls to the club's owner, Allan Pepper, but had been unable to get him on the phone. So he turned to a colleague he knew could be of help. "We called Sam Feldman, who's an agent in Vancouver, and who had an act called Doug and the Slugs," recounts Flohil. "Now for some reason that was beyond anybody's imagination, Doug and the Slugs were huge at the Bottom Line. So I called Sam and said, 'Sam, do me a favor. Call Allan Pepper, and ask him to pick up the phone the next time I call. And if you can, put in a good word about Kathy.' "

With Feldman's help, Flohil finally got through to Pepper, and sent him some press clips and a videocassette. Pepper was impressed, and offered to book the reclines as the third act on a bill called "Local Heroes," a series designed to showcase artists who weren't commercially known, but who had large grassroots followings. He wasn't offering a lot of money, but it was enough to get the band down to New York. After that, it was up to them.

It was then, in the spring of 1985, that luck and coincidence again crossed k.d.'s career path. It started when Bernie Finkelstein, a Toronto-based manager, was having dinner with a writer from *Rolling Stone,* and the talk turned to new artists. The reporter asked Finkelstein what was hot in Canada at the moment, and Finkelstein casually mentioned k.d. Then he called Flohil, letting him know that the seed had been planted and suggesting he follow up on it. Flohil promptly sent a press kit to *Rolling Stone* in Los Angeles, and within a couple of weeks, the magazine phoned to say they'd be sending a reporter to the Bottom Line gig.

To everyone involved it seemed that k.d.'s career was moving with the speed of a turbojet, but its destination was still unknown. Several Canadian record companies tried to sign the artist, but Stohn was holding out, not really impressed with the resources many of these companies were willing to commit. Of the bigger companies, the one that was the most interested was still CBS, but even they didn't seem willing to offer more than a development deal, which meant that they would give k.d. money to go into the studio, but they wouldn't promise to spend any money marketing an album. As is usually the case with a new artist, it wasn't easy for Stohn to turn down the offers being made. Yet he insisted that k.d. hold out for something he felt matched her potential. "There was not the slightest doubt in my mind that this was a major act, on the level of Elvis Presley," he explains earnestly. In his opinion, nothing but a superstar contract would be good enough for his artist, and at that point such an offer had not yet come along.

Stohn doesn't remember k.d. being too worried about what was going on around her. Instead, she maintained a very calm demeanor, as if she just knew that everything would naturally—perhaps karmicly— fall into place. "Kathy just had this sense that she wanted to go out and make the music that she loved, and that wonderful things would result because that was her destiny," he explains rather poetically. "That was her goal, and she allowed her conscious mind to be a flow-through mechanism for the unconscious part of her that was going to make it all happen."

The more time Kathy spent focusing on her music, the more it became obvious to those around her that what drove her was something far less tangible than mere material ambition. Her singing could not be talked about in simple career terms—to her it was a divine calling. "It just *wompph!* hit you like a truck," Stohn says. "When you were talking with her in those days, whatever she said, the details didn't matter. It was never like, 'Yes, I'll play the Bottom Line,' or 'No, I won't play the Bottom Line,' it was just this flow of energy, and it all seemed to lead to the ultimate goal."

On May 2, 1985, k.d. lang had her U.S. debut at the Bottom Line, and as Stohn reports, all the important people were there. Island Records, Virgin, even Warner Brothers had sent representatives, while CBS, thanks to Bendith, filled a whole table right in front of the stage. For k.d., the gig had the potential of being her only chance to win over the heavy hitters, and mid-show, she went in for the kill. "I remember a big bunch of guys sitting at the end of one of those long tables," says Flohil, "and at one point Kathy just said, 'Fuck it. Go for broke.' She ran right out on the table and stood right over these guys, singing and dripping with sweat. And she got 'em! Had them eating out of her hands."

The show garnered k.d. an invitation to return to the Bottom Line the following month. Better yet, the CBS executives were falling all over themselves to get a meeting with Stohn and Wanagas. They were hoping to convene the very next day, but Kathy had to leave to continue the rest of her tour. So the Canadians agreed to return in three weeks.

When k.d., Stohn, and Wanagas returned to New York, they did it at their own expense, so as not to feel any obligation to CBS. At the CBS offices, they met several people, including a producer who had worked with Cyndi Lauper. Everyone seemed excited and talked of a fairly high-budget album. But it was still being presented as a development deal, and no firm offer was made. After a forty-five minute meeting, they all shook hands, and the visitors were shown to the door. It was then that k.d. announced she would never sign with CBS.

As Stohn explains, k.d.'s decision was hardly based on any sort of rational business concerns, but rather, an intuitive feeling she had about the way they were being treated. "The meeting had been scheduled for twelve-thirty," he recalls. "Now, being from Canada, we hadn't been infected by the New York mentality of time. So here we were, having flown at our own expense quite a distance, and you sort of think when you're having a meeting at twelve-thirty in the afternoon, when it's over you might be invited out for a piece of lettuce, maybe a carrot, or a glass of water or something. You know, some kind of lunch." Stohn wasn't clear if the lack of hospitality meant that CBS wasn't interested, or whether the people were just too bound up in their schedules to take a break. But when Kathy came out of the meeting, her mind was made up.

Stohn tried to be calm, urging his client not to be too hasty, but it was to no avail. "We went across the street to some delicatessen, and as we talked about the whole thing. I was feebly trying to say, 'Let's not be too rash here,' " he says. "They were talking about a fair number of dollars—I think it was around $200,000, which in those days was a fair amount. But I can recall Kathy being very firm that this had not gone the way she had wanted it, and she just did not feel comfortable with it. I think Larry, too, wanted to be able to step back and look at it rationally, but more than that we all just really wanted to support k.d."

Stohn and Wanagas both knew that when Kathy felt *that* strongly about something, it was best to follow her lead. "The thing about Kathy was her directness, and her belief—which she expressed a little in her thing about the reincarnation of Patsy Cline—that she was merely a physical embodiment through which this music was happening. She had a tremendously unshakable belief—whether you call it the collective unconscious, a fourth dimension, a greater universe, or a god, and she believed it so strongly, and spoke with such conviction, that it was hard not to get caught up in it. She had been proven right so often, that you just had to carry on and say, 'Okay, logic is not necessarily the be-all and the end-all. Let's go with the flow on this.' "

Sure enough, it wasn't long after their meeting at CBS that the head of Sire Records, a subsidiary of Warner Brothers, fell in love with k.d. lang and the reclines.

■

Seymour Stein is part of a dying breed, one of last of the old-school music men in a business that has become increasingly corporate. A passion for music courses through his blood, and his good taste and acute foresight have built him a small empire over the years. He has signed artists who've defined one musical era after another, from the Ramones and the Talking Heads to the Smiths, Depeche Mode, and the Pretenders—not to mention Madonna.

When Stein received the package containing *a truly western experience,* he wasn't quite sure what to make of it. The picture, he says, looked like Buddy Holly in drag, but he immediately loved the music, and after hearing reports about k.d.'s Bottom Line gig, he was on the phone to Canada. "All of a sudden," says Warner's Bob Roper, "we were getting calls from Seymour and the Sire people saying, 'Listen, we hear this woman has a really interesting voice. Have you seen her?' And knowing that he had the finances and the resources to take on a project with a wing and a prayer, I said, 'Yeah, Seymour, and you have to see it. There's nothing I can tell you. You just have to see it first-hand.'" Roper knew that Stein had a penchant for quirky acts, and that he would go *anywhere* to sign the right artist. The next thing he knew, the guy was flying from London to Edmonton to see her perform.

When Stein arrived in Edmonton he was operating on very little sleep, having been up all night on his transatlantic flight. But his enthusiasm for what he saw on stage that night gave him one last burst of energy. Roper was there, too, and reports that Stein literally got up out of his seat, went to the front of the house, danced with k.d. for a couple of minutes, and returned to his seat saying, "I'm going to sign her." Then he sat down in his chair and fell asleep.

When the band finished playing, Roper saw Larry Wanagas making his way over to their table, and sensed a minor disaster about to occur. "I kept giving Seymour a really sharp elbow and saying, 'C'mon, wake up. You're going to be the height of embarrassment here if the manager comes over and you're sound asleep at the end of the set.'" Roper finally got Stein onto his feet, bundled him up, introduced him around, and sent him off to the hotel. The next morning Wanagas dropped by the hotel and took Stein out for a drive.

■

It had been just over a year since k.d. lang and the reclines had recorded their first homemade album, and the grueling exercise of trying to land a record deal was finally starting to wear Kathy down. She found a lot of stress in the process of trying to figure out who would be the best company and what they were going to do with her. Worse still was the simple prospect of becoming a commercial act, and what that would mean in terms of her artistic freedom.

Thankfully, when k.d. returned to the Bottom Line at the end of June, Stein stepped in and put an end to her worries. After the show, he followed a gang of well-wishers backstage to find a sweaty, breathless lang slumped on a tattered couch. She looked up, obviously exhausted, to find him grinning from ear to ear. "Do you know 'Ballad

of a Teenage Queen,' by Johnny Cash, and 'She's No Angel,' by Kitty
Wells?" asked Stein, showing off his legendary knowledge of pop's hit
parade. "Or how about Alberta Slim?"

"That's Montana Slim," k.d. shot back. "In Canada we call him
Wilf Carter."

"You're what country music would've been if Nashville hadn't
screwed it up," Stein beamed. Impressed, k.d. took an immediate liking
to him.

For Stephen Stohn, Stein was just the type of visionary k.d. needed
to cultivate her talent. "The man is brilliant," he says matter-of-factly.
Stein had a reputation for finding innovative people, and not expecting
huge sales, but working with people as artists. Yes, he had Madonna
on his label, and yes, it gave his company a certain flagship status. But
what really impressed Stohn and Wanagas were the other acts he was
working with, and the relationships he developed with his artists.

The difficulty, if there was going to be one, was that k.d. and the
reclines were just about to leave for Japan, where they would spend
nearly a month as part of the Canadian contingent of Expo '85. Nobody
wanted to wait until she returned to sign the deal, so Stohn, Wanagas,
and Stein immediately sat down to settle on a concrete offer. Then,
with six days left until k.d.'s departure, Stohn and Stein's lawyer ham-
mered out a contract.

Normally, negotiating a serious recording contract can easily take
three to six months. But as luck would have it, the lawyers involved
hit it off right away. Skipping all the usual back and forth that usually
goes into the process, Stohn laid out his artist's demands in straightforward terms: he wanted the first draft of the contract to be written
in superstar language, and if he liked it, he promised not to play
hardball on the particulars. It worked, and by Saturday morning, just
one day before k.d. was to leave for Tokyo, the entire group—Stohn,
Wanagas, Stein, and his lawyer—sat down with k.d. to review a document that most agree was one of the finest contracts ever negotiated,
promising k.d. the time, money, and promotional resources to make
at least three albums. With that they parted ways, agreeing to conduct
the actual signing of the contract on a party boat that evening, where
k.d. and the reclines were scheduled to perform one last time before
leaving the country. The scene that unfolded that cool summer evening
as the "Boating with Bud" party boat cruised Vancouver Sound is the
kind of thing legends are made of. Everybody was there, including a
host of k.d.'s friends and family, and a significant number of journalists.

But the secret still had not been revealed that k.d. was about to sign a record deal. At midnight, the interested parties climbed the steps to the captain's cabin, pens at the ready, and the ceremonious process began.

"We'd had this vision that we'd just sit down at a table and do a normal signing," says Stohn, "but we couldn't have the lights on, because that would have blinded the pilot. So we all got down on our hands and knees on this corrugated floor, someone held a flashlight, and everyone began signing the contract."

The last thing Stohn remembers about the evening was how radiant k.d. was as she gathered her family and friends around her. She had dreamed all her life of being a star, and now it looked like she was on her way. "I walked down the pier and looked back to wave, and I remember her standing up on the deck of the boat, all alone. The lights of the boat were shining down on her like the lights on the castle at Disneyland. She just stood there, looking around and soaking it all in."

5

"Fame is just a by-product of what I want to do,
which is sing."

BY the fall of 1985, k.d. lang had become Canada's newest national
hero. Within a three-month period she had toured Japan with the
reclines as part of Expo '85, performed with the Edmonton Symphony
Orchestra, and won her first Juno Award—the Canadian equivalent of

a Grammy. She had appeared in *Rolling Stone,* been reviewed in New
York's *Village Voice,* and made her U.S. television debut on "Late Night
with David Letterman"—all *prior* to recording her first Sire album. In
Edmonton, one of the local Honda dealers gave her a new motorcycle
in exchange for posing in an ad, and soon her face was plastered on
billboards all over town.

The speed with which Kathy's star had risen may have astonished
some people, but it didn't surprise Kathy one bit. "I've always known
this would happen," she boldly told more than one journalist. "Like
some people who always knew they would grow up to be a teacher
someday, I've always known I'd be a well-known performer." Fame,
however, was a mixed blessing, as Kathy soon found out. Sure, she
was thrilled to be onstage singing her heart out every night. It was
where she belonged, where she felt most comfortable, and what she
had dreamed of all her life. But with her newfound popularity came
more attention than she had ever imagined, and soon she found her
entire life being thrust into the spotlight.

At home in Edmonton, she could barely step out of her house

without being mobbed by fans. "I would try to take her out to clubs, and she didn't want to go, because she said there would be too many people there who would bother her," her friend Lin Elder recalls. "Even quite early in her career she was very concerned about that. I remember we went Christmas shopping, and here we were, carrying our bags through West Edmonton Mall, and kids were stopping her, and parents were stopping her, and there I was just twiddling my thumbs, like 'Come on, we've got a lot of shopping to do.' But people were on her, even then, and it drove her quite nuts, I think."

Flohil, too, remembers Kathy being rather distressed by all the fanfare. "I remember one time at a festival somewhere, sitting in her room with her, and she just turned and said, 'You know, I just really think this thing is gonna go crazy on me,' " he recalls. "And all I could say was, 'Kathy, don't believe your press clippings. You're a human being. Stay grounded.' " According to Flohil, the problem had nothing to do with bad reviews, since at that time there were no bad reviews. What concerned her was the adulation, the autographs, and the endless attention. She wanted to be famous, and she was focused on it, but with it came issues she wasn't sure she could handle, and she worried about the impact fame would have on her ego.

The media was hopelessly in love with k.d., which was no surprise to Denise Donlon, director of music programming at MuchMusic. "When a new artist bursts on the scene who has put together an independent product, who's great to look at, who's over the top in terms of excitement and enthusiasm, is alternative to the 'nth' degree, and is completely and refreshingly something that you've never seen before in your life, how can you help but not get behind it?" she asks rhetorically. "She had it all." It was true: k.d. was smart, personable, passionate, and talented, all important ingredients when it comes to making a star. Yet she wasn't at all accustomed to dealing with the press, and that alone brought a fair amount of trauma.

Part of what made it difficult for Kathy to play the part of a media darling was that she was practically making herself up as she went along. Her act walked a thin line between music and performance, comedy and passion, acting and real life, and she had yet to figure out exactly where Kathy ended and k.d. began. "Initially, she thought it was fun," explains Flohil. "Yes it was a put-on, and yes it was tongue-in-cheek. But at the same time, underneath the razzle-dazzle and the fun and games was the real thing. I can think of a couple of other artists who I equate in the same way, like Leon Redbone or Tiny Tim.

Yes, there's all the crap and shtick, but deep down, Tiny Tim loves that ghastly 'Tiptoe Through the Tulips' pop music." And k.d. loved that country music.

Consequently, journalists were always surprised to find that the character they saw onstage was very different from the woman they met when it came time to do interviews. One writer remarked in an article that, in contrast to her dynamic, free-spirited performance, the artist herself was subdued, sullen, and almost humorless. k.d. responded to such observations by explaining that she had become withdrawn as a result of her fame, saying that before she started performing she was extroverted, but now she had to conserve her energy, opting for anonymity during the day in order to shine at night.

She also began to understand that keeping Kathy separate from k.d. might be a way for her to maintain some semblance of sanity, as she struggled to keep fame from intruding too heavily on her personal life. She began to think more about how she dressed, careful to leave the flamboyancy of her country-punk outfits in the dressing room when she wasn't onstage. And to a certain degree, she began to retreat into herself.

As her publicist, Richard Flohil tried to make her interaction with the media as tolerable as possible. Because she wasn't good at interviews and didn't like doing them, he made a point of talking to media people before they talked to her, trying his best to help them understand their subject a little better. Sometimes this worked, and when the chemistry was right between k.d. and the interviewer, she often displayed a guilelessness that was naively sincere, blurting out even the most personal details of her life. But her openness and honesty worked as a double-edged sword, and when she was tired, troubled, or simply fed up with the situation at hand, she had the ability to seem snotty, aloof, or even downright arrogant. Although some of this has remained an integral part of k.d.'s personality over the years, she eventually learned to keep her moodiness more or less in check, at least where the media was concerned. But in the beginning, Kathy often put her publicist's patience to the test.

For example, Flohil cringes when he recalls the day he watched k.d. snub one of the most influential media personalities in all of Canada. "Larry and I and Kathy were up at the CBC doing some interview," he explains. "We had just finished, and were standing in the corridor, when suddenly, here comes Peter Gzowski. So I did my thing and said, 'Hi Peter. By the way, this is k.d. lang.' He looked at her, and shook her hand perfunctorily. Then she turned and walked away." Wanagas and Flohil were stunned. "Kathy was in one of her 'I don't want to meet another media person and I don't give a fuck who he is' moods," he says with a smirk. "And here was potentially the most important media person in the country. He was already supportive, and she just cut him dead. It was embarrassing."

k.d. later went on to do some marvelous interviews with Gzowski, and the two seemed to get along fine. But it didn't change the fact that where the media was concerned, she had a bit of an attitude problem, as she found herself torn between the requirements of her job and her need to be left alone. Liam Lacey, who came to witness many facets of Kathy's personality over the years, thinks that part of her reticence came from a very real need to isolate herself in order to concentrate on her work. But he also thought it had something to do her age. "When she wants to, Kathy can charm *anyone,*" he says emphatically. "But she sometimes gets sort of stubborn, and at that time I think it was partly just this teenage thing about her. You know, like, 'I'll be cool, 'cause that way I won't be rejected.' "

There are those who thought Kathy's detachment signaled something far more serious, and that perhaps she harbored some deep dark secret that was weighing on her mind. It was something Paul McGrath, a senior arts reporter for CBC television, noticed the first time he met her. "I remember someone from her record company leading me into the hotel room where we were to do the interview, and k.d. was sitting on the windowsill with the windows open, just staring out," he recalls. "When she looked over at me, she didn't really change expression. She seemed very weary that day, and I thought she seemed oppressed somehow—very out of sorts."

It could just be that McGrath was taken aback by the fact that in person k.d. lacked the kinetic energy he saw in her performance. But he insists there was more to it than that. "It has struck me since that she carries something around inside of her, and that there is a bit of a dark side to her," he says. "She wasn't being unpleasant to me by any means, but she was a little reserved, and a little dour. Maybe a little sad." McGrath won't speculate as to what might have been troubling k.d. But he claims it's been with her nearly every time they've met.

In particular, he remembers running into k.d. at the Juno Awards a few years later. It was right after Roy Orbison had died, and she was rehearsing "Crying" for the show that evening. After she finished the song, he tried to approach her to tell her how wonderful she sounded. But he sensed something was amiss. "She was backstage, behind the curtain, and I wanted to go back and say, 'Fabulous,' " he explains. "But it was like there was a force field around her. When I got about ten feet from her I just went *boom!* It stopped me dead. She was so inside herself at that point, in such a dark way—maybe thinking about Roy, or maybe the song meant something to her and one of her lovers. Who knows. But it was just so clear: Stay the fuck away. Don't try to talk to her. Even if you only want to say, 'You were fabulous,' just don't do it. It was a feeling that was inescapable."

Percy Adlon, the German director who would later spend several months working on a film with k.d., has an entirely different interpretation of what makes the artist tick, and says that if she sometimes seems unapproachable, it's because she simply doesn't care for superficiality. "k.d. has the wisdom of someone who grew up with nature," he observes. "She knows exactly what is false and what is true, and this is found in the way she speaks. She will not respond when she has nothing to say. Sometimes she's very short, and doesn't really answer, but this is because there's never any small talk with k.d. When it comes to important talk, she talks plenty."

To the extent that k.d.'s interactions reveal any sort of arrogance, Adlon just doesn't see how it could be otherwise. "She thinks very highly of herself," he explains. "She has a very, very high opinion of her qualities and her talents, and she *is* almost arrogant in this way. But the arrogance does not come from the surface, from a success that is just a success. The arrogance comes from her talent of knowing what quality is."

Another thing that made it hard for Kathy to deal with so much attention in the beginning was the fact that, in her own way, Kathy was a bit of a loner. "She was a very 'to herself' type of person when I knew her," says Lin Elder, reflecting back on the time they spent together. "Part of that is the confidence thing. I found her very strong, but it was also very strange that she would be so happy just being by herself." Elder remembers that Kathy spent an inordinate amount of time with nobody but her dog, who she took with her everywhere she went. This impressed Elder, as if it was a reflection of k.d.'s strength.

Yet she concedes that what impressed her the most about Kathy— her supreme self-confidence and the fact that she didn't ever seem to need anyone—might have also left the artist feeling a little lonely. "She once said something to me that has never left me," Elder says thoughtfully. "She told me that I would never be alone, but that I would always be lonely. And I thought, gee, that's a nice thing to say. But in a sense it's become very true, and I always wondered if she said it because that's the way she is too. She's surrounded by a lot of people, but I think in some ways she's lonely."

In terms of the day-to-day grind, k.d.'s biggest dilemma vis-à-vis the press seemed to be all the hype around her connection to Patsy Cline. "You may think Patsy Cline died in a plane crash in 1963, but she's living right here in my merry body, I tell ya," she used to announce during her shows. It was a wonderful hook, and in the beginning, it gave her a lot of notoriety. But after a while, k.d. started to worry that the Patsy Cline story was being misinterpreted, as if it were a joke. She became uneasy with the way her spirituality was being represented in the media, and where she had once brazenly referred to Patsy Cline in all of her publicity materials, by 1985 it was as if she wished she'd never mentioned the dead country star.

Unfortunately, the more she backpedaled on the Patsy Cline story, the more insincere it made her seem. And while on the one hand, she seemed annoyed when journalists wanted to discuss Patsy Cline, she couldn't disown the story without making it seem as if she had made the whole thing up. Lacey remembers one particular interview where she seemed to want to downplay the Cline connection, only to flip-flop again once the story appeared in print. "We had passed over the Patsy Cline thing because I didn't really get it," he recalls. But when Cline's name came up later in the discussion and k.d. grew defensive, Lacey called her on her apparent consternation, pointing out that it was *she* who had encouraged it in the first place. "Well, if some asshole interviewer asks me, 'Are you really the reincarnation of Patsy Cline?' of course I'm going to say yes," she snapped at him. Lacey asked k.d. if he could change "asshole" to "idiot," and proceeded to include the comment in the article he wrote. She complained to him later, saying, "Now everyone thinks I don't believe it."

"The funny thing is, she would get really irritated and snotty about it when some local DJ in some little town in Saskatchewan would ask her about it," says Lacey. "Like, 'Oh, can't they think of anything better to ask?' And I was sitting there scratching my head, thinking, 'Well, *you're* the one who keeps saying it.' "

Few thought k.d. would make up such a story simply for publicity purposes. On the other hand, there weren't many who thought she really believed herself to *be* the reincarnation of Patsy Cline, especially since Cline had died a good eighteen months after Kathy was born. "I think she was just speaking in a rather humorous metaphor," offers Paul McGrath. "I think if you said, 'Now do you *really* think you're the physical reincarnation of Patsy Cline?' she'd say, 'No, but you know what I'm talking about.' She did have the spirit of Patsy Cline in her. That, and a whole bunch of others. You have to give her some credit for having wit, and if a bunch of bozos at news desks around the country want to make her responsible for the literalness of it, well, fuck 'em."

It was a good lesson for Kathy to learn the weight and power of what she said to the press. "Fortunately or unfortunately, depending on how you looked at it, you become a product of what you create," says Denise Donlon, waxing philosophical. "Yeah, I think she felt a spiritual connection to Patsy Cline at the time, and I don't think she would have said so dishonestly. But then the media started to own it, and that's where she started to disown it."

Interestingly enough, it took a conversation with Larry Wanagas's wife, Cheryl, before Lacey finally felt he understood the situation. He was discussing the dilemma with her one day when she turned to him and said, "You know, I don't even think k.d. knew what reincarnation really meant." According to Lacey, Cheryl told him that she had given k.d. a copy of a Shirley MacLaine book with certain passages about reincarnation underlined, and shortly after reading it, she stopped using the term "reincarnation" and started referring instead to "a strong psychic connection." She also came to the conclusion that maybe people weren't ready to accept her sense of spirituality.

"At one point I felt very strongly about letting people know how I felt about my personal beliefs," she told a British journalist. "But North Americans aren't really that open-minded when it comes to things like reincarnation." Especially the North Americans she would soon be encountering in Nashville—people who had known and loved Patsy Cline on a very personal level.

■

On November 4, 1985, just as she was preparing to head into the studio to record her first record for Sire, k.d. found yet another excuse to make national headlines. She won a Juno Award for Most Promising Artist of the Year, and accepted the award in a wedding dress, getting her photo into every major newspaper in Canada. The joke was that weddings were meant to be full of promise, and she accepted the award by making a few promises of her own, including the promise that she would "continue to sing for only the right reasons."

On the surface, it seemed like k.d. lang was hamming it up again, and in a sense she was. "I was so excited to put on that wedding dress," she later teased Denise Donlon, "because I knew that was the only time in my life when I would be wearing one." But she also meant what she said, and people knew it, even then. "The moment she uttered those words—'I will continue to sing for only the right reasons'—a hush went through the crowd," recalls Paul McGrath vividly. "These were all people who have spent every day of their lives compromising, because that's what the music business is about. And here was some-body with a very clear vision, who was not going to compromise it in any way. It was a magnificent speech—a chilling moment almost, because you could sense that here was an attitude that was very rare in the business. Here was somebody who had almost a sacred trust with music, and who was not going to abuse it. Someone who believed in it, in all its depth and complexity, and was going to try to convey that in her work. And I'd say that 50 percent of the crowd said, 'Yeah!' and the other 50 percent of the crowd said, 'Uh-oh, this chick's gonna be trouble.' "

■

k.d.'s trip to Japan was three jam-packed weeks of festivities, including a concert and tour of the Yamaha instrument factory and a performance in a 1,000-year-old Buddhist temple. More importantly, it was in Japan that she met Ben Mink, a violinist who would become her songwriting partner, musical arranger, and long-term friend. At the time, Mink was part of Cano, another band on the Expo '85 tour, and a well-respected musician in his own right, known primarily for his work with artists like Bruce Cockburn and the progressive rock band FM. Ben and k.d. hit it off right away, and soon k.d. discovered something very significant and personal about Mink that simply delighted her. Harbored deep within the bowels of his electric fiddle lived a tiny plastic world, filled with miniature toys held together by glue and a lot of love and care. It reminded k.d. of the farm scenes that decorated her apartment back in Edmonton.

Once they were back in Canada, k.d. and Mink decided they would like to try working together, and soon Mink had become an official member of the reclines. According to Gordie Matthews, an original recline who was k.d.'s guitarist off and on for over six years, Mink was recruited primarily for his songwriting capabilities, which had always been a weak spot for k.d. She was known to procrastinate, and even confessed that when it came to writing, every song was a struggle. Mink, on the other hand, was brimming with ideas of what he could do with k.d.'s voice, and had even sent her a tape containing a couple of songs he had written. The songs sounded good, and with a new album just around the corner, and pressure from the record company to develop stronger material, Mink was assigned the job of playing guide to k.d.'s muse.

"She needed someone to help move her along," says Matthews. "She wasn't much of a writer at the time, and if there was ever a problem in the beginning, it was a shortage of original stuff. Ben Mink had a lot of experience with home recording, and with recording in general, and because of his musical background, he had a lot of options to throw at her."

Looking back, some might say that Ben Mink has been as responsible for k.d.'s success as the singer herself. She calls him her "other half," claiming that it is he who fills in where her talents fall short. He returns the compliments, calling her voice "a freak of nature," and he makes it his business to push her, challenge her, and give her creative support. From their very first album together, he urged her to reach beyond Patsy Cline toward her own personal style. "Ben pointed out something that hit home in a significant way," says k.d. "He said that Patsy and Owen Bradley didn't try to re-create. They tried to create. They were doing something new." But even with Mink as a permanent part of k.d's band, international success wasn't going to happen overnight.

■

In the winter of 1986, k.d., Larry Wanagas, and Sire's A&R executives set out for uncharted waters, their mission to turn a high-spirited, androgynous-looking country punk into a sustainable and perhaps even profitable artist.

The first step was to find a producer who could understand k.d.'s unique brand of western swing, rockabilly, and sultry balladeering, and translate it successfully in the studio. They considered Chris Thomas, known for his work with the Pretenders and Elton John, and also T-Bone Burnett. k.d. wanted Burnett or Elvis Costello. But at the top of Sire's list was Dave Edmunds, a guitarist whose own band, Rockpile, represented a funky and popular blend of British new wave and roots rock. In addition, Edmunds's work with artists like Johnny Cash, Carl Perkins, and the Everly Brothers gave him a credibility in the country music community they hoped would help k.d. break into country radio. The only problem was that Edmunds wasn't interested in doing the album.

"Choosing Dave Edmunds was not fun," recalls Flohil. "He was on a list of people they wanted, and basically, from conversations I recall, he had passed on the project completely." Eventually, Edmunds was persuaded to reconsider after a friend in the industry phoned him on k.d.'s behalf, and soon the band was on its way to England to record *Angel With A Lariat.*

The finished album confirmed what had been everyone's worse nightmare: that Edmunds, who had never seen k.d. live, didn't really understand where she was coming from. Her voice, which was meant to be the primary focus, he buried deep in the mix, rendering it barely audible on a couple of the tracks. And the souped-up, almost Abba-esque sound of some of the lighter songs was completely out of character for her. In short, he had absolutely failed to capture what they were looking for.

At first k.d. tried to remain enthusiastic about the record, and when asked by the press what it was like to work with Edmunds, she stuck to vague comments about how he had "given them lots of room." Others who knew the story were less polite. Mink, for example, made no bones about the fact that he found Edmunds to be thoroughly unimaginative, and mocked the fact that he didn't share their ideas of record making, which involved k.d.'s use of a hand-held mike in order to re-create the energy of her live performances. He also complained— perhaps a bit snobbishly—that nobody in England understood country music, and that their technology was not up to snuff. "It's a European country and the standard of living is a lot lower," he scoffed. "Technically they were far below our standards."

There are two sides to every story, of course, and as she later confessed, k.d. wasn't always the easiest person to work with, either. "Part of it was that Edmunds didn't understand what I was doing, and I was just so hyper and enthusiastic and overly emotional," she says, "I fought everything he said, whether it was right or wrong. I just wanted to be a big star right away."

"I don't think they really hit it off," says Gordie Matthews, looking back on the tension between Edmunds and k.d. "The guy was doing wonderful things at the time, and did well with a lot of other artists.

But it just wasn't a good match." Matthews also points out that because the band didn't have a lot of songs to choose from at the time, it made the job of producing an album a little harder.

In lieu of strong new material, k.d. had hoped to fall back on some old stuff, and had set her mind on rerecording "Pine and Stew," her favorite song from the previous album. But Edmunds didn't like the song. "He didn't think it was a good idea to include that song on the album," Matthews continued, "and you know, that's sort of a producer's call. But there was a lot of tension, and when he said he didn't think they should do that particular song, she got really mad and said, 'Well I guess I'm producing this track,' and went and sat in his chair."

Aggravating matters was that Edmunds seemed to have a very lackadaisical approach to the project, taking his time while the reclines were chomping at the bit. "Dave didn't start until two in the afternoon, and he didn't work weekends," Matthews recalls, "so we ended up doing a lot of waiting around." Then, when k.d. tried to take more control over the situation, Edmunds took issue with the fact that she was pushing him too hard. "I don't know why she's so uptight. It's only her first record," Matthews remembers him saying one day, to which she responded incredulously, "What do you mean? It's my *first record*."

Eventually, k.d. gave up the charade of pretending to be pleased with the album. "I wasn't too happy with Dave," she finally blurted out in an interview a few months after the album had come out. But she did concede that some learning took place as she worked on *Angel With A Lariat*. For one thing, Edmunds generally insisted on using first takes, a technique k.d. appreciated and would experiment with more on future albums to capture the energy and spontaneity of the performance. Also, the fact that Edmunds didn't seem to be in control meant that k.d. got more involved in the production. "If someone could convince me that Dave Edmunds's strategy was to get me wound up so I'd get involved in my album, then I'd say he was a great producer," she said sarcastically. "But I'm not convinced that was his strategy."

Looking back on that first big-budget album, Stephen Stohn has mixed feelings about what went on. He knew that Sire's decision to hire a well-known producer was meant to lend a stamp of credibility to the record. But in a way, forcing a match between Edmunds and k.d. revealed a lack of confidence on Sire's part, not to mention a tremendous waste of resources. "Is it right to take any artist and put a big-name producer with that artist?" he asks rhetorically. "It's a trap I see happening over and over again. You take a young artist who seems to show a lot of promise, you get a big-name producer who costs a lot of money, and then the record doesn't come up to people's expectations."

"The album stiffed," says Liam Lacey bluntly. In hindsight, *Angel With A Lariat* isn't a bad collection of music. It's just that there'd already been so much hype about k.d. by the time it came out—and so many people who had seen her live show and knew what she was capable of—that the album was a disappointment, and several music critics said so. "Lang is all over the place," wrote Jimmy Guterman in *Spin,* adding that many of the songs sounded "forced, as if the songs were built for a slower tempo and the reclines thought that the only way to put across a questionable tune was to play it as fast as possible." It was criticism not only of the album's production, but of the material itself.

Most critics were kind, though, noting that lots of artists don't do well the first time they go into the studio. And as Lacey points out, it wasn't really fair to expect k.d. to be an overnight success. "People forget that Bruce Springsteen did six records before he became a megastar," he says. "I think k.d.'s intelligent enough that she doesn't have to sit around thinking, 'I've got to come up with a hit record.' Since she's on Sire, Madonna can pay for her." The truth of the statement makes him smile.

Nevertheless, the lukewarm reception that greeted *Angel* was jolting for an artist who'd never received a bad review in her life. "I die when people criticize me," k.d. later confessed. "I totally fall apart." It was then that she learned another valuable lesson in surviving the sometimes fickle pen of music criticism: she stopped reading her reviews.

■

Even before *Angel With A Lariat* was shipped to critics, Sire had to come up with a plan on how to present the record to radio programmers and at the retail level. The big question was whether or not the record was going to be accepted by a traditional country crowd, or whether Sire's marketers should stick to the alternative-rock and pop outlets. Nick Hunter, who was the senior VP in charge of sales and promotion for Warner Brothers' Nashville office, remembers the first time he heard k.d. lang and the reclines, and the brief discussion that ensued. "I was in the Burbank office," he recalls, "and Charlie Springer, who was the VP of national sales, called me up and said, 'C'mon down here, I want you to hear something.' So I went in, and they played me 'Rose Garden.' And I loved it. So I said, 'Yeah, we'll put it out as country.' " He pauses for a moment before adding, "I don't know what they would have done if I'd said, 'No, that's not a country record.' It's not like one person's say-so should determine the whole thing, but sometimes that's the case."

On April 11, 1987, *Angel With A Lariat* debuted at No. 68 on Billboard's Top Country Albums chart. It peaked at No. 56, with a total chart run of 10 weeks—not great, but probably a lot better than anyone could have hoped for, given that none of the songs on the album got any radio play whatsoever.

Why Sire chose k.d.'s remake of Lyn Anderson's "Rose Garden" as the first single, after making such a big deal about the band needing more original material, can only be attributed to the weakness of the other cuts—or Sire's inability to see a market for them. "It was always *the* question and it continues to be *the* question," says Stohn of the ongoing problems that arise in trying to classify k.d.'s music. "I'm not sure that Sire, when they first signed her and put out the first album . . . well, let's just say that there was always a tug back and forth. Was this a country artist, or was this an alternative artist? There was a sense that it was country, but a very different kind of country, and if it worked, it would change the way people thought of country music." It was an inevitable dilemma for such a uniquely talented artist, making the round peg of creativity fit into the square hole of the music industry.

■

Once *Angel With A Lariat* was out, k.d. lang and the reclines were back on the road, touring the United States, Canada, and England as an opening act for Dwight Yoakam. It's customary for artists to tour when they've got a new album to sell, but in k.d.'s case it was imperative that people experience the exhilaration of one of her live shows. If her album wouldn't make her a star, her performances certainly would. And sure enough, she was soon back in the media spotlight.

"If Patsy Cline and Elvis Presley had conceived a daughter, her name would probably be k.d. lang," wrote Gerry Wood in *Billboard* on September 26, 1987. Others hailed her as country music's answer to Cyndi Lauper, hearing influences that ranged from Loretta Lynn to

Malcolm McClaren. She debuted on "The Tonight Show" in May—just after the album had come out—and Carson was so intrigued by her that he had her back three times that first year. "Carson just fell in love with her," reports Flohil. "He would always give her two or three cameras, plus let her bring her own band." Not only that, but it gave her the perfect opportunity to hone her wry sense of humor in front of the camera.

Nobody at Sire minded that k.d. enjoyed being such a cutup, but after a while both she and her advisers started worrying that her image was stealing attention away from her musical talents. Even before *Angel With A Lariat* came out, she had decided to ditched her lens-less glasses, a significant move marking the first step toward blurring the line that separated k.d. lang from Kathy.

Wanagas wasn't sure what to think of this new direction. Part of him questioned the wisdom of making changes in something that had already proven successful. He knew that k.d. could seduce almost any audience with her wit and charm. But Kathy wanted to be known first and foremost as a singer, and she began to feel that her goofy props were getting in the way. "The wacky, crazy, kinetic k.d. lang began to override the music," she explained when asked about the change. "My voice was playing second fiddle and I didn't want that to happen."

Some people, particularly the folks back home, worried that k.d. lang was selling out, an allegation she firmly denied. "I've already been criticized," she told a Canadian journalist. "They think I've lost my edge, but I think the edge is just my short hair and the glasses and doing novelty songs. That's where I was then, and now that I'm taking my music more seriously and buying newer clothes, they're telling me I've lost my edge. Well, it's still there. It's just not as blatant as it was before."

The fact that k.d. was now playing much larger venues also required that she make a few changes to her show, and the dance contests were the first to go. But not before she caused quite a commotion at a gig in Toronto. "She was performing at Ontario Place, which is a theater-in-the-round, and which has very uptight security," explains Richard Flohil gleefully as he remembers the scene that night. "Don't get up, don't cheer, don't stand, don't do anything, ya know?" About halfway through the show, as she had been doing for years, k.d. stopped the music and announced that it was time for the dance contest. It was then that all hell broke loose.

"First she made them stop the stage from rotating, which confused the hell out of them," Flohil chuckles. "Then she said, 'Okay, everybody up,' and the guards in their little red uniforms were like 'Ahhhggg,' as hoards of people hit the stage. Everyone was up dancing, the band was playing, and it was just hilarious. Then, at the end of the number Kathy said, 'Okay, that's it.' And what really amazed those Nazis on staff was that everybody went back to their seats, just like that. But the next year it was in the contract: 'No dance contests on stage.' "

Beyond the rules and regulations of the larger theaters and concert halls, the nature of moving from a bar environment to a venue where several thousand people sit passively in plushly cushioned seats meant that k.d. had to adjust her expectations as a performer. It was difficult at first, because it meant a much greater distance between herself and her new audiences, and the crowds didn't respond with quite the enthusiasm she was used to when she could get out and mingle with them. In other words, she had to work a little harder for less immediate gratification.

But in general she was happy to be reaching larger and more diverse audiences than the ones she had encountered on the Canadian bar circuit, and bringing different types of people together under one roof became one of her greatest pursuits as an artist. She took pride in the fact that her performances appealed to everyone from hardcore punks to 70-year-old country fans, and that her charisma seemed to attract both men and women, young and old. In a funny way, it was as though she offered something for everyone, and she was convinced that it was country music that helped her do it.

By the time she finished touring in the fall of 1987, k.d. had adjusted to the pop-star routine. Richard Flohil had faded from the picture, replaced by a team of record-company publicists who found her becoming more and more media-savvy. In fact, she was getting pretty good at spewing humorous or thought-provoking sound bites, and had begun using interviews to add a whole other dimension to her persona—a good thing, since at this point k.d.'s visibility in the press and on the television talk-show circuit stood in marked contrast to her lack of record sales.

She still wasn't particularly fond of the day-to-day music business, and looked askance at the possibility of living her life in the so-called fast lane. "I think Elvis was the 20th-century Jesus Christ," she theorized one afternoon as she sat chatting comfortably with Denise Donlin. "I think he basically sacrificed himself to teach young artists like myself what can happen to you in the music industry. His death has taught a lot of people a big lesson about excess, and the heavy-duty responsibility it is to be a public figure. It's very difficult to handle, and I think Elvis must have been devastated by the amount of responsibility." It was quite a bundle of wisdom for a woman who had yet to get a real taste of her impending superstardom.

6

*"We've entered a stage where music is very sterile
and synthesized and narcissistic. Country music
deals with real human emotions and I'd say that's
something we're all craving right now."*

NASHVILLE. Known to many who make a living there as Music
City, U.S.A., it's home to Loretta Lynn, Johnny Cash, and, until he re-

cently passed away, Conway Twitty. It's also the buckle of the Bible
Belt, hosting the headquarters of two major Protestant denominations
(the Southern Baptist Convention and the United Methodist Church),
the largest church-owned publishing operation in the world, and more
churches per capita than nearly any other city in the western hemi-
sphere.

In the minds of many Americans, for whom country music has
always seemed an aberration in pop culture—the bastard stepchild of
an otherwise forward-thinking music industry—this landlocked and
fairly homogeneous city, presumably full of nothing but hillbillies,
evangelists, rednecks, and racists, made perfect sense as the nexus of
the country music establishment. If country music was cornball and
ignorant, favored by southern Baptists, hicks, and "poor white trash,"
then Nashville, perched halfway between the Appalachian Mountains
and the deep, rural South, was the heart of it. And while plenty of
folks in Nashville are living high on the hog, raking in mountains of
cash churning out hillbilly hits and attendant paraphernalia to the tune
of $600 million a year, many agreed with Ben Mink when he com-

mented, "At its worst, Nashville is an inbred family that's won the lottery."

That was before Garth Brooks. By 1992, Brooks had sold over 30 million albums since his debut in 1989, outshining Michael Jackson as the highest-selling recording artist in the world. It was a tabulation that rocked the music world, hitting many unwitting sophisticates like a Mack truck. All of a sudden it became painfully obvious that hillbillies alone could not possibly account for Garth Brooks's success. Educated, city-slickin' rednecks like George and Barbara Bush once had their White House clock radio tuned to a country station, and so did lots of liberal yuppies, whose growing CD collections secretly harbored a number of country's leading lights.

It's true that country music has traditionally been a white, working-class music. A 1973 poll taken at the Grand Ole Opry showed that 60% of the audience had not completed high school, and that only 12.8% had received some college education. But a lot has changed since 1973, and today an enormous cross section of people who came of age in the sixties and seventies are turning to country music, not only as listeners, but as songwriters and performers as well. *Billboard* magazine reports over 2,500 country-western stations in cities as diverse as Detroit, New York, and San Diego—nearly double what it was in 1979. In fact, country music stations have become more abundant than any other radio format, including rock and news, reaching a combined market of over 28 million listeners.

With demographics like these, it's inevitable that the basic values and traditions of country music have also been put to the test in recent years. Explanations for why so many people are turning to country music are as bountiful as rawhide in a western dress shop, but Bill Ivey, executive director of the Country Music Foundation, thinks it has something to do with changes taking place in other forms of popular music, noting that a decline in rock's popularity over the last decade, coupled with R&B's move into rap, has caused a plethora of talented songwriters to turn to country music.

Amy Curland, owner of the famed Bluebird Cafe, a small Nashville nightclub that serves as a breeding ground for country music songwriters, has a more personal take on the matter. "Country songs are the best songs of any genre of music," she states unequivocally. "I can't even judge rock songs because they're so inane and repetitive— 'Oooh, I love you and I want to sleep with you, I really do, I really, really do, baby.' That's your basic rock lyric, and I could probably have a hit record with that. But country songs, although they talk about the most basic of emotions—love, hate, jealousy, hurt, disappointment—express them in simple but clever ways. There's a real story behind a country song."

■

It's hard to imagine that in 1984, a young punk from Canada could have anticipated the surge in Stetsons and rodeo belt buckles that would sweep the American Top 40 charts a mere six years later. Yet there she was, explaining her attraction to the music by noting that in such a high-tech, impersonal time, the corniness of country music gave her a way to reach people who yearned for stories of real life experience.

Maybe it was only natural that a Canadian would understand this. After all, country music has always been a central thread in Canada's cultural history, revered and respected in a way it's never been in the United States. Many of Canada's most beloved national recording artists—people like Anne Murray and Ian Tyson—have made their mark primarily in the country music industry. And while American country music has been charming Canadian listeners since the 1920s, when Chicago's "WLS Barndance," and later, WSM's "Grand Ole Opry," were picked up by radio stations in Toronto, Canada also has its own vibrant country-music scene, complete with a cast of characters and distinct regional flavors dating back to Don Messer's "Jubilee," the most popular show in Canadian television history.

k.d. may have hated country music as a child, but she couldn't have helped but hear country artists like Wilf Carter and Stompin' Tom Connors regularly. Nor was she oblivious to European folk styles, ranging from the polkas and fiddle music of the Slavic peoples who migrated to western Canada, to the music of the French Canadian peasants in the east. These were the same sounds that shaped American country music, and many of them showed up in the music she created.

Once k.d. announced her allegiance to the music of her roots, the Canadian country scene wasted no time claiming her as one of their own. In September 1987, the Canadian Country Music Association christened her twice, giving her their Rising Star award, and the even more prestigious Entertainer of the Year award. She was surprised, honored, and relieved to receive the CCMA's support, confessing her fear of rejection and vowing to live up to the honor. Her opportunity came in February of the following year, when she performed in the closing ceremonies of the 15th Winter Olympics, thrilling everyone in the 60,000-seat McMahon Stadium in Calgary, and serenading millions of people worldwide who watched the show on TV. It was a proud moment for most Canadians.

Nashville was a different story. Hardly known as a community open to outsiders, some might go as far as to say that if you aren't part of the family, you're just plain out of luck. After all, this is a town where Garth Brooks knows the waitresses at the Pancake Pantry by name, where Johnny Cash shops at Kroger, and where Dolly Parton can walk down the street any old time she chooses without anyone batting an eyelash. It's a well-accepted fact that if an artist wants to make it in Nashville, they ought to at least live there, just as sure as someone wanting to make it in movies might want to think about moving to Hollywood. But k.d. lang had no intention of moving to Nashville. Worse yet, she wasn't even American!

Then there was the issue of her looks, quite a lump to swallow in an industry where the rule of thumb for women has always been, "The higher the hair, the closer to God." There's no doubt that many in Nashville were shocked when k.d. waltzed in the door, not quite sure what to make of her cropped haircut, her high-top men's shoes, or her stockings with the holes in them. Which brings up the third dilemma: the question of k.d.'s intentions.

It wasn't hard to tell that, both on stage and in person, the girl could put on a damn good act, which made more than a few people suspicious. "A lot of times you see people who do music, but who find a way of distancing themselves from it at the same time," notes Ivey. "So they say, 'I'm going to do this for you, but I'm going to dress or act in a way that shows you I'm not really one of them.' And that doesn't play well with a real country audience. You really have to be part of the tradition, like, 'I'm going to be *one* of you, and we're all just friends and neighbors.' " k.d. may have *called* her audience "friends and neighbors," but in Nashville, her general defiance of protocol left people wondering just how much was a put-on and how much was really from the heart.

Hazel Smith, a Nashville-based columnist for *Country Music* magazine, was just one of many country-music afficionados who wasn't going to be happy if k.d. lang was trying to make fun of them, echoing a popular sentiment when she declared, "Country music is not a joke to me. It's my life, and I love it with all my heart."

k.d. knew she was in for a challenge, but she wasn't too concerned.

"I know I have to prove myself," she acknowledged. "But I'm not worried. I'm going to stick my neck out on that line. If they chop it off, well, I'll run around without it for a while." At the same time, she made it clear that she had no intention of making concessions for Nashville. In fact, if anything, she seemed to want Nashville to make concessions for her. Not only did she intend to be accepted, but she planned to set a precedent. "I'm going to change country music," she stated confidently a few months after her first visit.

Her first crack at wooing the American country music audience came in 1986, even before *Angel With A Lariat* came out, when Sam Lovullo, the executive producer of "Hee Haw," caught a stint she did on "David Letterman." Three weeks later, she was traveling to Nashville to do a taping with the weekly variety show.

To say that the people working on "Hee Haw" were taken aback when she walked onto the set would be an understatement. Whispers and gossip around the studio criticized Lovullo's choice of talent, with people's main concern being not k.d. lang per se, but whether or not she was "Hee Haw" material. "She is not a conservative by any means, as you well know," explains the producer. "And Nashvillians, and people in the South in general, are very religious and very conservative. To some extent that's also the 'Hee Haw' image." It's what's known in the business as 'Christian family programming.' "

As thrilled as k.d. was to be rubbing shoulders with the Nashville entertainment industry, she was hardly prepared to toe the Christian family line. When the producers of "Hee Haw" asked her if she intended to go onstage with holes in her stockings, she turned to them and snorted, "Would you ask Minnie Pearl to remove her price tag from her hat?"

Lavullo's perception was that k.d. never did care about what she wore or how she looked, except for her absolute refusal to wear makeup. Yet that alone was enough to cause commotion on the set. "After she sang three or four songs, and she sings her fanny off, bless her soul," Lovullo recalls, "I had some makeup people come in and dab her a little bit, because you just don't want to see too much of that perspiration floating all over someone's body. But she was very concerned about whether or not we were actually putting makeup on her while we were dabbing her down." To be safe, k.d. went and found her own little towel, and after that, she did the wiping herself.

Regardless of what the crew thought of her being on the show, k.d. lang was a hit with the "Hee Haw" crowd. "I'll tell you this," says

Lovullo, proud of being the first to formally introduce the young artist to Nashville. "When she came into the studio and sang those six or eight songs—and we just couldn't get her to stop singing—I have never found my studio to be so full of guests ever, for any artist that's done our show. Never. I mean, they were all over the rafters. The place was just jammed. People had just heard that this was a great new act, and it was something that Nashville had never seen before. And every television monitor in the complex was turned on when she was on. There may have been mixed emotions as to whether she was right for the show, but everybody was impressed with her singing."

■

k.d. had to keep pinching herself, she was so excited to be in Nashville. It wasn't just the chance to work with String Bean, Grandpa Jones, and all the other "Hee Haw" regulars she had seen on TV as a child. More important was the chance it gave her to soak up every nuance of the town Patsy Cline had once called home. She couldn't wait to get out and see the sights, and since the people at Sire Records were also eager to introduce her around, they paired her up with a Warner staffer and fellow Canadian by the name of Mary Martin.

Bob Oermann, a prolific entertainment journalist who's spent many years covering the country-music scene, remembers meeting the wide-eyed k.d. lang on that first visit. Mary Martin, who was very enthusiastic about k.d., called Oermann to fill him in on her new artist, and asked the critic if he would help to welcome her and show her around. Oermann agreed, and invited the two of them over to his house, where they chatted and explored his vast record collection.

Despite k.d.'s professed love for country, at the time she was rather naive about the music and its history beyond a small handful of her favorites. "She was very enthusiastic about Patsy Cline, as everybody is," he recalls. "But her knowledge of country music was not real deep. She didn't really know Tammy Wynette, and things like that, so I played a few records for her. And she was very receptive, very interested." Next Oermann offered k.d. a real treat, suggesting that she might like to see Tootsie's Orchid Lounge, a tiny, beat-up bar down by the river, where Patsy Cline had hung out after her performances at the Opry. k.d. knew all about Tootsie's, and of course she wanted to go see it, so they all schlepped into the car, and headed downtown to lower Broadway.

"She was like a kid," chuckles Oermann. "I took her into Tootsie's, and showed her where Patsy's picture was on the wall, over near the jukebox, up near the steps." It's the tradition at Tootsie's for every visitor to leave their signature on one of the walls, and so many names have been left over the years that most are barely legible. Nevertheless, when k.d. saw Patsy's picture she got a pencil, went right over to it, and signed her name. "She was really thrilled to be there," Oermann smiles, "because the place is exactly as it was when Patsy hung out there thirty years ago."

Then Oermann and Martin took k.d. by the hand and went down the street to the Alamo, a store specializing in the rhinestone suits and spangled gear that makes country music what it is. Again, k.d. could barely contain herself. "She was totally into it," says Oermann. "She just loved the costumes. And I had warned her that the store was run by a religious cult, and she was very intrigued by that idea as well."

Back then, k.d. was still a starving artist—albeit one with a recording contract—so she had no money to actually purchase anything. But Martin was having so much fun just watching k.d. that she decided to buy the youngster a treat. When k.d. wasn't looking, Martin picked out an orange satin cowgirl shirt with white fringe, and hid it in her purse. Later, when the trio was back in the car, she took the gift out of her bag and watched k.d.'s eyes light up in disbelief. Shopping at Salvation Army would never be the same again.

■

The following April k.d. lang paid a more formal visit to Nashville, introducing *Angel With A Lariat* at the Exit/In, a nightclub named after the fact that it used to have only one door (you had to come in to go out). It was a showcase event, and Sire had invited a long list of Nashville royalty to attend, including Bonnie Raitt, Juice Newton, Wynonna Judd, and a number of the "Hee Haw" regulars. It was an important crowd, and one that k.d. was determined to woo at all costs. She walked out that night with two standing ovations.

"It was just one of those moments when you knew she was a star," beams Oermann, who was sitting in the front row. He was surprised that Sire had been able to get so many old-guard Nashvillians to attend the show, like Minnie Pearl and famed country-music songwriter Harlan Howard, and even more amazed at their response to the young k.d. "They loved her," he says, delighted by the memory. "They thought she was absolutely marvelous, and unique and really cool. And the younger hipsters in the industry really dug her a lot, too."

One woman who worked with Harlan Howard recalls that he was so impressed by the show, he suggested to k.d. that they do some writing together. But she also remembers that a few stuffed shirts were put off by her presentation. "I remember after the show about twelve of us went next door to a restaurant and were talking about her," she recalls. "Some of us, like me and Harlan, loved her energy and her performance. But some of the others were just like, 'I don't get it,' and one of them was even an artist. I just looked at him and thought, 'Well, you just stand up there and sing, so of course you don't get it.'" Others were hesitant. To them, she had one of the most incredible voices that had ever turned up on a Nashville stage. But when they looked at her, a lot of them had problems putting it all together. Perhaps they sensed that what separated k.d. from the artists they were used to was more than just the scuffs on her sawed-off boots.

She has said that "Three Cigarettes in an Ashtray," one of Patsy Cline's vintage tearjerkers and a song she covered on *Angel With A Lariat,* is one of the most pathetic songs ever written. Yet she loved it because it was a great vehicle for her voice, not to mention a great excuse for some hokey props.

When it came to her own songwriting ideas, however, tradition had no place in the mix, and Harlan Howard soon found that this was not the type of girl he could collaborate with. "I remember him saying, 'I want to know what makes her tick,'" recalls Howard's assistant. "But when they got together, she wanted to write about things that didn't make any sense to him. I don't remember exactly what he said the differences were, but after a while he just gave up and said there was nothing for them to write about together."

■

The younger Nashville crowd was excited by the prospect of k.d. bringing something sorely needed to the country scene: a fresh new approach that would give a kick in the butt to an industry bogged down by Kenny Rogers clones and other urban cowboys who'd ridden in during the late seventies. As reviewer Michael McCall wrote in his *Angel* review in the *Nashville Banner,* "The startlingly original debut by k.d. lang and the reclines gives country music a tornado of a twirl that could send a few rhinestones flying into the 21st century. Put away the telescopes, Music Row. This angel from left field just tossed a lariat around the future and pulled it into view."

There was no doubt that k.d.'s music heralded a new way of approaching country, and that *Angel* conveyed a curious attitude about what a country song was supposed to be. Her lyrics were ambiguous, arty, and even convoluted, with vague metaphors and meandering phrases that brought to life a far more complex series of emotions than the standard country fare. Less subtle but equally significant were her arrangements, which were often jazzier and much more quirky than most of what was gracing country radio. She had rediscovered the *western* in country and western, and her interest in polkas and western swing came at a time when those styles were more or less dead.

As k.d. had hoped, these stylistic differences were generally applauded by the artists, journalists, and record company executives who made up the Nashville circuit. But the country radio programmers, as her album's chart activity showed, weren't as hot for her music as Sire's promotions department would have liked. Not that anyone was surprised, given radio's tendency to shun anything even the slightest bit unusual. "Let's just hope that the label of taste knows how to keep lang and her reclines from getting pigeon-holed into some marketing wasteland," wrote one reviewer who gushed over k.d. "She may be a radio programmer's nightmare, but she's a listener's dream."

There was one group of people that had not yet cast its vote on k.d., and Oermann, sitting spellbound in his seat at the Exit/In, knew it was a group clearly missing from the handpicked audience around him. "My question," he recalls, "was whether the *fans* would go for something that was so clearly left field."

■

Following k.d.'s stunning show at the Exit/In, a strange incident occurred that seemed to mysteriously foreshadow her next few years in Nashville. She had just finished at the club, and had gone into the drugstore next door to buy a drink. In her hands were some balloons that had been given to her by a fan, and as she came out of the store, she looked up at the sky and said, "Patsy, this is for you," releasing the balloons.

At that moment a man walked by. "What'd you say?" he asked.

"I was just letting go of my balloons and sending them to Patsy Cline," she responded.

"Well, I'm Charlie Dick," he said, sticking out his hand. And in meeting Patsy Cline's widower, she discovered what a small town Nashville really was.

■

Gaining the support of a few key veterans of the Nashville scene was important to k.d., and an integral part of Sire's strategy for cementing her position and reputation in town. One of k.d.'s personal favorites was Minnie Pearl, the zany backwoods character whose tattered hats, curtsies, and "How-deee"'s have kept many a "Hee Haw" audience in stitches. Pearl's humor spoke to, and in some ways even shaped, k.d.'s own comic sense, but unfortunately, Pearl was absent from the set the day k.d. taped her "Hee Haw" segment. When she returned to Nashville the second time around, Sire made sure the two women were introduced.

The meeting was a staged encounter at the Country Music Hall of Fame, a museum, library, and all-around tourist attraction sandwiched between Barbara Mandrell's Museum and a string of record company offices that dot the main vein of Music Row. Tagging along to document k.d's country-music history lesson was a field crew from "Entertainment Tonight," who witnessed her glee as she came upon the Patsy Cline exhibit. Awestruck, she was so overwhelmed to see Cline's fringed and studded purple skirt-and-blouse ensemble, with its cut-out horses and rodeo riders and matching leather cowboy boots (circa 1960), she convinced a guard to open the vault and allow her a closer look.

Pearl, meanwhile, was in love with k.d., and the two quickly formed their own mutual adoration society. "This child, as far as I'm concerned, sings right along with the best of the women who've come along," Pearl told Roy Clark when they later appeared together on "Nashville Now," a country music version of "Arsenio Hall." Pearl loved k.d.'s look, and the mischief in her eyes. More importantly, she was captivated by her voice. "You know, there's an old fellow up home, and they used to say about him, 'He *would* take a drink,'" she teased. "Well, let me tell you, k.d. *would* sing."

The country television matriarch told everyone she knew about the not-so-little "little girl from Canada," including Judy Bryte, a booking agent at Opryland Talent. She phoned Bryte day and night, urging her to pick up a copy of *Angel With A Lariat,* and eventually Bryte complied. Although she wasn't terribly impressed with the album, in June she found herself, at Pearl's insistence, on a plane to Houston to catch one of k.d.'s gigs. As Pearl expected, Bryte was blown away by the live performance, and she returned to Nashville a committed fan. Soon k.d. was booked as part of an afternoon matinee at the Grand Ole Opry.

■

The Ryman Auditorium, built in 1889 and situated in downtown Nashville, not far from Tootsie's and Ernest Tubb's Record Shop, had been the venerable home of the Grand Ole Opry since 1943. Year after year, up to 3,000 people turned out nightly to hear the living legends of country music sing, dance, and yuck it up, until one day, bursting at its seams, the rickety old building could bear to have its rafters lifted no more. On March 15, 1974, one last Opry show filled the Ryman.

Today the Ryman Auditorium is a museum, and tourists eager to hear their favorite stars perform must drive—or board one of the air-conditioned buses—to Opryland, twenty minutes outside of town, where a $15 million concert hall, a theme park, a hotel, and the obligatory Shoney's Restaurant pay tribute to the staggeringly profitable relationship between Nashville music and commerce. It's not as romantic as the Grand Ole Opry of yore, but the new and improved version, with its 4,400 cushioned seats filled to capacity, was perfect for k.d.'s ultimate test: to prove herself to the authentic, record-buying, country-music public, without whom she would go nowhere fast.

"It brought the house down," said Judy Bryte of k.d.'s two-song set, sharing the bill that October afternoon alongside Minnie Pearl, George Hamilton IV, and Opry host Roy Acuff. "It slaughtered them."

Backstage, Acuff told k.d., "You look like a boy, dress like a girl, and sing like a bird." Overwhelmed by the response, she grabbed her things and was meekly headed for the door when Pearl grabbed her and shoved her back onstage for a roaring, crowd-pleasing encore. From then on, word traveled fast around Nashville, and soon k.d. was invited to participate in two other very prestigious events: performing with Hank Williams, Jr.'s band for the Country Music Association Awards show, a program akin to the Grammys and broadcast on national television; and an invitation to join Loretta Lynn, the Judds, Randy Travis, and a long list of Nashville dignitaries performing for the CMA's 30th-anniversary celebration, also taped for national television.

■

The Nashville Network is a huge recording complex on a "special access" lot just behind the Grand Ole Opry. On the air since March 1983, it's one of those stations that is frequently skipped over by cable-surfing couch potatoes oblivious to its existence and skeptical of its importance. Unless, of course, that couch potato is one of a growing legion of country music devotees, in which case the station, which delivers an unexpectedly sophisticated array of music videos, talk shows, news, and special features, is only a recall button away.

A TV the size of Texas sits in The Nashville Network's lobby, right below an enormous mural depicting a cross between a barn dance and a back-porch barbecue. The guests at this barbecue run the gamut, from Roy Rogers, the Carter Family, and Gene Autry, to Johnny Cash, the Union Gospel Tabernacle Choir, a few guys fishing, and an old lady in a rocking chair. During the fall of 1987 and on into 1988, that giant TV, which is forever stuck on The Nashville Network, started monitoring a hell of a lot of k.d. lang, since just like Johnny Carson and David Letterman, country television went gaga over the Wild Alberta Rose.

Lorraine Crook and Charlie Chase, whose daily program "Crook and Chase" might be a Christian family version of "Regis & Kathy Lee," were the first to invite k.d. to be interviewed, for a show that aired October 13, 1987. As usual, k.d. spared no energy hamming it up, beginning by entering the stage backwards, stumbling through the curtained backdrop as if she were lost. The joke, of course, was a question: Was she in the right place? No doubt it was a question that ran through the minds of at least a few people in the audience.

"We've never had anyone come out backwards before," said Lorraine Crook as she marveled at k.d.'s standard-issue sweatshirt, jeans, and high-top sneakers.

"Well, I always like to approach my career a little differently," she grinned. Then, craning a glance back at the curtains, she cracked, "You know, my mother used to make me things out of old curtains, and those would make a doggone nice dress." Laughter filled the audience. k.d. won another round.

k.d.'s entrances became a running joke on "Crook and Chase," and the next time she visited she greeted the audience by sticking her head—with a really bad haircut—out from under the infamous curtains. "You are the craziest person I know," said Crook, honestly shocked.

"Well, I think that's a compliment. Thank you," replied k.d., adding mischievously, "I should have just stayed there, and really made you sweat."

By her third visit the following May, Lorraine Crook nervously anticipated k.d.'s emergence from behind the stage. It turned out to be just a normal stroll. Relieved, Crook confessed that she had come to expect something more outrageous and unpredictable from her Canadian guest. "Expectations and I get along like a cow in a Texas gate," the artist snorted. "So whenever people expect me to do something, I do the opposite."

Most of k.d.'s visits to "Crook and Chase" were spent pitching her hybrid musical style to the audience. In response to questions about her music, she dodged the label "new traditionalist"—a term being bandied about to describe some of the newer, more rootsy country artists like Rosanne Cash and Dwight Yoakam. Instead she said she considered herself a "new progessionalist," rejecting the term "cowpunk" and coining the phrase "torch and twang" instead. "I've been influenced by punk and that whole movement, but I don't feel necessarily a part of it," she explained. "I came up with 'torch and twang' because I'm very influenced by torchy jazz singing, and also by hillbilly twang, so I put the two together."

As for her look, which to many seemed more of a gag than a fashion coincidence, she offered no real explanation, except to say, "That's the way I am." Then, to soften the blow, she offered a joke and a bit of reasoning: "I think country music has a tradition of promoting honesty, and honest, down-to-earth people, and although I might not be from this particular earth, I'm just being honest."

■

In between the sweet talk and sweat of k.d.'s multiple Nashville engagements, she took time out to accept another invitation that would seal her career as one of the world's great singers. She agreed to join Roy Orbison to record a duet of his classic song, "Crying."

It was late 1987, and Orbison was working on the soundtrack for the movie *Hiding Out* when he was asked by one of the film's producers, who'd seen k.d. perform in Los Angeles, what he thought of the idea of a duet. Orbison had never even considered rerecording

"Crying," since he'd always been happy with the way he did it the first time around. But he conceded that the sound of he and k.d. singing together could be quite remarkable, so he agreed to ask her into the studio.

Ironically, Orbison was one of the few artists who had managed to successfully straddle the fence between country music and the larger pop world. He lived part of the time in Hendersonville, a suburb of Nashville, right next door to his good friend Johnny Cash, and to many in the town, he was one of their own. But he was also considered one of the greatest songwriters in pop-rock history—"Pretty Woman," "Blue Bayou," and "Only the Lonely" being only a few of the many gems that had flowed from his pen. In many ways, what Orbison had done in bridging these two worlds was exactly what k.d. had in mind for herself, and presumably, she stood to learn a lot from him. Yet amazingly enough, when asked to work with Roy, she almost turned it down.

"They wanted it to be a duet and I said it should be either Roy singing or me singing," she confessed. "I didn't think it should be a duet. But then I started to wake up and go, 'It's Roy Orbison that you'll be singing with, you goon.' "

k.d.'s involvement with Orbison was brief but poetic: she flew to his home in Boston to record her vocals, and he flew to Vancouver to record his. A few of the parts they recorded together, and it was really only then that she realized the power of the moment. As they stood there, side by side, singing, she became so engrossed in what was going on that she forgot her lines. But the story she cherishes most was when she actually brushed cheeks with Roy. "We were both leaning really close to the mikes," she recalls. "Now, you have to understand, when you're standing that close to a vocalist, you can feel the air move, the body resonating, and everything. And Roy was very operatic, so he had a great deal of air moving, and even though he may look meek, he used his body a lot to get that projection. Our cheeks were touching, and we were singing, and his cheeks were just so, so soft, and yet his body was providing this enormous sound, and it was just like two different worlds. It was an overwhelming experience."

Hiding Out bombed at the box office and quickly disappeared, but not before "Crying" had a chance to climb to No. 42 on *Billboard*'s Top Country Singles chart in January 1988. In the spring of that year she performed with Orbison in his HBO special "A Black and White

Night," along with Elvis Costello, Tina Weymouth, Bruce Springsteen, and Bonnie Raitt. The single sold more than 50,000 copies in the United States, and would later earn k.d. her first Grammy nomination. Since then, the song has become her showstopper; it was eventually released on Orbison's posthumously released album *King of Hearts*.

k.d.'s work with Roy Orbison took on a real air of poignancy when the musical legend passed suddenly into the world of the spirits the following December. Saddened, but blessed, she would remark years later, "Everything I did with Roy brought baskets of horseshoes. He was like a Midas to my career." In 1989, k.d. would perform a rendition of "Crying" that would become one of the most enduring and passionate moments of her entire career. But for now she intended to take that basket of horseshoes and make it work for her in Nashville.

7

*"When I was criticized for what I was saying about
Patsy, I consulted her and got my answer."*

IN 1948, Patsy Cline, her mother, and a family friend trekked across
the Blue Ridge Mountains from Virginia to Music City. Patsy was only
sixteen at the time, but she was determined to become a star, sleeping
on picnic benches in a Nashville park because she couldn't afford a

THE HOUSE OF
THE SPIRIT

hotel. Not long after her arrival, Roy Acuff heard her sing and offered
her a gig, but the job didn't pay enough to live on, and when the
money ran out, she headed back home. It would be eight more years
before Patsy Cline returned to Nashville and hooked up with Owen
Bradley, the man responsible for what has since become known as the
"Nashville sound."

The "Nashville sound" was created by Bradley and fellow record
producer Chet Atkins in the mid-1950s, when Decca Records approached them to "smooth out" a couple of the label's more important
artists, most notably Red Foley and Ernest Tubb, in an effort to make
them more commercially viable. Using full, string-laden orchestras,
choral arrangements, and other pop music techniques, Bradley and
Atkins soon developed a rich, polished style that would become a
crossover formula for early sixties singers like Eddy Arnold and Brenda
Lee. Soon country music was moving out of the honky tonks and into
the mainstream, putting Music City on the map for the very first time.

Some say if it wasn't for Owen Bradley, there might not be a Music

Row. As a producer, he was the one who helped shape and define some of Nashville's most important artists of the fifties, sixties, and seventies. His arrangements, which were complex, lush, and flowing, but never overpowering, were perfectly designed to highlight the human voice; thus, Bradley worked with many of the finest crooners of the period, including Kitty Wells and Loretta Lynn. But of all the records attached to his name during his long and illustrious career, the crown jewel on Bradley's resumé was Patsy Cline. Once k.d. realized this, she was determined to work with him.

The people at Sire Records loved her idea of hooking up with the esteemed producer, knowing that Bradley's name would lend their artist an instant credibility in Nashville. It was something they felt she needed after *Angel With A Lariat*'s poor showing; moreover, it would be a great learning experience for k.d. to work with a true country-music veteran. Unfortunately, Owen Bradley had retired in 1980. Worse yet, in the spring of 1987 he suffered a massive heart attack, which left him weak and unable to consider going back to work.

Even before his heart attack, k.d. had tried to contact Bradley several times, both on her own and through mutual acquaintances. Bradley never responded. Then one warm June evening, as he lay languishing in the hospital following his heart attack, Owen Bradley saw k.d perform "Three Cigarettes in an Ashtray" on "Johnny Carson." Staring at the TV, he sat bolt upright in bed, astonished at the strength and energy behind this young woman's voice. Suddenly, he knew what would make him recover faster than anything the doctor had prescribed. He made instant plans to reopen Bradley's Barn, the famed recording studio with the tin roof on his farm in Mt. Juliet, Tennessee. Then he called Sire Records.

"Mary Martin, who knows him, called me and said, 'There's a twinkle in his eye. Call him,' " k.d. remembered of the news that Bradley had decided to bring her in. "So I ended up going down to Nashville to see him. We sat down and played some songs at the piano, and before I knew it, we were in the studio, recording."

■

Originally k.d. and Owen were under no obligation to produce an album, since the people at Sire wanted to give the two artists time to get to know each other musically. If, after spending some time working together, an album came of it, then fine. If not, then at least k.d. would have had the learning experience. Either way, they didn't want to rush the process, so they sent them into the studio, and sat back to see what would evolve.

Interestingly, when the two sat down at the piano together, it was not in country but in jazz that they converged. Bradley, who had been a band leader before becoming a full-time producer, harbored a fondness for smoky nightclub standards, and k.d., who'd always dreamed of singing jazz, had her own predilection for the steamy drama of Las Vegas–style lounge music. Eventually, they each selected a couple of favorites to work on, like "Black Coffee" and "I Wish I Didn't Love You So"; "Shadowland," a piece Bradley's own band had enjoyed playing years earlier; and an old Roberta Sherwood number called "Tears Don't Care Who Cries Them."

They began by arranging the songs on piano, Bradley playing and k.d. singing by his side. They'd practice these songs only two or three times a day, spending the rest of the afternoon listening to great jazz vocalists like Carmen McRae, Ella Fitzgerald, and Peggy Lee. They also listened carefully to a number of hillbilly singers and saxophonists like Jimmy Hidges and Ben Webster. With each artist they would discuss at length what they liked and didn't like about each vocal style. Then, after several weeks, they emerged from the studio with a demo tape containing six cuts—not a single country song among them.

When k.d. played the tape for Sire's A&R team, they instantly fell in love with it, and eagerly agreed that what k.d. held in her hand was the first half of a hit record. Excited, the artists went back to the studio, this time taking with them a handful of country standards, including Roger Miller's "Lock, Stock and Teardrops" and Slim Willet's 1953 hit "Don't Let the Stars Get in Your Eyes." They also recorded two newer songs: Chris Isaak's "Western Stars," and "Busy Being Blue," a piece penned by former recline Stu MacDougall and originally recorded on *a truly western experience.*

■

While k.d. was spending all her time in Nashville, her band was fading farther and farther from the spotlight. Not that there was ever any question as to who was the star of the show, but in Canada her musicians carried their own weight as minor celebrities. Such was not the case south of the border, where they were completely unknown. And especially not in Nashville, where the singer was considered all-important, the band members largely interchangeable. Nevertheless, it was a difficult moment when k.d. realized that Bradley had no intention of working with her band. All along she had planned to use the reclines on her next record, but her producer just wasn't up for having to learn the communication system between five new musicians. Besides, using the reclines would have defeated the purpose of working with Bradley in the first place, since a large part of what made up the "Nashville sound" lay in using the session musicians Bradley had always relied on. Like it or not, they were key ingredients in the formula.

When she broke the news to the band, they took it pretty well, understanding that they really had no choice. "I remember her going to bat to get everyone on the record," says Gordie Matthews. "But you know, when you work with someone like Owen Bradley—I mean, he was a bigger star than she was at that point, and we could have never made that record the way they did. To get the record he wanted, it would have been very awkward for him to work with a bunch of guys like us, who, for the most part were pretty inexperienced. So I don't really hold that against him at all. Sure, I would have loved to play on that record, but I understand why it happened the way it did."

In place of the reclines was a lineup of musicians and vocalists that had worked with Bradley off and on for over thirty years, including Hargus "Pig" Robbins on piano, Buddy Harman on drums, and Owen's brother, Harold Bradley, on bass. Backing vocals were provided by two choral groups, the Jordanaires and Tennessee, with the Nashville String Machine providing accompaniment on several cuts. Last but not least, Buddy Emmons brought along k.d.'s favorite instrument— the steel guitar.

These session musicians, seasoned veterans all, were impressed with k.d.'s musical talent, even though they were a little shocked by her appearance. "She had such a wide variety of things that she could do," says Emmons. "Even before I met her, Owen had given me a tape of something he had done with her that was sort of jazz-oriented, and it sounded as good as any jazz singer I'd ever heard. Then, when she came in to do country, I was really surprised." His biggest surprise of all was that he wasn't sure at first whether k.d. was a boy or a girl. "I didn't know what k.d. stood for, so I didn't know what to say," he laughs.

■

Unlike k.d.'s work with Dave Edmunds, her time with Bradley was calm and relaxed. For the most part she was content to quietly observe, soaking it all in. She did make another attempt to sneak "Pine and Stew" onto her new record, hoping to win Bradley's support after losing the fight to include it on *Angel*. But Bradley thought the song was a novelty piece, and wasn't interested in having it be part of the collection. "He's really into straight-ahead lyrics, and subject matter everyone can understand," k.d. explains. "It's almost a totally different school from where I come from. As a kid I studied Joni Mitchell as a lyricist, and hers is a very introspective type of writing. The type of lyrics Owen goes for are very generic and publicly applicable."

As for his studio demeanor, k.d. found Bradley to be attentive, accommodating, and jovial. He preferred to sit back in the control room and listen, interjecting his thoughts only as they were needed to keep the mood of the project intact. "Owen was trying to keep it in the direction he thought was best, but it also appeared to me that she had quite a bit of input," says Emmons of their collaboration. In fact, the musician was a little surprised by k.d.'s assertiveness. "She stopped several times, just about on the edge of demanding things," he continues, "and I thought it was a little soon to be pulling that kind of thing. But that was her style. She wanted things a certain way musically, which is not all bad—all artists have a right to do that. It's just the way she went about it. Let's just say she was a little more aggressive than most artists, especially at that point in her career. She was headstrong, and she wanted us to do it her way."

k.d. was stubborn, and as those who worked with her knew, she wasn't one to compromise. But Owen was used to strong-willed women. Patsy, too, had been very determined, and her drive was often mistaken for pushiness, earning her a reputation for being hard to handle. Part of Bradley's talent rested in the fact that he was as good at smoothing out artists' egos as he was at smoothing out their sound, and he never allowed fights in the studio. "Owen's been doing this long enough to know how to keep the tone of the sessions at a level that everybody can be comfortable with," Emmons explains. "If there were problems, they were something that got talked about after we left. You can't let that happen during a session. You can't argue back and forth, because it disrupts everybody's thought processes."

Besides, most who worked on the album agreed that k.d.'s aggressive nature and her desire to have things her way were no different from the way most artists behaved in the studio. It was something that went with the territory.

When it came to laying down tracks, the actual recording process took only six days, the mixing another four. Things moved quickly thanks to Bradley's insistence on recording the sessions live—a technique born of the days when producers had nothing but a two-track stereo and a mixer, with egg cartons hanging from the ceilings in place of acoustic tiles. He liked the old technique of recording everyone together because he felt it preserved that special energy that occurs between a singer and the musicians. "You just can't build that magic into a session," he marvels, noting that "When you work on a track for three months, the only feeling you get is 'I'm sick of hearing this.' "

"Tears Don't Care Who Cries Them" and "Black Coffee" were recorded completely live, including the strings, and Emmons agrees it's a method that's hard to beat. "Generally, when I do a session, my best work happens in the first two or three cuts," he says. "If it takes much longer to do it, then I go downhill." In this setting, if a musician needs more time to get a cut that's acceptable to the producer or the singer, he usually has to come back later and do an "overdub" without the band. Unfortunately, thanks to k.d.'s perfectionism and her obsession with the slide guitar, Emmons, in particular, found himself working a lot of overtime.

"She was a big fan of the steel guitar, but the problem was she kept wanting me to play it like I quit playing about thirty years ago," he laughs, referring to that characteristic sliding sound associated with a time when musicians were only beginning to experiment with the instrument. Since then, artists like Emmons have developed a much more subtle technique, one that relied very little on the slide bar itself. "Really, the style she wanted was typical of the early years of steel playing," he explains. "In other words, she wanted me to sound like an amateur."

■

On April 4, 1988, Bradley and k.d. enjoyed one final historic moment before wrapping up what would soon be christened *Shadowland: The Owen Bradley Sessions*. It was a breezy Monday at Bradley's Barn, and the place was abuzz with lights, cameras, and the smell of hair spray.

"Are you girls ready?" someone shouted above the din.

"Well, I didn't get a chance to put my nail polish on, but what the heck. Let's go," answered a familiar voice in a soothing Southern drawl.

Four women moseyed over to four empty bar stools and slid in behind four vocal mikes. Loretta Lynn, Kitty Wells, Brenda Lee, and k.d. lang exchanged warm smiles, and nodded yes, they were ready. The cameras started rolling, and soon four of Owen Bradley's favorite female singers were recording the video for their new song, "Honky Tonk Angels' Medley." Off to the side, a bevy of news reporters snapped, clicked, and scribbled, feverishly documenting every glance and quiver that passed between the four stars. Amid all the commotion, Minnie Pearl sat quietly beaming as she surveyed the scene.

It was Owen's idea to bring the legendary singers together, creating a delicious new slice of country diva history, not to mention a great story for the press. None of the three elder songstresses had ever worked together before, nor had any of them worked with Bradley for almost a decade. When he suggested that they consider coming together to record with k.d., all signed on without giving it a second thought. First Wells, whose honky-tonk hits in the 1950s had earned her a crown as the "Queen of Country Music," then Lee and then Lynn—not only did they relish the idea of working with each other, but they had heard enough about k.d. to be impressed. It was an opportunity nobody wanted to miss.

The medley they recorded was built from a trio of country standards Bradley had unearthed: "In the Evening When the Sun Goes Down," Ernest Tubb's "You Nearly Lose Your Mind," and the Delmore Brothers' "Blues Stay Away From Me." The title of the piece came from Wells's 1952 hit "It Wasn't God Who Made Honky Tonk Angels," and it was a fitting description of the four characters who reveled in each other's company. "We had a few drinks and said hello for an hour, cut the record in an hour, and listened back for an hour," Bradley laughs, recalling the afternoon they spent gossiping and laying down tracks. "That's the union way of making a record in three hours."

k.d. was visibly charged to be in the company of such important country artists, especially Loretta Lynn, whose photo had hung in her vocal booth for most of the *Shadowland* sessions, snatched up as inspiration from a stack of memorabilia she found lying around Owen's studio. Each of the women had made their own contributions to the way k.d. had come to view country music, and to be accepted as a peer by such great women left her nearly speechless. When asked by the press what it felt like to be involved in such an amazing project, all she could do was recall the magnificent bouquet of personalities that had gone into the experience: "Brenda is a very technical singer, Kitty is so serene and maternal, and Loretta is exactly what you thought she'd be like," she said reverently. "She came into the studio with a pound of bologna and a loaf of white bread, and everyone had bologna sandwiches. I'm a vegetarian, but I almost ate one. I thought it was blessed food."

At the video shoot, Wells, Lynn, and Lee affectionately returned the compliments, none of them the least bit bothered by k.d.'s unorthodox approach to country music. They paid no mind when a journalist pointed out that visually, k.d. didn't seem to fit in. "She's a great singer, she's really uninhibited, and she's not afraid to try new things," explained Lee. "She's very campy, and that's something we've missed from this business for a long time. It's refreshing."

When asked if she felt intimidated being surrounded by such greatness, k.d. barely had time to utter a polite "No," when Lee jumped in. "If you've ever seen k.d. in the studio, you know she doesn't get intimidated," she insisted.

"When you have k.d.'s talent, you don't have to be intimidated," added Wells.

Bradley, meanwhile, could hardly contain himself amid all the excitement. k.d. teased him, saying he was "like a young boy at Christmas," as he basked in the glory of having "his women" together in the studio. "These are all gals who've made their mark," he told the crowd that had gathered. "If you say Kitty, you know it's Kitty Wells. You only have to say Brenda or Loretta, and you know who it is. And now I think you'll just have to say k.d. and you've got a new star."

Then, with a twinkle in his eyes he added, "You're lucky if you find someone like that once in a lifetime. I guess I'm a very lucky man."

■

The collaboration between k.d., Wells, Lynn, and Lee made a huge splash in Nashville, and soon a video of the making of "The Honky Tonk Angels' Medley" worked its way onto country-music television. It's ironic, looking back, that k.d. had initially tried to thwart the whole idea of bringing three such familiar voices into the studio, presumably fearing that their collective fame would somehow distract from the album. "Actually, we had a big fight about it," she later confessed, adding that when she and Bradley first discussed the idea she actually stormed out of the studio. "I stomped out to the lake and had a talk with Patsy to find out why he was so stubborn," she explained. "And of course he was right."

It wasn't the only time Patsy Cline's name came up during the making of *Shadowland*. In the beginning, k.d. had vowed to keep her feelings for Patsy under wraps, conscious of the fact that Bradley, Lynn, and others had been extremely close to the singer. She worried, and rightly so, that folks might take offense at her claiming to be in communion with the great spirit. But ultimately she just couldn't help herself, and soon there were rumors of studio sessions suspended while k.d. went off on her own to consult with her spiritual guide. Nobody seemed to think much of it, though.

"People in the South don't believe in no reincarnation bullshit no way," says columnist Hazel Smith when asked what she thought of the k.d. lang–Patsy Cline connection. "Nobody here paid any attention to that. They just thought it was some new-world something or other, and they just ignored that, 'cause they knew better." Then again, Loretta Lynn believes she's psychic, and once told a *Rolling Stone* reporter that she can look at someone's eyes and know what has passed. She claims she once saw her grandmother's coffin floating above a pigpen near the house she grew up in. She has also said of Patsy Cline, "There's nobody like her, and never will be."

k.d. tried to be careful not to step on any toes, and when people questioned her about Patsy, she generally downplayed the subject. When asked by a reporter if she felt Patsy's spirit had been present during the videotaping, she coyly pointed out that it had affected *all* of the artists on the album. "If you're going to talk about the Patsy Cline thing, you have to say that every country singer, female and male, has been greatly influenced by Patsy. We all have a great empathy for her."

In private, however, k.d. was constantly begging Bradley to share with her every detail regarding her heroine. To a certain extent, he got a kick out of telling k.d. stories about Patsy Cline, but he saw a danger in it as well. "I wouldn't want to make fun of k.d.," he chuckled, "but I'm afraid she had a few of her own ideas about Patsy, and I probably destroyed some of them. Your imagination is usually so much better than the real thing."

He also tried very hard not to let k.d. get carried away with her obsession. "Owen and I talked about never wanting to emulate Patsy," she explained a few years later, "but her presence was so strong, it was just impossible to not be immersed in her energy. My obsession with Patsy was a very real thing, and I was never joking when I talked about it. Doing that record was just so close to being on the edge of something—some area of life and death and energy. It was extremely,

extremely emotional and really shook me up, and it took me awhile to adjust after I made that record."

Ultimately, *Shadowland* served as a catalyst for k.d., a final convulsion of empathy and adulation that got the ghost of Patsy Cline out of her system once and for all. "I know it sounds weird," she confided to Liam Lacey, "but when I finished that album, the whole Patsy thing somehow came to an end. She'll always be important to me, but it's not the same obsession it was. I think, in a way, that *Shadowland* was the whole reason for that Patsy obsession, and now I can just go back to being k.d. lang."

Besides, her new album proved that k.d. didn't have to emulate Patsy Cline any longer. She was as good a singer as Cline ever was. Many said she was better.

■

"What a difference the right collaborator makes," proclaimed Jimmy Guterman, who had panned *Angel With A Lariat* less than a year before. "*Shadowland* is much more vivid and loose-limbed than the earlier album by the Canadian country siren."

"Bradley uses his prowess to bring out what's best in lang," added Holly Gleason in *Musician*. "She drapes her voice convincingly around the proffered material and illuminates the darkest corners of desperation and heartache with a few exhaled syllables."

It was just as everyone had hoped: Owen Bradley captured k.d.'s voice in a way that no previous recording had, and the results were magnificent, garnering accolades in magazines ranging from the youth-oriented music trade publication *College Music Journal* to *Truckers* magazine, which warned, "Anyone who lets this gal's mannish appearance deter a close listen to her singing is a damn deaf fool." In Canada, country-music radio stations jumped on the album's first single, "I'm Down to My Last Cigarette," an overripe weeper penned by Harlan Howard. More importantly, American country radio finally seemed to be warming to k.d. lang, with enough stations adding her to their playlists to push the single to No. 21 on *Billboard*'s Top Country Singles chart. It was the first time k.d.'s name had appeared in the U.S. Top 40, the closest she'd ever come to a bona fide hit.

The album did even better than the single, appearing on *Billboard*'s Top Country Albums charts on May 21, 1988, and rocketing to No. 9 before disappearing from the lineup a strong 121 weeks later. Better still, the album crossed over to the pop charts as well, hinting that yes, it was possible for k.d. to have it both ways—appealing to a hardcore country audience while retaining her pop/alternative edge. It seemed that she had finally arrived.

By now k.d. had been in and around Nashville for a little over a year and a half, and with *Shadowland* creeping determinedly up the charts, it was time to pull out all the stops. There's a saying in Music City that an artist hasn't ever really made it until they've been mobbed at Fan Fair, that annual down-home but highly commercial week-long cattle call designed as a tribute to the country-music fans.

Over at the fairgrounds, k.d. was scheduled to perform smack-dab in the middle of a long and very hot day, and Bob Oermann was anxious to see how it would go. "She was just about to go on," he recalls, "and normally I stay backstage and schmooz, but for k.d. I decided to go out into the audience to see how this was gonna work. And it was one of those moments when you realize how much the industry underestimates the tastes and the intelligence of its fans. I mean, these were the people who went to Baptist church in Indiana every Sunday—what you might call 'regular ol' Americans.' And *they went bananas.*" k.d. worked up the biggest sweat she had in quite a long time, and soon she had an entire arena full of the world's most traditional country fans falling all over themselves to get a better look. "Middle America loved her," Oermann repeats in amazement. "This is a group of fans who watch 75 hours of country-music shows in a week. They've seen it all, and yet they stood up, they left their chairs, grabbed their cameras, and went to the front of the stage, en masse, to check it out."

■

Shortly after Fan Fair, k.d. embarked on a very limited *Shadowland* tour, this time opening for Lyle Lovett in a few key cities like London, New York, and Los Angeles. But for the most part she stuck to TV and radio appearances and interviews with the print media, since she really didn't have a band, per se, who could re-create *Shadowland* on the road.

In June she made her fourth "Carson" appearance in just over a year, and performed as part of the HBO special "Country Music: A New Tradition." The show was entertaining proof that k.d. wasn't the only one calling for change on the country-music front, as new faces like Rosanne Cash, Rodney Crowell, and the Judds came together with an older generation of artists that included Waylon Jennings, Carl

Perkins, Merle Haggard, and Bill Monroe. Highlights of the performance included k.d. and the Jordanaires on "Lock, Stock and Teardrops," and k.d. and Rosanne Cash doing a passionate duet of Loretta
Lynn's "You Ain't Woman Enough to Take My Man."

In September, as "Lock, Stock and Teardrops" danced on the lower
rungs of *Billboard*'s Top Country Singles chart, she returned to Canada
for a hero's welcome and to join the eastern Canadian leg of the
Amnesty International Tour, performing next to Sting, Peter Gabriel,
Tracy Chapman, and Youssou N'Dour. In October it was back to Nashville to participate in the "22nd Annual Country Music Association
Awards," a live two-hour broadcast seen across North America on CBS.
Then, in December she switched gears again, appearing in a live national telecast of "Pee Wee Herman's Christmas Special."

k.d.'s performance on *Shadowland* and her duet with Roy Orbison
also earned her another spate of awards, including two Canadian Country Music Association awards for Entertainer of the Year and Female
Vocalist of the Year. From there she went on to win two of the Canadian
music industry's highest honors, taking Junos for Best Female Country
Vocalist (for *Shadowland*) and Female Vocalist of the Year (for
"Crying"). The country title was stolen from Anne Murray, who had
reigned as queen for the previous seven years. But it was the award
for "Crying" that hit k.d. the hardest. As she walked to the podium to
accept the honor she was overcome with emotion. "Thank you," she
said, choking back the tears. "Roy deserves part of this."

In January came news that shook the Sire offices, as k.d. discovered
she had been nominated for three Grammy awards: Best Female Country Vocalist for "I'm Down to My Last Cigarette," and Best Country
Music Collaboration both for "Crying," and with Wells, Lynn, and Lee
on "Honky Tonk Angels' Medley." The nominations were unexpected,
and while she was bewildered, she graciously accepted them as a vote
of confidence from her music peers out in L.A. "I never expected one
nomination, to be quite honest," she said. "Awards are something I
could never figure out anyway. It's partly political, partly record sales,
and partly artistic merit. Most of all, it's a great motivation and very
good publicity." She also didn't expect to win, and when she took the
award for "Crying," she was flabbergasted. "Life astonishes me sometimes," she said in awe. "Here I am being rewarded for one of the
most incredible experiences of my life, sharing a microphone with
Roy Orbison."

k.d. wasn't the only one who was surprised. Coming as it did from

California, her win elicited a slight but audible grumble from the country-music establishment, who, despite k.d.'s obvious talent and charm, were not at all convinced she was the next big thing. Owen Bradley may have had his name attached to *Shadowland*, but that didn't mean k.d. had earned her keep, and she knew that unless she straightened up and played by the rules, there was no guarantee that life as Nashville's little darling would continue.

"Politically, this album is very correct," she said, acknowledging her dilemma. "I mean, I was working with Nashville session players, in Nashville, with Nashville's most celebrated producer. But it's going to be very interesting to see how they swallow the next reclines record." She also knew that while *Shadowland* was very mature and subdued, appealing to an older and more influential crowd, she still possessed a wild streak that scared some people. As much as she wanted to be accepted by the country audience, there was a stomping-mad polka queen still inside of her.

8

*"on them shiny pages
all that hairdo
it ain't me
i am showing just what i am"*

WHEN k.d. recorded a song called "Miss Chatelaine" in 1992, there wasn't a self-respecting fan outside of Canada who didn't run to their dictionaries in an effort to discover the meaning of the song's title.

HERE'S LOOKING AT YOU

Close attention to the lyrics left no doubt that she was singing about love. But what was the significance of becoming "Miss Chatelaine"? The *Random House Dictionary of the English Language* says "chatelaine: 1. the mistress of a castle 2. a hooklike clasp or a chain for suspending keys or trinkets." The king's wife ... Was it a reference to some obscure piece of literature?

Not exactly. Call it a private, Canadian joke, dating back to January 1988, when k.d. was nominated by *Chatelaine* magazine as their Woman of the Year, joining the ranks of such highly elevated heroines as Canadian astronaut Roberta Bondar, gold medal figure skater Elizabeth Manley, and the entire Ontario Government, which one year had the largest number of women holding elected office in all of Canada's history. Each year another woman was chosen to be *Chatelaine*'s celebrity cover girl. Nineteen eighty-eight was k.d.'s year.

Chatelaine is the type of magazine that might sit next to *Self* or *Redbook* on the newsstand, a fashion-oriented journal that features articles ranging from profiles of career women to cooking tips. According to its editors, this decidedly unhip magazine reaches one in five Canadian women, including k.d.'s mom, who k.d. remembers always had a copy of it on her coffee table. Ivor Shapiro, *Chatelaine*'s features editor, describes it as *"Vanity Fair* meets *Good Housekeeping* meets *New York* magazine," and puts the periodical's circulation at nearly a million copies a month in a country of 25 million people. It's amazing that such a prominent, mainstream women's magazine would choose an anomaly like k.d. to grace its cover.

Surely somebody on the magazine's editorial board must have noticed that k.d. bore no resemblance to a king's wife—or anyone else's wife either, for that matter. She was androgynous, even butch, and fiercely and defiantly so, bowing to none of society's notions of the ideal female. Yet she was a star, as Shapiro ardently points out, in a country that doesn't have a lot of stars. At the time she may not have been a huge success in international terms, but she was certainly a success in Canada. More importantly, she just had that *star quality—* a certain something that captured people's attention and imagination, making her by far the most interesting woman nominated for *Chatelaine*'s Woman of the Year in a long, long time.

What the other editors at *Chatelaine* found most appealing about k.d. was her "don't mess with me" personality. "She's got a real persona, and a sense of 'take me or leave me,'" Shapiro explains, "like this unique character that she just invented as she went along. She was interesting, she was quirky, she had her strange, funky kind of way about her and she was definitely an individualist. And I think everyone just loved that."

From an American point of view it seems incredible that in the "post-feminist '80s" (as the media was so eager to dub it), someone like k.d. lang would be chosen for the cover of a major women's magazine. After all, individuality, quirkiness, and defiance were hardly the kinds of things publishers looked for in the women whose faces were meant to sell magazines. What was even more amazing was that *Chatelaine* stuck with k.d. even when she announced that she would not be wearing makeup for her photo shoot, a stunt that could have easily gotten her bumped from the cover of most American magazines at the time. Nevertheless, in the winter of 1989, her face was gracing newsstands across Canada.

"That was a very interesting paradox to my career," the artist ruminated a couple of years later. "It was in some ways the arrival of k.d. lang on the mainstream—at least in Canada—and I felt really proud of the fact that I had gotten there doing everything I wanted to do. I was still wearing secondhand clothes, I was still not wearing makeup, and I was still cutting my own hair at that time. And there I was on the cover of *Chatelaine*, which had been in my mother's house for years. It had always had pretty women on the cover, and there it was with this goofy tomboy on the cover. It was a pretty big deal."

Given such a high-profile opportunity, k.d. was determined to milk it for everything it was worth. "Will *Chatelaine* let me talk about why I think it's a triumph to be 'Woman of the Year'?" she asked Jay Scott when they sat down for the interview. "First, I don't wear makeup, and if I were going to do one of those 'before' and 'after' makeover shots, I'd show me 'after' as being much prettier without makeup. It's about accepting yourself and not striving to be an image invented by other people. I'm a very androgynous-looking woman, and my goals are not to be a wife or necessarily a mother."

Woooah, this kind of talk in a fashion magazine?

"You have to understand," explains Donna Alexander Zaica, *Chatelaine*'s fashion editor, "our magazine is not really a fashion and beauty magazine. We're a women's magazine that deals with all different types of issues, and we really pride ourselves in reflecting a broad spectrum of Canadian women. Besides, k.d. lang *is* beautiful. She takes incredible care of herself and her body, and I don't know if you've ever seen her up close, but she's got an amazing complexion. She didn't *need* makeup."

Maybe not, and yet a funny thing happened to k.d.'s photo on the way to the printer. For all the lip service given to the artist's prerogative—and Alexander Zaica did say that k.d. was given free rein to dictate her own look—when the magazines rolled off the presses and bundles were loaded onto the distribution trucks, a ruby red-lipped face grinned up from the stacks. A gasp must have risen from k.d. when she realized the change that had occurred. The makeup she had so adamantly refused had ended up on her lips anyway—presumably airbrushed on in the photo lab!

Chatelaine editor-in-chief Mildred Istona denied that the photo had been doctored, and suggested that perhaps it was a printer's error—an excess of red ink on the presses, or something to that effect. k.d., of course, didn't think so. "They *did* airbrush lipstick on me," she insisted during a MuchMusic interview. "I was mad about that." Not only that, but it wasn't even a good airbrush job. Instead of lipstick, it looked like a goofy red splotch where her lips should have been.

Years later, k.d. and lipstick would become a running joke. When Madonna met her labelmate at a reclines concert one evening, she immediately whipped out her MAC color stick and applied it to k.d.'s kisser. "I looked like a drag queen," the androgyne later laughed. "Trust me when I tell you, I don't look good in makeup."

■

By the time k.d. rolled into Nashville in the late 1980s, winds of change were already sweeping through town, fueled in part by a strong and growing women's movement. Despite constant media proclamations that feminism was dead, the truth was that it had burrowed deep into America's body politic, spawning a new generation of women who were simply too young to have ever known a world without Gloria Steinem. Even women whose mother's weren't active in the feminist movement knew that there was more to life than being barefoot and pregnant, Southern and rural women included. In country music, the image of female singers with towering hair and billowing gowns— the women writer Neil Hickey glibly referred to as looking like "fugitives from the court of Louis XIV"—was fading fast, and in 1988, an article by Hickey in *TV Guide* heralded a new breed of female country artists. His proof was K.T. Oslin, Patty Loveless, Kathy Mattea, and Rosanne Cash, all part of a crop of new singers like who looked more like their pop or rock contemporaries—or for that matter, the average woman on the street—than the country divas of yore.

Still, none of them looked quite like k.d. lang. As Burt Kearns wrote in *Spin* magazine shortly after *Shadowland* came out, she was "an enigma in a genre that likes to know the boys from the girls without having to reach down the front of their pants." Confusion followed her everywhere she went, like the day she wandered into the Lawrence Brothers' Record Shop on Nashville's lower Broadway. She had been out roaming the streets with a photographer from *Vogue* magazine, looking for a good place to snap some photos. As they passed the store, with its tattered collection of vintage country singles, k.d. knew the scene was ripe for a photo opportunity. She sauntered in and introduced herself.

Ted Lawrence, the shopowner's son, is a friendly fellow who loves to tell stories about the Nashville celebrities who have visited the store, and judging from the autographed pictures on the walls, there's been plenty. But it's k.d. who really sticks out in his mind. "We was

HERE'S LOOKING AT YOU

just standing there talking, and a few minutes later she says she's gotta go get her friend, and she went out the door and come back with Randy Travis," he says. Impressed by the company she kept, he told k.d. that she and her crew could snap all the photos they wanted. He snickers at what happened next.

"She had some fancy outfit with her, so she went back in the back to change her clothes, and she had this girl with her, too. My dad was back there working, and as soon as he saw the two of them go back, he come up to the front and told my mom, 'Some girl's in the back with that guy.' Mama said, 'Why, there ain't no guy back there. That's two girls.' And he didn't know what to say."

The elder Lawrence, blushing, relives the story as he tugs on his cigar. Then he reaches for his own worn copy of *Vogue,* which he keeps tucked handily under the antique cash register, and rifles through the pages until he gets to the photo of k.d. He stares at it contentedly for a moment, then zeros in on a record she's turning in her hand. "She bought some old Patsy Cline singles," he remembers, pensively tapping the page.

■

Kathryn Dawn Lang was used to being called "sir." There was an evening in 1983, at the Longhorn Saloon in Calgary, when a guy approached her to settle a $200 bet he had riding on whether she was a boy or a girl. But even before she got famous, she had already accepted that being a big-boned gal would forever be her blessing— or her curse.

Kathy recalls having been delighted as a child by the fact that her mother told her she was "handsome," which not only nourished her self-esteem but also encouraged her to stand tall in the face of societal pressures regarding women's beauty. As an adult, k.d.'s homemade haircuts and bizarre grooming regimens gave others the impression that she cared very little about her looks. Yet at the same time, her vibrancy and natural beauty intrigued people. "She never used soaps, and she didn't use shampoo or traditional toothpaste, or any of that sort of thing," Lin Elder recalls. "It was all some organic stuff. And she *never* washed her hair, yet she had the most beautiful hair." Elder was impressed by the apparent ease with which k.d. ignored the most basic dictates of what it meant to be feminine.

But there are some things a kid can't escape, and Kathy, like all women, did have issues when it came to her own image. At age thirteen she weighed 170 pounds, inciting her siblings to taunt her with the nickname "Mama Kath Elliot." She admits that ever since, she's never been fully comfortable with her body size. "k.d. always seemed so strong and full of confidence, and I always thought that if I could be any bit as confident as her I'd be on my way," remarks Elder. "But I realized after a while that she did have some insecurities about her appearance. She confided in me once that she wished she didn't look so much like a man, and that it really bothered her. She seemed extremely concerned about it at the time, and I remember looking at her and thinking that it was odd she felt so insecure that way, because really, she was quite beautiful, and she's gotten even more beautiful as her career has progressed."

Had she chosen a less ostentatious career path, perhaps Kathy's size and overall appearance would have never been an issue in her life. But as it was, her name rarely turned up in the press without some mention of the way she looked. It was ironic, because her fashion choices—long skirts, baggy suits, jeans and sweatshirts revealed little about her figure and even less flesh—seemed designed to draw attention *away* from her body. Yet in the end, her bizarre getups gave people the perfect excuse to discuss exactly that.

The fact that everyone was looking at her made Kathy a little crazy in the beginning, and on one occasion it went to her head—literally. "I started to feel this weird change in my personality and I was getting vain and very concerned about the way I looked," she said of an incident that occurred shortly after she had signed with Sire Records. "Then one day I needed to give myself a haircut, and for some reason I just kept cutting and cutting and cutting. When I finally looked into the mirror, I was bald. I had to perform that night in front of 3,500 people, which was huge for me at the time. So I wore a hat, but in the middle of the show, I took the hat off, and 3,500 people gasped." It was just the reaction she needed to snap her back into shape. "I just went, 'Yeah,' because it gave me this incredible feeling of breaking through."

Overall, Kathy worked hard at loving and accepting the way she looked, and decided early on that others would just have to accept it too. She knew she could never maintain her sanity wearing high heels and a dress every day, so she didn't bother to try. Rather than pretend to be something she was not, she chose a style and image that represented a natural response to how she felt, giving her both comfort

Young Kathy Lang always knew she would be famous. By tenth grade she decided to make it official by signing her name with a star. (Courtesy of Consort High School)

A rare fashion moment in k.d.'s life was when she donned a dress for the high school prom. Even then, the hiking boots remained firmly on her tomboy feet. (Courtesy of Consort High School)

If she were known for anything, it was her outstanding athletic abilities. Pictured here as Consort's senior volleyball team are coach Larry Kjearsgaard, Kate Tait, Cahrlene Schetzsle, Margaret Deagle, Debbie Vincett, Joanne Neumeier, Marilyn Mohr, Noraine Symes, Lila Kyfiuk, Cheryl Meier, Wanda Deleff, and Kathy Lang. (Courtesy of Consort High School)

*Kathy's friends were shocked to see the emergence of k.d.
lang. Yet her sawed-off cowboy boots and plastic skirt
accessories soon became her trademark.* (Tom Braid)

She invited her audiences to have a "wing ding daddy-o of a good time" as she tore up the stage, spraying everyone with sweat in the process. (Tom Braid)

Once she recorded
Shadowland: The Owen Bradley Sessions,
k.d.'s obsession with Patsy Cline ceased. It remains one of her
finest albums. (Dean Dixon)

k.d.'s collaboration with Loretta Lynn, Kitty Wells, and
Brenda Lee signaled her desire to be accepted into the
Nashville family circle. (Dean Dixon)

When k.d. posed with Lulu to protest eating animals, some Albertans fought back, defacing a sign at the edge of Consort with slogans like "Eat Beef Dyke." But not everyone in Consort agreed. Here, local supporters attempt to clean the sign while showing support with posters reading "Help Support k.d.'s Freedom" and "We Still Love k.d. and We Still Love Beef." (*OPPOSITE: Courtesy of PETA; ABOVE: Courtesy of* The Edmonton Sun*)*

When k.d. played a lesbian in the movie Salmonberries, *she knew it would be hard to ignore the bearing it had on her real life.* (Courtesy of Lenora Films)

Once k.d. came out, Sandra Bernhard, Liza Minnelli, and Wendy Melvoin were just three of the many women gossip columnists tried to pair her with. (*LEFT: Nick Elgar*/London Features; *BELOW: Vinnie Zuffante*/Star File)

*You know times are
changing when women
begin dressing up as gay
men who dress up as
women. (Nick Elgar/*
London Features; ACROSS:
Brett Lee/Starfile)

*Who could possibly top the Donna Summer/Barbra Streisand duet version of "Enough Is Enough," except possibly k.d. lang and Andy Bell? (David Fisher/*London Features*)*

In 1993 k.d. lang won a Grammy for Best Female Vocalist. Recognized as the best voice of her generation, she also became the first out lesbian to win such an award. (Ron Wolfson/ London Features*)*

More than family, friends, or fans, k.d.'s true passion is reserved for the animals in her life. (Stephen Danelian/Outline)

and confidence. For a time in the late eighties she even cultivated her boyish image, wearing clothes and hairdos that made her look more like a young Martin Sheen than a female country-music diva.

By 1989 she had upgraded her wardrobe from bargain box hand-outs to Nudie suits, those garish, rhinestone-covered inventions named for their designer, Nudie Cohen, and immortalized by artists like Porter Wagoner, Gene Autry, and Elvis Presley. The suits further enhanced her gender ambiguity, and for a time she almost became like a North American female Boy George—a cross-dresser, a woman in drag. Not that drag was rare among entertaining women: from Marlene Dietrich to Liza Minnelli to Annie Lennox, sassy babes have always loved playing boys for a day. The difference was that unlike most of these otherwise glamorous women, k.d. wasn't playing. Nobody waited at the end of the day for her trousers to come off and the mascara to go back on. Were it not for that unmistakable voice, it would be curious to know how many people actually thought she *was* a man as she waltzed across their TV screens.

Will it play in Peoria? It's always the question nagging at the back of a marketer's mind, and one that the Sire team could hardly have ignored. For all intents and purposes the label resisted the temptation to toy with k.d.'s image. Still, her music already presented a serious marketing dilemma, and having people hung up on her looks only complicated the matter. If the message was never spelled out to her, it was implied nonetheless: she'd sell more records if she would play by the rules. But she was convinced that such compromise would be detrimental to her work. "I sing because of the way I am," she says without hesitation. "I don't want to endanger my soul and my voice because of my physical looks. It wouldn't be worth it."

To offset people's criticisms of the way she dressed and to help put them at ease, k.d. often cracked her own jokes about her masculine appearance—and the inherent implications. When, for example, TV host Lorraine Crook seemed skeptical of her assertion that she had driven a grain truck as a teen, k.d. teased, "Wait—you're looking at me and saying you're shocked I drove a grain truck? I don't buy it." After pausing for a beat while the speechless Crook pondered the retort, she chided: "Oh, you just didn't think I could actually hold a job, is that it?"

To a certain degree, the humor worked, and by 1989 k.d. seemed to be winning the image battle. Despite her scant exposure to radio, she *was* selling records, and the exuberance with which people received her in concert helped build her following even more. But it wasn't just her breathtaking talent that was attracting this growing legion of fans. In no small way, what k.d. represented was more than great entertainment. She was a refreshing glitch in the pop music machine, embodying wit, charm, and a down-to-earth realness that her fans simply adored. She knew this and she wasn't about to do anything that might jeopardize it.

Years later, when a journalist asked k.d. if her androgynous look was calculated, she denied it. But she did concede that her sexual ambiguity gave her the freedom to move beyond the boundaries of her body, and that her use of theatrical cross-dressing allowed her to transcend her sex while still remaining sexy. "Elvis is alive, and is she ever beautiful," cooed Madonna with typical flourish, recalling the erotic charge that was often part of an Elvis Presley performance. k.d.'s gender may have been in question, but her sexual energy was not, and if people were shocked by the way she looked, they were even more shocked by the way she made them feel.

"I always found her really attractive in a very strange way," Lin Elder confesses. "She has an appeal about her—a charisma, especially onstage, and especially as she's gotten older and removed all her gear and it's just her up there. She has that ability to turn on a female audience *and* a male audience, which is a bonus for any artist." Part of k.d.'s allure has to do with a certain physical grace and sense of her own body, traits that reflect not only her athleticism but her sheer and abundant energy. Some say k.d. transcends sexuality, but that doesn't account for the multitudes of men and women who have fallen in love with her over the years. Far from avoiding sexuality, what k.d. really seems to do is sidestep sexual boundaries, calling forth a balance of male and female energy that enhances her sex appeal.

Few people who've witnessed a k.d. lang performance have been able to avoid her spell. Nashville shopkeeper Ted Lawrence, for example, tells a story of a young man who couldn't stand the fact that k.d. looked like a guy. In fact, it bothered him so much he could barely stop talking about it. But eventually the poor guy got dragged along by his parents to one of her concerts. "Now he says he can't get enough of her," Lawrence laughs.

The controversy over k.d.'s looks really had little to do with whether or not she was attractive. Sure, there was the stodgy old editor of *Alberta Report* who, in 1983, balked at the suggestion of putting her on the cover of his regional news weekly because he thought she was "too ugly"—an argument he lost after his staff pointed out that if cows were attractive enough to be on the publication's cover, then so was k.d. But in truth, what bothered people, and particularly those in power, was not k.d.'s biological features. The problem was the message her 'look' conveyed.

"I hate to sound like a feminist," says Nashville-based singer/songwriter Janis Ian with complete sincerity, resorting to a rhetoric whose efficacy she questions. "But the music industry, in the upper, upper echelons, is basically controlled by white men who are over fifty. Someone like k.d. lang scares the shit out of them. She doesn't look like she's an *ingenue,* to use a play on words. And in the case of Nashville, she walked in here with that haircut and that androgynous look and said, 'I'm cooler than you are.' That's a rough one to follow, especially if you're a record-company person."

What made k.d. seem so cool to some while earning her the cold shoulder from others was her refusal to bow to industry expectations. Such assertiveness was hard for some to swallow since, as she herself explained in conversations with American journalist and talk-show host Connie Chung, "Assertiveness and self-confidence are viewed as male characteristics, which is bullshit."

"But why do you have to dress like that if you are assertive anyway?" asked Chung, moving beyond the question of fashion to the far more complex issue of k.d.'s "in your face" approach.

"I don't see why you shouldn't dress any way you want to," k.d. responded, obviously bored with the entire line of reasoning.

Unfortunately, outward appearances have always played a significant role in how female entertainers are perceived, both by the general public and the entertainment industry. In this regard, Ian, who moved from Los Angeles to Nashville in 1988, doesn't think country music is that much different from any other form of pop entertainment. "Country music is very carefully defined," she says, conceding that most of the country women she knows spend an inordinate amount of time grooming. But she's not sure that women in other genres of music fare a whole lot better. "If I were a man, I would have never had to go through a lot of the stuff I've been through, including arguing with people about wearing dresses," she says. Not sure whether to laugh or cry she adds, "Have you ever tried to play the guitar and look cool in a dress?"

Amy Curland, owner of the Bluebird Cafe, agrees that there are certain expectations governing how country-music women are sup-posed to look, but an attempt to define those rules and parameters leaves her at a loss for words. "What that look is, exactly, I can't describe," she says hesitantly. "Obviously Wynonna Judd doesn't por-tray home and family very well. The last time I saw her on TV, she was wearing what looked to be a black leather harness. But she's gotten past image, and doesn't have to deal with that anymore. She already was the good girl, so now if she wants to be a rebel, everyone says, 'Oh, isn't that cute. She's a rebel.' And then you have Tanya Tucker, who's a single mother, and extremely blatant about it, and yet she got to go sing the national anthem at the Republican National Convention."

The difference is that unlike Wynonna or Tanya Tucker, k.d.'s image defied classification. She represented neither virgin nor whore, and that alone made people nervous, especially amid the traditionally conservative realm of commercial radio. "The image she projects scares the living hell out of country radio," observed Warner's Nick Hunter of k.d.'s inability to get her music played there. "She doesn't have hair piled on top of her head. She doesn't look like the rest of them, and that intimidates people."

Inherent in k.d.'s rejection of traditional standards of womanhood was what it implied about her sexuality, since it was clear she wasn't out there looking for a husband. Asked if he thought it was k.d.'s music that posed a challenge to country radio programmers, Nick Hunter responds with a resounding "No," standing firm in his belief that the problem had *everything* to do with her image. "I would say that people taking a look at her decided that her sexual preference was not the way it should be," he states, "and I guarantee you, it held her back."

Issues around gender and sexual orientation are always closely linked, and in k.d.'s case it was hard to tell where the sexism ended and the homophobia began. But there was no denying that even when her music did get played on the radio, it was rarely without some sort of accompanying wisecrack from the on-air peanut gallery. "I remem-ber the first time I heard her on the radio," says journalist Michael McCall from Nashville. "*Shadowland* had just come out, it was late at night, and I heard one of her songs and thought, 'Gee, that's the first time I've heard her on the radio.' And at the end of the song the DJ made some remark about her haircut, like, 'She looks like she went to my barber.'" Comments like these were not necessarily nasty. Still, it was frustrating for k.d. to realize that her gender and her appearance carried so much weight in an industry that was supposed to be about music.

If there's one thing that distinguishes the world of pop music from its country cousin, it's the inherent need to be cool and cutting edge. People in Hollywood may not have understood k.d. anymore than folks in Nashville, but they certainly weren't about to admit it. Instead they played along with the joke, and as more and more people came to appreciate her talent and her charm, many stopped laughing at her, and started laughing with her.

In December 1989, *People* magazine indulged the sartorial renegade by inviting her to be one of the judges for their year-end roundup of celebrity style, "The Good, The Bad, and The Ugh-ly." In a glorious bit of fashion lampooning, k.d. delightedly took aim at a photo of Jackie Onassis. "It looks like she managed to get enough velvet off her old Elvis paintings to get a dress," she quipped. A year later she was savoring the irony of having her name on the season's best- *and* worst-dressed lists, noting that perhaps her interpretation of women's wear was finally catching on. "I did notice that Cher was looking very k.d. lang this year," she grinned in a MuchMusic interview, pointing out that Cher had been seen wearing little black jackets with rhinestones and baggy pants. "She was dressed just like me, but her hair was higher."

What was really catching on was not so much her look, but the attitude represented by k.d.'s willingness to buck the system. Consider it a quiet revolution, as people began warming to the idea that women could refuse to wear makeup and still be both alluring and successful. She may not have gotten the radio play she deserved, making it harder for her to reach people, but for those she did reach—particularly women—she became a role model. The result was a growing fan base of people extremely loyal to the artist, and who took it personally whenever they found her subjected to unwarranted attack. There was public outcry, for example, when the odious fashion dictator Mr. Blackwell tried to dismiss her, making the venomous claim that "as a woman, she rates a zero." One angry woman summed it up in a letter to her local newspaper, declaring, "As an intellect, Mr. Blackwell rates the same, and he can't sing."

By the end of the decade k.d. had developed quite a "crossover" following, despite the fact that Sire was still marketing her primarily as a country artist. In addition to attracting an alternative-music crowd who loved her spunk and her outrageous stage energy, she was becoming quite the darling among other artists in the pop music industry. In Los Angeles, Madonna, Sandra Bernhardt, Warren Beatty, and Jennifer Grey were a few of the many celebrities who turned up frequently at her shows. In the East, Bernadette Peters, Johnny Lydon, and Debby Harry were self-declared fans.

k.d. enjoyed hobnobbing with the entertainment elite, particularly when it meant meeting idols. She appeared with Peggy Lee in a photo for *Rolling Stone,* where the two sported matching black leather jackets for a spread about artists and their role models. She sang a duet with childhood hero Anne Murray for a Canadian country-music retrospective. And eventually, she even got to meet Joni Mitchell, her songwriting inspiration and the only person she says has ever made her star-struck. And contrary to the ambivalence she had felt just three years earlier, she was finally starting to realize and accept how much she loved all the attention she was getting, even though it could sometimes be draining. "Fame brings this unconscious pressure that you're constantly being observed and judged, that your energy is wanted," she confessed. "At the same time, if you go for a certain period when you're not recognized, this animal inside you goes, 'What's happening?' " As all celebrated artists must, she was learning that fame could not only be exhausting, but addictive as well.

■

Despite the attention and recognition she was getting from her peers, the one thing k.d. lacked more than anything else in 1989 was her very own hit—a signature song that would anchor her forever in the soundtrack of pop culture. She wouldn't have that hit for another four years, but on May 10, 1989, she gave a performance that became the next best thing, when she sang "Crying" as part of a tribute to Roy Orbison at the 20th-anniversary celebration of the Songwriters' Hall of Fame.

It was no small honor that k.d. had been asked by Orbison's widow, Barbara, to be part of the all-star celebration. It would be an evening filled with some of the entertainment world's most beloved stars, ranging from Quincy Jones to Liza Minnelli, and she prepared for nearly four months to make sure that her performance would be deserving of the honor. Nevertheless, she had to take a deep breath when she arrived on the night of the show to discover that she was the only one given a dressing room that had neither bathroom nor mirror, a stark reminder of her position in the evening's celebrity pecking order. Her response? She stole the show.

As was her way, k.d. prepared for her performance with a total mind-and-body workout—one which she would perfect in great detail over the years, to the amusement of her fans. The regimen, as she describes it, is as follows: "First I take a washcloth, pull my tongue out a little bit—not to where it hurts, just a little bit—and then wiggle it back and forth. What it does is like a physical stretching of the vocal chords, a sort of reflexology. Then I take a long shower. I'll have eaten just once in the afternoon so that my sinuses are clear, and I won't have eaten dairy. I chew a lot of these Swiss-made cough drops, which are eucalyptus, sugar-free. Then I stretch, and sometimes I get a little bit of a shoulder massage. I'll drink something room-temperature, water maybe, and then I'll do some sort of aerobic thing to get my adrenaline and my heart rate up. And then I get cocky. Look in the mirror a lot. Be kind of dirty. Because the voice is many things. There's a physical side, and there's the attitude side—the spiritual, the sexual. So it's only fair to exercise both of them."

If k.d. wasn't well-known among the guests at Radio City that night, she wasn't soon to be forgotten. Her performance earned her a ten-minute standing ovation—quite an achievement given the audience—and would become one of the hallmarks of her career. "I have never seen a singer who calls on every part of her body like that," says CBC's Paul McGrath, echoing what many in the audience experienced that night. "From her toenails to her hair follicles, she seems to draw this whole energy up through her legs and down through her gut, all at the same time. It's astounding to watch, and it's scary to watch, the extreme physical nature of what she does. She has to, because to summon up that kind of power in your voice, you've got to be using your body in a way that most people don't. It's almost like I can feel it in *my* throat when she sings, and to watch her gets *my* body doing the same thing. Like, 'C'mon, you can hit it,' and it's so involving that you feel yourself pushing for her, tensing your muscles, hoping she's going to hit the top note on key."

It was just what Liam Lacey had experienced when he saw her very first performance in Toronto five years earlier. And once again, it seemed that the more pressure that k.d. was under, the better she performed. "She didn't fuck up when an opportunity presented itself," assures Lacey, ticking off the times when k.d. had found herself in a situation that could make her or break her. "Edmonton, Toronto, New York, Nashville, 'The Tonight Show.' When it was a key performance, or a showcase, she nearly always did really exceptional work, and she seemed to know everything she had to do to make it work. She just had this great capacity to rise to the occasion."

There were a lot of reasons why the Radio City performance was special for k.d. Being the underdog, getting bottom billing, with so many egos flying was a big part of it, and the challenge fueled her determination. "I really do get up for those big shows," she concedes. "I think it's the high-school athlete in me coming out. I'm a naturally competitive person, and I find a lot of affiliations between sports and performing." But more than that, her Radio City performance was k.d.'s personal gift to Roy Orbison's legacy.

Later that night, as she sat recovering in her tiny dressing room, there was a knock on the door. She rose to greet Liza Minnelli, who gushed that she wanted to meet the young woman who had so magically taken her breath away. k.d. returned the compliment—after all, it was Minnelli who had received the only other standing ovation of the evening. The two hit it off immediately, and became instant friends, sparking a relationship that has only grown with time.

◼

When k.d. returned to Vancouver following the close of her work with *Shadowland,* the reclines—or at least what was left of them, namely Ben Mink, Michel Pouliot, and Gordie Matthews—were thrilled and relieved to finally be invited to return to the studio together. Understandably, they'd been a little nervous about their place in k.d.'s band while she was away, but once they were reunited, k.d. noticed a renewed energy among them. To round out the unit, John Dymond was recruited to replace Dennis Marcenko on bass, while Greg Leisz added the sound of whining steel that k.d. had become so fond of. It was a tight unit, with k.d. firmly at the helm, a more mature and experienced artist than she had been when she left them two years earlier.

Of the many things she learned from Owen Bradley, one was how to get what she wanted from her musicians without jeopardizing the harmony of the group. She had always tried to be a good band leader, but there were inherent challenges in working so intimately with so many other people. "It's very hard, because you're so self-absorbed half the time and so many people are demanding everything from you," she confessed. "It's like a marriage with seven other people, and you have to treat them like lovers or family. You live with them and each one is a relationship."

Matthews, k.d.'s guitarist, remembers her as being a pretty good team player, and says she treated her musicians very well. "You can't work with anybody and not have sparks," he points out. "But overall, she would definitely listen, and if there was ever a real problem, she would deal with it. Some people just freak out and leave the room, but she was pretty reasonable. She knew what she wanted, and she'd work with people until she got it."

As jobs go, Matthews feels that working with the reclines was a pretty good gig while it lasted. The money was decent, if not overwhelming, and he enjoyed the kind of music the band was making. Yet by 1989, he couldn't help feeling that the pressures of the industry had greatly altered what had once been the k.d. lang experience. "I think things really changed once she started working with the record company and trying to get into Nashville," he says in hindsight. "We really lost some of that energy that we'd had when we were still a more alternative band, and there were some exciting things happening in the beginning that never got truly captured in the studio." As far as Matthews is concerned, k.d.'s much-heralded recording contract and the constant pressure put on her to write songs took a lot of the fun and spontaneity out of what they were doing. He also feels that Ben Mink's arrival permanently altered the dynamic of the group. "After that, there was a whole different energy there," he says with a hint of melancholy. "All of a sudden, k.d. wasn't really hanging out with anyone else as much."

Nevertheless, he concedes that despite the fun and excitement of those early years, k.d. was still in the process of flushing out her identity as an artist, and therefore needed to make whatever changes she thought would bring her closer to that ideal. It wouldn't be easy, since she didn't really know exactly what stood between her and a really great record. All she knew was that none of her first three albums had been able to capture the true nature of what she was doing as a performer. Her first project, *a truly western experience*, had been a test run, long on effort but short on planning and production. *Angel With A Lariat* was a lot of the right ingredients in the wrong doses, and *Shadowland*, for all its brilliance, had been a borrowed affair, fueling many people's suspicions that k.d.'s talent was as an interpreter, and that she shouldn't bother with her own songs. Her hope was that her fourth album would bring together all that was good in the other three, creating a package that would put her over the top.

Sire's A&R department was convinced that k.d.'s real problem remained a lack of strong original material, and the team spent considerable time pondering options for strengthening her overall concepts. Part of this involved discussions with the band, in which Seymour Stein asked them what they thought they needed to come up with some good songs. Matthews thought they needed time together away from the road. "I said, 'Geez, you know, we never really have time to write songs, because everybody lives all over the country. What if we had a month in a rehearsal studio just trying to write some tunes?' Everybody seemed to think that was a great idea."

Unfortunately, those conversations denied the reality that Mink and k.d. had become the songwriting team, and that the others were really nothing more than musicians for hire. Matthews got the impression that everyone in the band was going to be given the chance to bring in their own material for the group to work on together. But when k.d. and Ben showed up with a demo tape of twelve new songs, he knew it wasn't going to happen. "I was under the perception that things were going to proceed in a different manner than they did," he says regretfully. "If they would have just said flat-out that Ben and Kathy were going to write all the material, then fine. But they all seemed to think our working together was a great idea, and I was kind of expecting it to happen. Then, when we got the tapes with the songs already on them and were told we were going in to record them, well, I improvised some solos here and there, but at that point, we definitely weren't included."

Matthews's disappointment was enough to tempt him to quit the group, but since he didn't have any better offers at the time, he decided to stick it out for the duration of the new album's tour. Nevertheless, he realized then just how much things had changed in five years, and he knew his time with the reclines was coming to an end. "I had definitely become a side guy at that point, and I knew it wasn't the best place to be," he says, adding that he understands the professional decisions k.d. had to make and doesn't hold any grudges. "I never assumed it would last forever," he says wistfully. "It would have maybe been nice to bail out after a few more bucks had come my way. But those things happen all the time. People need to change and try different things until they find whatever it is that they're looking for. That was her call, and I can't hold it against her."

Besides, even Matthews concedes that when *Absolute Torch and Twang* was unveiled, it was clear k.d. and Ben Mink had finally found what they were looking for.

9

IT was May 16, 1989, and up on the monitor at The Nashville Network, k.d. lang, with her rosy cheeks, tousled hair, and torn jeans, was looking just as farm-fed and boyish as ever. But the changes showed in the eyes, and in the oh-so-subtle smirk that curled out of the corners of

PLANTATION RADIO

her lips. It was another visit to "Crook and Chase," and this time k.d. was fielding questions from the audience.

"How come they're not playing your records on the radio?" asked Bob from Pennsylvania.

"Bob," she heaved with thinly veiled disgust, "I don't know."

k.d. was tired of asking herself that same question, tired of banging her head against the walls that seemed to fortress Nashville's Music Row, and as her patience waned, so did her ability to cheerfully persevere in the face of such hostile misgivings. An acerbic sarcasm began to wash through the jokes that had once deflected people's criticisms and mistrust as she struggled to get her point across. "This is the newest k.d. lang single," she told the crowds during her *Torch and Twang* tour. "Which, of course, means to program directors: Do Not Play this Record." Her audience may have been her "friends and neighbors," but her relationship with country-music radio was becoming much more "us" and "them."

k.d.'s frustration was enhanced by the fact that *Absolute Torch and Twang*, which she co-produced with Mink and the newly re-

125

cruited Greg Penny, was nothing short of a brilliant album, combining the liveliness of her first record with the quietly seductive emotion that enveloped *Shadowland*. Some of the songs, like the enduring "Trail of Broken Hearts" and "Pulling Back the Reins," had a stark, haunting quality to them, the result of a "mood-setting" trek k.d. and Ben took through the badlands of Montana. Others, like "Big Big Love," and Willie Nelson's "Three Days," were more upbeat, although they too reflected a sense of style and arrangement that came directly from the Owen Bradley sessions. Overall, the record constituted a substantial nod to the classic sounds of Top 40 country music, and even revealed a lilt in k.d.'s voice which suggested that maybe she *had* been dipping into Loretta Lynn's bologna sandwiches after all. At the same time, the new album represented a graceful but firmly planted affirmation of k.d.'s own big-boned self, as the weepy artifice of *Shadowland* gave way to a more starkly revealing exploration of the artist's inner being.

Her fans ate it up, and three weeks out of the chute, *Absolute Torch and Twang* had sold over 200,000 copies, carrying k.d. nearly half the distance towards her first gold record. On June 17, 1989, the album debuted on *Billboard*'s Top Country Albums chart, where it stayed for 104 weeks, stopping just two short of the Top Ten. At the same time the album also appeared on the Top Pop Albums chart, where it peaked at No. 69 during its 56-week run. On July 4th k.d. and the reclines hit the road, kicking off a tour in Jacksonville, Florida, which would cover 40 stops in 75 days (and that was just the first leg). One week later, "Full Moon Full of Love" was climbing the country singles chart, signaling that more than a few radio stations had added the song to their playlists.

For a moment that summer, it looked like all of k.d.'s hard work was about to pay off. The record company quickly sold the 250,000 units they needed to break even on the album and coasted comfortably into the profit margin. Royalties from radio play would soon be flowing in. And night after night, in city after city, critics and fans alike were falling head over heels in love. At her sold-out show on August 11 at New York's Beacon Theater, the crowd dragged k.d. back for five encores. As a local journalist gushed, "Those who witnessed it were baptized. k.d. is God." It was the same everywhere she went.

But something still wasn't right about the way things were progressing down in hillbilly heaven, and one had to look no further than the Country Music Association to see it. Unlike the Los Angeles–based

Academy of Country Music, which has no real clout with people in Nashville, the CMA, boasting 6,800 members in 31 countries, is the only club in town for country-music artists, and considered the only true clearinghouse for all things country. On July 26, 1989, k.d. was nominated for a CMA Horizon Award, an honor given to an artist who demonstrates significant creative growth and development in terms of sales, chart activity, live performance, and critical media recognition. Yet she never, in all her years in country music, received a single nomination from the CMA membership for the general awards given out each October. Like a Grammy in the pop-music world, a CMA award would have meant that an overwhelming number of her peers— every one of them professionals working in the country-music industry—recognized her talent and were willing to cast her as one of them. But such was not the case.

■

Past the cash register, the maps, and the velvet ropes leading into the dark, cool chambers of the Country Music Hall of Fame, a photo hangs in honor of the Grand Ole Opry Family. Out of nearly a hundred familiar Opry legends whose faces appear within the frame, there are eighteen women in the photo. Among them, there's not a short-haired head in the bunch.

Women have always played a vital role in the country-music business, but until recently, the only place they've ever gotten much recognition has been as consumers. "The historical thinking, or the line you always hear, although it's never really been proven, is that women account for 70 percent of all albums and tickets sold," says Lon Helton, the country-music editor of the music trade magazine *Radio and Records*. "They either buy them, or they're the driving force behind the purchase. Consequently, country music has almost always been dominated by male artists, in order to appeal to those women."

The assumption, of course, is that women would rather see and hear male performers than they would other women. "Sales have always seemed to back that up, although it's hard to tell how much of it is a self-fulfilling prophecy," continues Helton. He says it was a long time before Dolly Parton had a hit record. "And even Tanya Tucker, who's been out there for twenty years, just had her first gold and platinum records in the last two or three. Historically, women artists just never sold a lot of records, and aside from Loretta and Tammy, who everybody knows, very few of them could actually sell hard tickets either. They were always on the labels as a nice balance, but it's only in the last few years that female acts have proven a viability at the cash register."

Helton has no explanation for why female country artists are suddenly so popular, except to point to changes in society in general, and the fact that more women are working in country-music radio. But Beverlee Brannigan, Director of Programming Operations of KJJY in Des Moines, Iowa, doesn't see the changes taking place at the radio level. "There may be more women on the air, but if you look down the list, I think I'm still one of two women program directors in country music," she says. Instead, she thinks that changes have taken place within the record companies. "I've never sensed that men programmers have had any prejudice against women artists," she says tentatively. "More than anything I think it just took a successful woman or two to make some money for a record company. Then they said 'Oh, that's interesting, we can make some money with these women,' and they started paying more attention to them, giving them better songs and better producers."

Others on Music Row agree. A recent spoof in *Close Up,* CMA's monthly magazine, asked the question, "What would happen if women held 50 percent of the top jobs in the music industry?" One response was: "Male record execs would be subjected to public hanging for disguising a lack of marketing savvy with the old adage, 'Female consumers just don't buy girl singers.' "

Sexism clearly played a hand in what was happening to k.d., which hardly took her by surprise. "The contradiction of playing the strong female within what is basically a submissive role I found extremely exciting," she acknowledged of the battle she seemed more than willing to wage vis-à-vis country music. But k.d.'s problems were not the result of an inattentive record label. And although she didn't seem to understand it at the time, they had little to do with Nashville, either.

"Nashville, for all intents and purposes, is a songwriting town," explains *Country Music* columnist Hazel Smith. "It's the Tin Pan Alley of the South, and has been for years. The thing is that recently some miracles have happened around here—miracles in the form of Garth Brooks and Billy Ray Cyrus. They came in here, the timing was perfect, and now we've got an artist who can compete with a Michael Jackson, and who can take the cover of *Rolling Stone.* It's one of the coolest stories that's come out of this hillbilly town, I guaran-damn-tee ya.

But what I'm trying to say is that a lot of times Nashville gets blamed for stuff that they shouldn't be blamed for."

Bill Ivey, executive director of the Country Music Foundation, agrees that there are limits to how much control Nashville has over what goes on in the country music industry. "The artistic community in Nashville has as its core the singer/songwriter," he explains. "It is not genre-specific, although it's generally in the categories of pop, rock, folk, and country. The country part of the Nashville community has to do with selling records, and they do it primarily through radio."

k.d. lang was, as many have said, one of the greatest singers to pass through Nashville in a long, long time. But Music Row's ability to make her a star only went so far. Sure, the industry movers and shakers could put her on TV, on talk shows like "Nashville Now" and as part of their music video lineups. And they could spread word about her throughout the industry. All of these things, and more, they did to help insure her success. But when it comes to country radio, Nashville's primary function is to provide stations with the music that fills the space between commercials. Beyond that, it's up to the radio programmers to decide who they're willing to play.

k.d. assumed that Nashville wasn't prepared to accept a woman who challenged so much of what country music was about. But as far as a lot of Nashvillians were concerned, her problems had nothing to do with them. "Where does she live? Up there in Canada. Out there in L.A.," snaps Hazel Smith, emphasizing the disconnected nature of the business. "They got country radio stations out in Los Angeles, and in Canada, and New York City, too. There's a lot of artists who can sell albums, but can't get their songs on radio. Now, who's fault is it? It ain't the fan's fault, and it ain't Nashville's fault either."

Nick Hunter and others in Sire's marketing department knew whose fault it was, and it frustrated the hell out of them that they couldn't do anything about it. "When she did her showcase for *Shadowland* here in Nashville," he recalls, "I was sitting right next to the music director of one of the local country radio stations. The album hadn't been out very long, maybe a month at best, but everybody in that place knew every song she was singing. So I turned to him and I said, 'Now doesn't that bother you a little bit? Here's an audience that, age-group-wise, you want your radio station to appeal to, and you want to have listening to you, right?' And he said, 'Absolutely.' So I said, 'Don't you think it's odd, considering your station's probably never played a k.d. lang record, that this entire audience knows every one of her songs, and are singing along?' " The radio man had nothing to say.

Oermann was equally dumbfounded and angered that country radio could ignore someone as talented as k.d. "I knew from personal experience that even the squarest country crowd really dug what she was doing," he said incredulously. "But it was those fucking programmers, misinterpreting their audience, and their complete lack of faith in people's abilities and people's tastes." It was a disgrace, given k.d.'s strong sales and growing fan base, that country radio wasn't willing to give her that added boost that would have pushed her over the top. And Oermann was proud that the print media wasn't so ignorant. "Never let anyone tell you that the printed word doesn't sell records," he insists, "because she wouldn't have sold record one if it hadn't been for us." Nevertheless, until she could get her music onto the radio airwaves, there were limits to how far k.d. could go.

■

It was 1940, and Todd Storz, who ran radio station KOWH in Omaha, Nebraska, had pulled up a stool in the local watering hole around the corner from his office. There he sat with a colleague, marveling at the rapid growth of FM radio, and discussing a programming dilemma that had nagged him for some time. How, he wondered, could he keep a handle on the myriad freewheeling DJs who were going crazy with all the records streaming their way from companies eager to get their artists on the air? It was then that he and his drinking partner noticed the waitress standing over the jukebox, dropping nickel after nickel of her hard-earned tips into the music machine. Much to their amazement, the young women chose the same song over and over again. An epiphany went off in Storz's head, and he ran back to the station. It was at that moment Top 40 radio was born.

In the half century since, an entire science has been built around defining audience listening patterns, as radio programmers attempt to figure out just what attracts listeners and what chases them away. Caller requests, telephone polls, Arbitron ratings, and local record retailers all provide information to stations regarding their potential listener base. Smaller stations that lack the resources to conduct their own market research often glean this information secondhand, by looking at the national record charts to see what other stations are playing. "A successful radio act is one that's selling albums, is charting, and has songs that people call for and request," says Beverlee Brannigan as she explains the process of choosing which artists get the most airplay at her station. "And we look to other markets to see who's playing it."

It doesn't take a genius to figure out that if most stations are waiting for other stations to tell them what to play, a few negative programming decisions can kill an artist's chances at radio. Brannigan concedes this is true, pointing to black cardiologist-turned-country-singer Clive Francis to illustrate the point. "There are a certain number of radio stations in the South that won't play him because he's black. And I suspect that there were also a certain number of stations that wouldn't play k.d. lang because she looked gay. Whatever the reason, if you've got five to ten major-market radio stations that won't play her, that could affect her chart activity a lot." Which, in turn, impacts on the radio play she'll get at radio stations who follow the charts.

On the subject of polling audiences, which often involves calling people on the phone, playing them a snippet of music, and asking them what they think, Oermann scoffs at the notion that this is science. "Of course audiences are going to hear a familiar voice and go, 'Yep, I like that one.' " As he sees it, this form of research only supports a commercial radio station's desire not to take chances airing any material that might alter its established listener base. "In the old days stations were like newspapers, owned by families—mom-and-pop operations who were like, 'Well, I like it,' and the music got on the air," Oermann observes. "But what has happened to radio, and country radio in particular, is that these FCC licenses have become increasingly valuable, and each time they've been sold it's been into larger and larger corporate hands. And as radio became big business, and the station licenses escalated ever higher in value, the whole situation became more conservative."

More important is the far more basic but oft-ignored fact that, much to the chagrin of the recording industry, radio is simply not in the business of selling records. Its business is to sell advertising, and to that end programmers will do whatever they need to in order to deliver the biggest possible market share to their clients. Usually, the way a station ensures the largest listening audience is by pandering to the lowest common denominator in consumer tastes. What it boils down to is not so much what listeners want to hear, but what they want *not* to hear.

In this context, the relationship between the music industry and radio is a strange one indeed, as Bill Ivey of the Country Music Foundation is quick to point out. "I think it's almost unique in the world of business," he says, baffled. "Here you've got an industry that goes through the whole process of creating a product, and then, instead of figuring out a way to sell that product, they say, 'Okay, now we're going to petition this other industry—namely radio, which has its own values and its own needs that are completely different from record production—and hope that maybe, if they're nice to us, they'll market our product.' You wouldn't sell shoes that way and you wouldn't sell cars that way. In any other industry you'd take your product all the way to the consumer."

It's a reality directly at odds with any creative ambition a record label might have. "Record companies thrive on innovation and novelty," Ivey continues. "They're always trying to break new artists, and they're always trying to get new material out there. Radio, on the other hand, thrives on repetition and familiarity." In the end, what this creates for the people making country music is a big, big funnel, with all the creativity of Nashville going into it. As the funnel narrows once, some of that creativity makes it onto a record. But then the funnel narrows again at radio, leaving very little end product available to the consumer." It's a dilemma that record companies have begun to get around with the rise of music television, which, for some reason, seems more willing to take chances. But even then, it's an uphill battle.

"I really do not understand what radio is looking for, nor what it takes to be categorized," says Lyle Lovett, who has had his own struggles with country radio. "I just try to write the best songs I can and do the best job recording them that I can. I don't know why one song gets played and another doesn't."

Unfortunately, neither does anyone who works in country radio. "I don't think you could get 225 radio programmers to agree that today is Wednesday," laughs Lon Helton. "There's no way that you can get them to agree on what to play, so I don't know if I could give you a blanket statement as to why they didn't play k.d. lang."

■

Nobody thought much of it when Clint Black, standing on the steps of the Vanderbilt Plaza Hotel in Nashville on a cool January day in 1990, announced k.d. lang's name among the list of five women who'd been nominated as Best Female Country Vocalist for the year's Grammy Awards. After all, nobody really expected her to win. But when, on February 21, she waltzed away with the award after a stunning performance at L.A.'s Shrine Auditorium, the gatekeepers of country radio quickly closed ranks.

"Here in Music City we have three awards shows of our own every year," Bruce Sherman of WSM-FM in Nashville told *Billboard*. "As far as our listeners are concerned, those are the real awards for country artists."

As far as country radio programmers were concerned, the Grammys bore no resemblance to what was really going on in country music. "Consider the people who vote for the Grammy nominees," said Russ Schell, of WFMS in Indianapolis. "Some are guys who produce rap records, some are from the world of classical music, and they're all asked to vote on genres in which they're unfamiliar. If Kool Moe Dee's producer is looking at a list of country nominees, he checks off the names he recognizes." In 1989, two country artists whose names had commonly appeared in the mainstream press were k.d. lang and fellow country renegade Lyle Lovett. And sure enough, it was Lovett who snagged the award for Best Male Country Vocalist.

In hindsight, it seems as though 1990 was a portentous year for country music, foretelling changes that would have never before been imaginable. But at the time, country radio programmers simply felt they were being railroaded. "I've tried every single that lang's released and I just haven't gotten anywhere," protested program director Don Christi of KRST in Albuquerque, echoing the common belief that *real* country-music fans would have never chosen lang and Lovett as their queen and king. "It's not as if people don't know who they are, but for whatever reason, country listeners have not embraced them."

The Grammys did stir things up, and a few stations tracked renewed interest in k.d., as *Absolute Torch and Twang* went gold, with sales of over 500,000 units. Even the half-baked *Angel With A Lariat* re-debuted on *Billboard*'s Top Country Albums chart immediately after her Grammy win, presumably because people were curious to discover what they had missed. But most country radio executives refused to acquiesce, maintaining that their audiences just weren't interested in k.d. lang's music. "The awards don't change too much for us," said Charlie Cassidy, program director for KKCS in Colorado Springs. "We're very research-intensive and neither artist has ever researched worth a darn in this area."

The Canadians, meanwhile, were appalled at the fact that American country radio continued to shun k.d. when it seemed so clear that the general public loved her. "She's being banned in the States by some major country stations because of her androgyny," declared one dismayed MuchMusic correspondent. "I was absolutely devastated when she was not up for Female Vocalist at the CMA awards. She could sing through her nose and sound better than most of those people, and it's beyond belief that they could close their ears to someone who sings like she does."

But even Mark Lewis, program director for WYNE in Appleton, Wisconsin, and an early k.d. fan, maintained that although she had struck a popular chord among much of his listening audience, people in the American heartland still seemed to have difficulty with her image. "I was watching the Grammys in a little hick bar, and you could see the cross section of people," he said. "There was a couple that were clearly our listeners and they cheered when lang won. But there were also two guys at the other end of the bar asking if that was a guy or a girl on-screen."

By winter, k.d. was at the height of frustration. She still wasn't doing all that well financially, between the lack of royalties from radio play and her need to support her staff—eight band members and a road crew of twenty-two, not to mention her manager and other office personnel. More importantly, it stood to reason that if she could sell half a million records and fill mid-sized concert halls without any radio play—enough quantifiable success that in March 1991 the National Association of Recording Merchandisers named *Absolute Torch and Twang* the year's best-selling female country album, based on 1990 sales figures—she could probably do double or even triple that with decent broadcast support.

"Radio is still the place where most country fans hear new music first," confirms Helton. "By and large, it's still the primary place where people are able gain exposure to the music, and most of the records that are being sold are being sold by country radio." Yet he hedges when asked how much further he thinks k.d. could have gone had radio programmers gotten behind her. "Radio airplay is just like ad-vertising hamburgers," he reasons. "You put your ad on the air, and hopefully somebody comes and buys your hamburgers. In terms of selling music, radio gives them a taste before they have to buy it, so that when people go to the store and see that record, they know what it sounds like. That's why record companies create hit singles. It's the advertisement for the album."

Helton balks at the suggestion that radio ignored k.d.'s records, claiming that just because she didn't appear on the country singles charts, it doesn't mean country radio's vast audience didn't hear her music. "There are roughly 2500 country radio stations in the U.S., and for the charts we select about 225 of them and ask them every week what they're playing," he explains. "I don't really recall where k.d.'s records peaked, but let's say at any given point they were on half of our playlists, or 110 stations. Then let's project that out and say they were on half of the rest of the stations. That's 12–1300 stations around the U.S. that could have been playing her records, and that's a lot of airplay." Helton's logic is flawed, of course, if you believe Beverlee Brannigan, who has already explained that a lot of smaller stations rely on the charts to tell them what to play. But questionable mathematics aside, Helton does admit that a record which appears on the singles chart has a much better chance of selling than one that doesn't. "It's probably a label's biggest frustration when an artist gets limited airplay and sells, because you think, 'My god, what would happen if they got huge amounts of airplay?' "

■

"I think the time has come for me to let go of the idea of being a country singer," k.d. sighed, kicking off her boots as the *Torch and Twang* tour finally ground to a halt in mid-1990. After six years of nearly nonstop touring, writing, and recording, she was ready to admit that she was thoroughly exhausted, and tired of the country scene in particular. "Country will always be a major influence on me," she insisted. "But I've also been influenced by everything from opera to Ofra Haza, and I'm not prepared to make the kind of compromises that would be necessary for me to be accepted by those people. At one time I did very much want to prove to them how much I honestly loved country music. But they make their own assessments whether you're honest or not."

With that, her Grammy win became a bittersweet victory—one that would allow her to walk away from Nashville with her head held high and her dignity intact. Yet, in perfect keeping with the myths, legends, and high-camp drama of country lore, there could be no final divorce settlement without a knock-down, drag-out fight.

10

*"I don't eat meat, I'm not a Christian, and I don't
have big fluffy hair, which basically stands against
a lot of the fundamentalist values on which country
music is based."*

IN June 1989, between the release of *Absolute Torch and Twang*
and its concomitant yearlong tour, k.d. found time to return to Red

STEERS, BEERS, AND QUEERS

Deer, rolling through town in a borrowed blue pickup. She was headed
for tiny, lazy Sylvan Lake, a resort community just a stone's toss west
of her old college town, where a crowd was gathering amid the clamor
and din of a ticker-tape parade. Native dancers, clowns, and the usual
civic roundup of local politicians cleared a path down Main Street,
making way for the tractor trailor carrying their beloved Alberta Rose.
As the saying goes, There's no place like home.

Rarely, if ever, had Albertans been so proud to claim someone
who had sat so many nights with Johnny Carson. Country music was
big in these parts, and k.d. was the first Canadian country artist in two
decades—since Anne Murray was first discovered—to achieve such
stardom beyond the national border. For the second year in a row,
the Canadian Country Music Association had honored k.d. as both
Entertainer of the Year and Best Female Vocalist, along with which
had come an award for Best Album for *Shadowland*. On this particularly sunny afternoon, the xenophobia threatening to thwart k.d.'s
American career must have seemed a million prairie miles away, as

the warmth with which her fellow Albertans greeted her rose to a fevered pitch. These people understood what others refused to: that *Absolute Torch and Twang* was one of the best country records available (it would appear six months later at No. 44 on *Billboard*'s list of the year's Top 50 Country Albums); that headlines raving about her talent and charm would draw capacity audiences for the *Torch and Twang* tour; and that k.d.'s star, regardless of the odds, would only continue to rise.

The occasion for the parade in Sylvan Lake was the taping of "k.d. lang's Buffalo Cafe," a CBC television special produced by Sandra Faire and featuring Dwight Yoakam, comedian Susan Norfleet, and Canadian folk hero and renowned eccentric Stompin' Tom Connors, who was making a comeback after a lengthy retirement from country music with a song called "Lady k.d. lang." The show took its name from the Buffalo Tavern, a murky, cockroach-infested Chinese/western diner in downtown Red Deer, where k.d. and her friends had shared gossip and a cheap cup of soup on many a quiet evening back in the early 1980s. The idea was to return to the Buffalo Tavern to celebrate those days. But alas, so quaintly run-down was the Buffalo Tavern that, rather than taping a live concert in the faintly powered lounge, Faire's crew sought to re-create the scene in the Quality Inn down the block— elevating the "tavern" to the status of "cafe" in the process.

For k.d., the show that aired on Canadian national television on November 12, 1989, was the culmination of many months of rejecting close to a dozen television proposals, not to mention rewriting Faire's original script, which had her performing in a studio in Toronto. "They came to me with a completely different idea," she said, "where I acted in someone else's script. That was fine, but I just didn't feel it was right for me. I wanted the show to be real and have the roots of my experiences in it. This is where I'm from, and this is where I get most of the imagery and visualizations for my music and performance. It's sort of coming full circle to come back," she waxed, recalling the days when she, Drifter, and a few other friends were convinced they held the world in their hands.

Getting the legendary Stompin' Tom to make his first television appearance in over a decade took some maneuvering on k.d.'s part, and it was clearly the highlight of the show. At the time, Connors was retired from music, having quit the industry in a huff after becoming disenchanted with the drab commercialism and regional politics that seemed part and parcel of the business. But for k.d., who cited him as a strong inspiration when she won her first Juno back in 1985, he was willing to step back into the spotlight. "If it hadn't been for k.d., I wouldn't have come out of my semi-retirement to do a show like this," he said. "I want to let Canada know that I'm certainly on the side of Canadian performers of the cut of a k.d. lang. She's a unique talent, and she's good for Canada."

The chemistry between them was splendid on stage and screen. k.d. beamed from the sidelines when Connors sang, "She jumps around like a 'rangutang/ Lady, k.d. lang." Later, the two did a rousing duet of another Connors favorite, "C-A-N-A-D-A," both of them crooning as she stomped around the stage in all her maple-leaf glory. But Connors wasn't the only guest enamored of k.d., and as Faire explains, he wasn't the only one who got treated like a king. "She's extremely modest about her own talents," the producer observed. "She told me that she wanted all her own standing ovations to be cut from the show, but to leave in the ones given to Stompin' Tom, which I refused. And she went out of her way to make her guests feel comfortable on the set."

Clearly, all her time spent hobnobbing with the entertainment elite in New York, Los Angeles, and even Nashville hadn't rubbed much of the country shine from k.d.'s proud, Canadian profile. A couple of years earlier she had returned to Consort to do an outdoor concert which drew almost 3,000 people and raised $10,000 to build a new recreation center. She had also participated in similar benefits for the Edmonton Symphony Orchestra and other local arts and civic groups in and around Alberta. Unlike many famous Canadians who had gone south and never looked back, k.d. wasn't about to let the world get away with assuming she was American, nor was she going to pass up opportunities to work with other Canadians whenever possible. The video for "Trail of Broken Hearts" was shot on the Albertan prairie, and it was the same backdrop that graced her album cover. "I thought it was very important to shoot it in Alberta because that's so much a part of what I am and what I do," she told a VJ at MuchMusic. "All the little Canadianisms, and the sky, of course."

But if, in 1989, k.d. could do no wrong, 1990 would test Alberta's love for their wild-eyed darling. Trouble lurked on the broad horizon.

■

There are few things about life on the road that live up to the romantic images it evokes, least of which is the ordeal artists go through to get their mouths on a decent meal. It's even worse for those who eat neither meat nor dairy, like k.d., who's vegan save for butter and, according to Percy Adlon, an occasional bite of St. Andre's cheese. Vegetarian artists often have riders attached to their booking contracts requiring that ample amounts of carbs and veggies be served between rehearsals and show time. But when it comes to refueling at highway truck stops, there's only so many french fries a person can eat. "I went to Denny's and I was trying to order a toasted cucumber sandwich," k.d. recalls of one of her many mobile dining experiences, this one occurring just outside of Graceland. "The waitress said, 'I don't think we can do that,' and my friend said, 'Look, it's just like a BLT, but you put in a cucumber instead of the bacon.' " She finally got her sandwich, but was a little disappointed to find that they had grilled the cucumber.

Road food or not, k.d. has always believed that animals were far too worthy to be considered food. As a child her family had plenty of pets, and friends remember k.d. tooling around on her motorcycle with her dog sitting on the gas tank. It didn't take long after she left Consort before her brother John convinced her to stop eating meat. "He made a great deal of impact on me with the concept," she recalled. "Growing up in Alberta you don't really have the choice because you don't know that there's such a thing. And I think that I always wanted to be a vegetarian as soon as I got out from my family situation."

Working as a teenager on her neighbors' farms gave her plenty of long hours in the blazing sun to consider the economics of raising cows for beef. "One day I was on a 15-mile cattle drive over 250 acres," she recalls. "We were rounding up about 50 head. And I'm throwing comments to the ranchers like, 'Oh, these poor cattle. I wonder if they know what their destinies are.' And these ranchers thought I was a wacky cult member or something. Then it just occurred to me that if you planted 250 acres of soybeans, how many people you could feed. It's just too evident, and when I'm there and I see all this, it's very alarming."

Aside from the economics of it, k.d.'s compassion for animals is part of her overall spirituality, which is very much tied to the land. In some respects she's like a feral child, claiming that while others study books, nature teaches her everything she needs to know. She says she learned to dance by watching the prairie crows, convinced she herself was a crow in another life. In her current incarnation as a human, her closest friend for much of her life has been a little Benji-like mutt named Stinkerton. "I'm an almost militant vegetarian and animal rights activist," she confesses. "Even my dog's a vegetarian. Eats couscous, soy protein, garlic, and broccoli. I'd bring her on the road—it'd be like a piece of God running around—but it would be too hard on her."

Despite her views and her dietary practices, some of which she shares with her sister Keltie, k.d. used to say that she would never try to force her views on others. "When I go out to Consort with my cowboy friends from childhood and round up cattle, I lecture them a little on vegetarianism, but at the same time, I can't lecture," she said in 1988. "I believe the strongest example is a silent example." But her friend Lin Elder rolls her eyes and laughs when it's suggested that k.d. kept silent on the subject. "She was the first one to introduce me to eating vegetarian," she says, adding that at times her friend could get a little preachy about it. "And then, of course, I smoke, which didn't help matters at all."

A staffer from her record label remembers a group dinner in a Chinese restaurant following a show in Colorado. "No MSG for the whole table please," k.d. commanded the waiter, offering dietary advice to anyone who would listen. And to this day, even her mother doesn't escape her daughter's watchful eye. "She grew up on pop and chips like the three older kids," Audrey Lang relates. "I used to try to get her to eat better. Now, when she comes home, she scolds me about what's in my fridge."

Her art, too, has sometimes been used as a means to express her strongly held views on eating animals, although it hasn't shown up in her music. "One of my paintings is an acrylic on canvas with a chicken wearing overalls and tossing feed out to these humans running around in a field," she notes, adding, "Lots of people will say, 'I'm a vegetarian, but sometimes I'll eat chicken and fish.' That sounds so funny to me."

Enter Dan Mathews, head of special projects for the grassroots organization People for Ethical Treatment of Animals (PETA). Mathews had heard that k.d. was a practicing vegetarian, and managed to get a meeting with her to discuss the possibility of her involvement with his group. He had a couple of specific ideas in mind, and showed up to the meeting with a plan.

PETA, which was founded in 1980 and boasts a membership of over 300,000, developed a reputation throughout the Reagan years for its creative, media-grabbing stunts used to raise awareness about animal rights: fashion shows where models would strut down the runway with "blood" dripping from their faux-fur coats; theatrical and vividly graphic mock slaughters of cattle at environmental confer-

141

ences; even taking undercover jobs in animal testing laboratories in order to spy on the cosmetic industry. They had grown particularly deft at working the entertainment industry, releasing two star-studded albums, *Animal Liberation* and *Tame Yourself,* and garnering many celebrity endorsements. All this and more made PETA one of the fastest-growing animal rights groups in the world.

"We knew k.d. was very popular, and since she grew up in cattle country, we thought she would be a very credible spokesperson," says Amy Bertsch, Mathews's assistant, as she rifles through the press files in PETA's barely converted warehouse headquarters just outside of Washington, D.C. They also knew she would fit in perfectly with Mathews's new and most ambitious idea to date: "Meat Stinks," a campaign designed to directly challenge the notion of eating meat. "There are a lot of different animal rights issues," explains Bertsch. "Some celebrities choose fur, some choose animal testing. k.d. felt really strongly about vegetarianism, and was enthusiastic about doing something for a vegetarian campaign, so Dan thought perhaps a commercial would work." k.d. thought so, too, and soon she was on her way to Los Angeles to visit a retirement ranch for old animals.

Cut to a crowded video set, where k.d. stands mugging for the camera as she hugs a tan cow named Lulu. Crews bustle around them as k.d. runs through her script, trying her best to keep Lulu from wandering out of the frame. "We all love animals. But why do we call some 'pets' and some 'dinner'?" she reads. "If you knew how meat was made, you'd probably lose your lunch. I know. I'm from cattle country. That's why I became a vegetarian. Meat stinks, and not just for animals, but for human health and the environment."

It was a historic moment designed to bring vegetarianism to America's dinner table, and PETA was media-savvy enough to know just how to play it. They contacted the press and invited a camera crew to videotape the shoot as a news event, the hook being the first time a vegetarian commercial had ever been produced. The next day, "Entertainment Tonight" aired "The Making of the First-Ever Vegetarian Commercial, with Country Singer k.d. lang." Immediately, the story blew wide open.

PETA had intended to buy ad spots for the commercial on both cable and network television, an ambitious move for a group that relies almost entirely on donations. "Public service announcements are usually free," Bertsch explains, "but they have to be very generic and mild so they don't jeopardize the ad revenues the station gets from its other sponsors. So in the past the ads usually featured someone saying, 'Hi, I care about animals, and I bet you do too. Write us for more info.' But here we were dealing with a specific issue, and with someone who says in the commercial, 'I'm from cattle country and I know what I'm talking about.' It was just such a strong message that we thought it was worth buying commercial time for."

PETA had miscalculated the amount of free publicity they would receive from their media coup. On June 21, 1990, just hours after the "Entertainment Tonight" segment had aired, the *Edmonton Sun* picked up the story as it went out over the AP wires, and within twenty-four hours "Meat Stinks" was creating quite a stink of its own.

"Going against the grain has always been country singer k.d. lang's way," announced a correspondent for CBS Nightly News. "The hair, the wardrobe, the act. But now southern Alberta's big-boned gal and Grammy award–winner has rubbed cattle country the wrong way." The initial reaction was strongest in k.d.'s home territory, where her popularity had previously found her ranked with the maple leaf flag and ice hockey. From there it fanned out across North America, as journalists began contacting the Canadian government looking for quotes from representatives in the beef industry, who, by this point, were howling like wounded animals.

"We're getting pretty fed up with these celebrities who think they're experts in areas where they have no expertise," scowled Dennis Laycraft, general manager of the Canadian Cattlemen's Association, estimating that the U.S. market for Canadian beef and cattle was $300 million a year. Almost immediately, the American beef industry offered their own feeble attempt at damage control, as John Lacey, a California rancher and president of the National Cattlemen's Association, issued a statement claiming that PETA disseminated false information. "There are no credible scientific facts to support the campaign's message that beef is bad for human health and the environment," he said.

It was the moment country radio had been waiting for. "Under no circumstances will anyone on this staff be allowed to play any music by k.d. lang until such a time as she publicly renounces her ties with the People for Ethical Treatment of Animals and her fanatic anti-meat philosophy," read an internal memo circulating the halls of KRVN radio station in Lexington, Nebraska, dateline June 26, 1990. It was the first of what quickly grew into a firestorm of bannings, burnings, and a host of other PR stunts aimed at stunting the popularity of Alberta's newest and biggest outlaw.

Other stations in the "beef belt" quickly followed suit. On June 28, five radio stations in Montana joined the boycott, with Hugh James, program director for KBOW in Butte saying, "If she's going to boycott one of our state's major industries, we're going to boycott her music." The next day, six Kansas radio stations agreed to stop playing k.d.'s current single, "Ridin' the Rails," which she had recorded with Take 6 for the *Dick Tracy* soundtrack. Joining them were stations in Wyoming, Nebraska, and Missouri, including one that claimed to base their decision to join the boycott on a 45-minute listener poll, during which time they received 3 calls in support of k.d. and 175 against.

By July 4, over three dozen stations had actively embraced the boycott, including several small stations in Alberta and the giants, CFCW in Edmonton and CKDQ in Calgary. Most not only refused to play k.d.'s music, but aggressively pumped people's emotions around the issue, scratching needles across her records or breaking them over the air, as DJs encouraged their listeners to write angry letters which the stations would forward to the artist. In almost every case, spokesmen for the stations involved in the ban—and yes, all the people quoted were men—insisted that they didn't mind the fact that k.d. was a vegetarian. What they objected to was what they saw to be her attack on one of rural America's biggest industries. "We don't have any problem with her music and lifestyle," claimed Rich Hawkins, farm service director for KRVN. "We have vegetarians on the staff. She is simply involved with a campaign that could destroy some of our listeners' livelihoods."

Larry Steckline, owner of several Kansas radio stations, agreed. "She can eat what she wants," he said. "My problem is somebody with a name in this industry coming down hard on the number one industry in our state. If she can say that meat stinks, then I can do the same for her records. And if she thinks meat stinks, she hasn't had the opportunity to smell cauliflower that's been in the refrigerator too long."

Many stations jumped at the opportunity to stir up their own bits of publicity around the issue. In Boise, Idaho, for example, where beef accounted for an estimated $680 million in revenues in 1989, a DJ from KF-95 organized a record swap, broadcasting live from under an Idaho Beef Association billboard that read, "Put some taste in your life." From his outpost the radio jock urged his listeners to bring him their k.d. records, along with those of other known vegetarians like Paul McCartney and Chrissie Hynde. In return he would exchange the records for those of artists who were supposedly less militant. In Alberta, meanwhile, station CFAC started a "Where's the Beef?" campaign, with listeners calling to win prizes whenever they heard a specially inserted "moo" interrupting a song. And at KXRB in Sioux Falls, South Dakota, DJ Dan Christopher poked fun by giving away steaks to people who called in during a k.d. lang number.

There were plenty of levelheaded people who steered clear of the controversy, recognizing that the issues it raised regarding freedom of speech were just too important to ignore. "I can wholeheartedly say we wouldn't get involved in anything that stupid," assured Jesse Raines, program director at KLFM in Great Falls, Montana. "We stand firm on the ground that we don't care who eats meat and who doesn't." A lot of listeners seemed to agree it wasn't an issue worth getting worked up about. Calgary's CKRY-FM reported receiving only one negative k.d.-related call, and a station representative there reiterated that what the artist did in her personal life had absolutely nothing to do with her music. And Great Empire Broadcasting Inc., a Kansas-based chain of ten stations, decided not to join the ban when 60 percent of listeners polled said they were against it.

"Our position is that we support the beef and cattle industry and that we disagree with her position," said John Speer, director of operations and programming at KFDI in Wichita, echoing the sentiments of Great Empire CEO Mike Oatman. "But it will not affect her airplay on KFDI. She is entitled to her opinion and banning her records wouldn't accomplish anything. She's an unusual person in lots of respects, but she is a very good singer." Upon hearing the statement, k.d. called Oatman to personally thank him.

As for the print media, a *Globe and Mail* editorial questioned the sanity of giving the issue any play at all, saying, "Amid contemporary music's mean-spirited diatribes against women, gays, and various ethnic groups, a dispute over animal rights feels like the sunny uplands of civil discourse."

Needless to say, PETA never had to spend a dime on advertising for their "Meat Stinks" campaign. In fact, the organization was deluged with calls requesting copies of the commercial from broadcasters eager to use it as part of the news story. Additional publicity was generated by other animal rights activists, who, along with anticensorship types, used the opportunity to do even more consciousness-raising. On June 29, the Kansas Prairie Society spearheaded a protest outside Steckline's office in Wichita, blasting k.d. lang music from a boom box for over an hour. Farther south, a message going out over the hotline for the Texas Society for Animal Rights urged callers to bombard local radio stations with requests for k.d. lang.

"Americans don't like it when things are banned," Dan Mathews observed, echoing a statement made by Paul McCartney in *USA Today* that when the Beatles were banned in the 1960s, it only made the group more popular. Other celebrities also joined the fray, sending letters of support to k.d. and phoning PETA to see how they could help. Chrissie Hynde, who had always been an animal rights activist but never been involved with PETA, called to proclaim her support, saying, "They'd have to put a gun to my head and pull the trigger to get me to stop promoting vegetarianism." Funny enough, Hynde later remembered having met a young Kathy Lang when the Pretenders were doing a gig in Edmonton in the early eighties. Still odd-jobbing it at the time, k.d. had been backstage, chopping carrots for the vegetarian caterer.

It was everything that PETA could have hoped for, and then some. All across North America the pros and cons of vegetarianism were being debated on the radio, TV, and in the press. Some journalists made light of the subject, putting their own sardonic spin on it. "Cows just stand around and do nothing except 'beef up' for their intended purposes," reasoned one newspaper columnist. "There's no such thing as watch cows, seeing-eye cows, or police cows. They can't be ridden, and they won't even pull a plow."

Toronto Star's Craig MacInnis got a good laugh when, after sympathizing with the young animals growing up in "maximum security cow prisons," he wrote, "It's a little-known fact that dogs, given the opportunity to express their own political views rather than toe the party line of their masters, are almost always left of center.... The majority of Canadian dogs support lang because she is the country's first popular performer to come out of the closet to promote couscous for canines."

Others took a more pseudo-intellectual approach: a letter from publisher Link Byfield in the July 1990 issue of Alberta's *Western Report* tried to argue that killing animals helped save them from the cruelties of starving in the wild. He also sounded the alarms, exclaiming that if the animal rights activists had their way, the cattle industry could "suffer a beating almost as savage as the one Miss Bardot and her sentimental think-alikes inflicted on Newfoundland's seal hunt."

As wildly right-wing and ill-reasoned as the rest of Byfield's commentary read—inspiring one reader to write a letter to the magazine begging him to "try not to sound like such a redneck"—he hit the nail on the head when he recognized it was the animal rights movement's previous successes that terrified the beef industry most. Even without PETA's efforts, and despite the beef lobby's claims to the contrary, more and more North Americans were developing health concerns regarding the consumption of red meat, and it was hitting the cattleman where it hurt most: at the bottom line. It didn't help matters when James Garner, spokesman for the Beef Industry Council's "Real food for real people" campaign, had to be dropped from the drive after undergoing quadruple bypass surgery to unblock his arteries. Add to this supermodel-turned-actress Cybil Shepherd's loss of a beefy endorsement contract after confiding to a fashion magazine that one of her beauty secrets was not eating meat, and things were not looking good for the cattle industry.

The fall of Cybil Shepherd and James Garner in the beef belt gave animal rights activists a good chuckle. But few were laughing in Alberta, where red-meat producers were generating nearly half of the province's $1.4 billion in farm income. "The campaign against k.d. lang in her prairie hometown has turned nasty," announced the *Edmonton Journal* on July 9, reporting that the sign at the edge of Consort declaring it the "Home of k.d. lang" had been plastered with "I Love Alberta Beef" stickers and spray-painted with the slogan "Eat Beef Dyke." The controversy erupting in Consort had particular impact on Audrey Lang, who still lived in the tiny rural village, and who became the target of hate mail and harassing phone calls before packing her bags and leaving town to join her daughter in seclusion. "It was like you'd imagine a TV movie about something hateful in a small town in the South to be," sister Keltie described.

For many in the area, k.d.'s participation in the "Meat Stinks" campaign seemed a direct attack on their livelihoods. "It doesn't take a degree in psychology to presume that lang, represented on her albums as a cowgirl when she is, in fact, the daughter of a pharmacist and a schoolteacher, is in some ways getting even, as so many of us do privately but so few of us have the opportunity to do publicly, with her roots," assumed Jay Scott, a *Globe and Mail* journalist. "She's economically biting the hand that may have refused to spiritually feed her."

k.d. tried hard to convince people that she had never meant ill will towards her fellow Albertans. "What got people is that they felt it was an attack on my home, on Alberta, on my upbringing," she explained. "But it wasn't. I love Alberta, I love the prairies, I'm very, very happy I grew up there. It's just that I don't believe it's necessary to eat meat anymore. I don't think it's a necessary part of human nature. We're evolving, and we have to grow with the changes."

Yet even some of her biggest supporters were shocked that she would do such a thing. "It was stupid," says CBC radio personality Peter Gzowski, shaking his head at the suggestion that k.d. was taken aback by the controversy. "I don't mean stupid, I mean ill-considered. To take that kind of active stance against your own culture is not necessary. I don't deny anyone a right of expression. But it really hurt the people in Alberta, because that's their lives and livelihoods she was talking about. It was an aggressive gesture."

Not everyone in Consort was pissed off at k.d., however. On July 8, about fifteen people, mostly teenagers, showed up for a rally in her support, organized by a local woman named Marjorie Hannah and her 15-year-old daughter Mary, a vegetarian and member of Greenpeace. The young people carried signs reading, "We still love you k.d., and we still love beef," and proclaiming, "Yeah k.d. Your voice is great. Your words are true!" They also endeavored to clean up the "Home of k.d. lang" sign that stood as testimony to the battle.

Watching the young people marching around, a bystander whose husband worked as a ranch hand gave k.d. a tacit nod of support when she mused, "If beef is so good, why the hell are they making such a fuss? They are just small-minded people around here, and gutless wonders." And indeed, some took k.d.'s remarks in stride. "It's a big country," rancher Roger Buxton told the *Calgary Herald.* "There's lots of room for ding-a-lings to do whatever they want."

■

"I think k.d. was genuinely surprised by the reaction," says Amy Bertsch in hindsight. "I mean, *we* were surprised, and we deal with strong opposition every day. But we were surprised that there was so much resentment, because frankly, it just doesn't seem like that radical of an idea. I mean we weren't trying to overthrow the government or anything."

Clearly k.d. had not expected to be dragged into the world of populist politics. There had been no real conversation with her manager before she embarked on the "Meat Stinks" campaign, and afterward, she seemed completely unprepared to deal with the fallout. "I knew there'd be adverse reaction, but I didn't know it'd be so immense," she admitted several months later. "My God, I mean, I just had to totally hide for the summer—not hide, but just say 'Later.' It was really, really stressful, especially because it was affecting my mother." Her record company, on the other hand, didn't seem too ruffled by the incident, perhaps because by now they had given up on country radio anyway. "When this broke, I don't really recall anything happening with Sire," says Bertsch. "We've always worked pretty closely with them, and we've always had pretty good support from the label." k.d. confessed that the label had expressed concern for her record sales, but they should have known, as Paul McCartney pointed out, that publicity sells records.

"The press made a bigger deal about it than it actually was," says Nick Hunter in retrospect. "There were some stations out there that gave us trouble, but they didn't have much of an impact. I guess after working with people like Hank Williams, Jr., and all the strange stuff that comes up with people, you just kind of say, 'Hey, they're artists, they're individuals, they have a right to their own views.' Besides, most of the people in radio have to be told what their views are anyway, because they don't seem to have any of their own."

In the end, k.d. had no choice but to stand by her political statements, and despite the pressure she felt from her family and friends to keep quiet, she stood her ground with characteristic boldness. "She has a broad cross section of support and, with all due respect to the rural people, the farmers, and the agricultural people, they are just one part of her base," Wanagas responded for his client. "Unfortunately those people will be upset, but there is no way around it, due to her beliefs."

Eventually the people of Consort grew weary of the attention the "Meat Stinks" imbroglio had brought to their quiet lives, and hoped for nothing more than for the story to go away. "The quicker this entire situation dies down the better," read an editorial in the *Consort Enterprise* on July 11. "The media is having a ball interviewing everyone and their dog." At the same time, k.d.'s campaign left a bitter taste in the mouths of many, including some who had previously been close friends and admirers.

"She really caused a lot of trouble around here when she made that anti-beef commercial," says Mark Laye, a rancher who many in Consort remember as one of k.d.'s most intimate childhood friends. Laye kept in touch with the singer long after she had moved away and become famous, and even appeared with her in a TV special when the two were videotaped riding horses together in the mid-eighties. Yet he hasn't spoken to her since her involvement with PETA, and says that if she ever bothers to call him, he will probably tell her off. "I'm not interested in talking about her or even thinking about her," he hisses. "I don't agree with her views, and I don't think she ought to be sticking her nose in other people's business like that. I'm a rancher, and the last thing I need is for someone to be going around doing a thing like that."

Others, like Murray Tetlock, manager of the one and only Consort Hotel, just chuckle when asked about k.d. and her involvement in the beef brouhaha. "She always was an individual and always had her own mind," he says with a twinkle in his eye. "I don't know why anyone would think she wouldn't still have her own mind when she left here. She ticked off a few ranchers in the area with that anti-meat thing, but nobody else gave it too much thought, I don't think."

Larry Kjearsgaard, k.d.'s old volleyball coach and the current principal of Consort School, agrees. "Personally, I was a little upset with the controversy," he confesses. "Not her statement—which probably wasn't the brightest thing to do, but that's her privilege. But as for the uproar, who cares? I'd like to think that most people feel that way. Unfortunately, not everybody does."

When asked about the k.d. lang sign that used to be at the edge of town—the one that a local rancher supposedly had cleaned and repaired in a gesture of conciliation—Kjearsgaard sighs. "It was never put back up," he says, speculating that it's probably sitting in a village shop somewhere, hidden away in an effort to avoid attracting more trouble. "It's really unfortunate, and a little small, I think," he says of the decision not to return it to its post. "It's a very conservative area here—some people might say redneck—and I think that most people tend to want to avoid controversy, rather than jump into it. So I think the feeling was probably, 'Let's just leave well enough alone.'"

■

The "Meat Stinks" controversy became quite a learning experience for k.d., forcing her to consider the political implications of some of her deepest personal beliefs. It also underscored the power of her celebrity status, which provided her with a platform unavailable to most opinionated people. She had always known that PETA sought her endorsement for the same reason Pepsico dangled millions of dollars in front of Michael Jackson: for some insane reason, America listened to its stars. But she seemed to underestimate just *how much* weight her voice carried, and correspondingly, how vociferously her opponents would respond.

The commotion also revealed how eager some people were to be rid of k.d. once and for all. "That whole business with the boycott was bullshit," says Bob Oermann emphatically. "All those programmers saying they weren't going to play her records anymore, when they had never even played them in the first place." It was a fact not lost on Bill Flanagan, editor of *Musician* magazine, who responded to country radio's call for a boycott with an illuminating commentary in *Billboard*. Noting that radio station KRVN, who initiated the boycott, had rarely played lang's records to begin with, he wagered that "they were presumably motivated less by devotion to carnivorousness than by a hunger for publicity. Censoring somebody for their ideology is bad enough. But here we're on to something new: censoring somebody for promotional purposes." He also wondered aloud whether country radio, intent on censoring artists based on their beliefs, would also try to tackle George Jones's drinking problem, Merle Haggard's history as a convicted felon, and Waylon Jennings's use of cocaine, concluding that if such were the case, "there will be a lot of dead air on the radio dial."

Country radio, and commercial radio in general, has always gone out of its way to avoid airing things that might be deemed controversial, as Garth Brooks was reminded when he released his 1992 single "We Shall Be Free," with its lyrics, "when we're free to love anyone we choose/when this world's big enough for all different views/when we all can worship from our own kind of pew/then we shall be free." Shunned by radio, it was the first Brooks single in three years to fall short of the Top Ten charts, even though the album sold better than Madonna's *Erotica*. It wasn't the first time Brooks had run into such trouble, either; "The Thunder Rolls," a single addressing the topic of wife beating, with a video in which a woman shoots her abuser, was banned from The Nashville Network in 1991. The difference between Garth and k.d., however, was that—aside from the somber cut "Nowhere to Stand" on *Absolute Torch and Twang*, a song which was never intended for radio—k.d.'s music could hardly be considered controversial. Never had she used her music as a political vehicle, nor had any of her lyrics ever become a grandstand for any cause.

When Charlie Brogan, program director at KRVN and the mastermind behind the k.d. lang boycott, made the assertion that the artist had "the right to say anything she wants to, but we're not obligated to air her political beliefs," it became clear what really bothered him— somehow, k.d.'s mere existence represented political controversy. Perhaps Larry Steckline said it best when he sniffed that k.d.'s comments about beef were "not what I call ladylike." Or the guy who wrote a letter to a farm magazine suggesting that the beef industry take out a full-page ad with a picture of k.d. lang and a caption reading "Eat meat or this could happen to you."

Comments like these revealed the dubious nature of the boycott, and proved that the boys at country radio didn't appreciate a woman who wasn't willing to play their game. But they also served to reinforce support among those who loved k.d. precisely *because of* her strong convictions. "There is talk, among Alberta ranchers, of a lynching substitute—record burnings—to eradicate the offending existence of a pop star who dares to win a Grammy and also reveal an intelligent brain," wrote author and poet James Strecker in the *Ottawa Citizen* on July 12. "But k.d. lang is a country-and-western woman star of her own making. She doesn't feel compelled to love Waylon and Willie 'in spite of their wicked ways.' In getting palsy with Lulu, Ms. lang is a real, not fake, outlaw."

"I think that in some ways people were waiting for something to attack me on," k.d. agreed. "I just thank God that it was something I truly believe in."

■

"I really have to hand it to the cattle people for launching the whole vegetarian campaign for us," gloated Dan Mathews a few months later. "Without their reaction, we wouldn't have received the response we've had." PETA's membership increased dramatically in the months following the "Meat Stinks" incident, as people from around the world wrote to find out more about the group. Some letters were from people who said they had heard about the ad and wanted to know about k.d. Others called to say that they had always loved her music, but didn't know she was a vegetarian. Still others came from people who were neither animal rights activists *nor* k.d. lang fans, but who were so outraged that somebody was trying to censor her and ban her records, they just wanted to see how they could help.

More importantly, it soon became apparent that the anti-lang crusaders had shot themselves in the foot, as k.d. watched her album sales climb from roughly 250 a day to nearly 1,200 a day over the next few months. Canadian cattlemen might have been miffed by her forays into international politics, but the Canadian Recording Industry Association didn't seem to mind. On November 11, 1990, she was honored, along with Bryan Adams and Rush, with one of the CRIA's most distinguished awards as she was named Canada's Female Artist of the Decade.

"Do I regret it?" she asked rhetorically after the controversy died down. "The only thing I regret is that it affected my mother in a negative way. I don't regret it on a spiritual level, and I don't regret it on a business level since, let's face it, I sold more records during that period than I did at any other time. But the fact that it hurt my mother really made me mad."

To those who tried to catch k.d. in a compromising situation, pointing out that her tastes in clothing weren't as pure as her tastes in food, she conceded that yes, she had fallen prey to the dictates of fashion. When Craig MacInnis discovered "our lady of legumes" wearing leather boots in a Gap ad that same year, all she could say was that she was trying. "I've gotten it down to one pair of boots and one belt," she said earnestly. "But it's like 'No, not my boots.'" As for allegations that she was more talk than walk, she sighed, "I wish people would realize I'm no angel, but I'm also not a hypocrite. I spoke out about not eating meat, and I've been a vegetarian for ten years. It's not like I came up with this out of nowhere."

■

On September 15, 1990, the People for Ethical Treatment of Animals honored k.d. for launching its "Meat Stinks" campaign and inadvertently putting her career on the line. Guests attending the group's tenth-anniversary gala, held at the Willard Inter-Continental Hotel in Washington, D.C., noshed on a vegan menu of melon soup, sautéed potato-and-corn cakes, and giant raviolis filled with ratatouille-and-shallot confit, while k.d. sobbed as she was presented with PETA's Humanitarian Award. "This is the first time I've sat down at an awards dinner and haven't had to choke down a baked tomato," she smiled through her tears. It was the beginning of a long-term relationship with a group of celebrities and activists who shared annual thanksgiving fund-raising dinners, and media appearances for the animal rights cause.

k.d.'s involvement with PETA also gave the gossip columnists something new to write about. "There she was, Ms. Anti-Meat, dining at the Nowhere Cafe late last week," read a sample entry in the *New York Daily News* a few months later. "We wanted to know if she practiced what she preached, so we sneaked a peek at what was on k.d. lang's plate. We're relieved to report that lang ate barley and wild rice, corn risotto and wild green salad. Oh, and a beer (nobody's perfect)." Other intrepid journalists—and a few undercover fans—trailed her when she showed up at Erewon, a Hollywood-based natural food boutique, hoping to gain insight into what pleased her palate by peering into her shopping cart.

In 1991, k.d. finally traded in her leather fashion accessories for a plastic belt and a pair of plastic combat boots she found for $25 at Payless. The boots, in particular, have become her trademark, and are replaced with a new and identical pair each time they wear out. "Now we have to be concerned with environmentalists," she whined half-jokingly. "Plastic's not kosher with them."

*For more information about People for Ethical Treatment of Animals, contact the PETA Action Hotline at (301) 770-8980.

K.D.'S RECIPE FOR
CHILI CON TOFU

1 lb. tofu, drained and crumbled
½ tsp. garlic powder
¼ tsp. salt
2 cups tomato sauce
2½ cups cooked (or canned) kidney beans and 1 cup bean
  broth or water
½ cup water
2 tbsp. vegetable oil
1 onion, diced
1 clove garlic, minced
4 tsp. chili powder
1 tsp. cumin
pepper

In a bowl, combine tofu, garlic powder, and salt. Set aside.

In a large saucepan, combine tomato sauce, kidney beans (and juices), and water. Bring to boil; reduce heat to medium-low; simmer 5 minutes.

Meanwhile, heat oil over medium-high heat in skillet. Add onion and garlic; cook, stirring 2–3 minutes or until tender. Stir in chili powder, cumin, and tofu mixture; cook, stirring 3 minutes or until tofu is lightly golden. Stir tofu mixture into simmering tomato sauce; cook uncovered, stirring frequently, for 10 minutes. Makes 4–6 servings.

11

"Nashville is an ugly little city. They hate blacks and there's nobody there but white Christians and blacks."

I F k.d. was waiting for something to give her one final push toward country music's front door, "Cattlegate," as one journalist dubbed it, was it. "Country music was a part of my life; now it's not," she said

D . I . V . O . R . C . E .

with some resignation, likening her relationship with Nashville to that of a pair of lovers whose love had gone sour. That summer, k.d. announced the end—it was over, she was leaving—slamming the door on the only chapter of her career that she or anyone else had ever known. She had survived the storm of controversy; now it was time to move on.

But she didn't leave quietly.

■

"I think I have some empathy with the British country audience because they have a very romantic view of it all. But I've seen the reality, with all the rednecks, the injustice, the religious intolerance, and so on," k.d. said with uncharacteristic bitterness, discussing her reasons for quitting country music with a journalist from London's *Melody Maker*. Ironically, it was comments like these—blanket statements that stereotyped rural American life—that gave credence to the accusations by her critics that she had never really understood country music, and moreover, had never really tried.

The story k.d. presented, and the one the press is fond of repeating, is that Nashville flatly refused to accept her. Yet many in Nashville say that this is simply not true. Instead they suggest that k.d. lacked the understanding, patience, and respect for country music that she needed in order to carve her place in it. "I can tell you right now, if she felt like an outsider, it's because she made herself an outsider," says Hazel Smith pointedly. "Nashville is an attitude, and if you get in there and you hang out—go to the Bluebird, go to the clubs—and you 'heart to heart' with people, then you'll get along just fine." If not, then it's not much different than any other town where "who you know and who you blow" is the cardinal rule of success.

The Bluebird Cafe is a perfect example. Nestled between a children's clothing store and a Century 21 in one of the many strip malls dotting the relatively upscale Green Hills section of Nashville, you'd never guess that this tiny cafe, the size of a large living room, is where country music often begins. "Garth played our open-mike night," says owner Amy Curland. Kathy Mattea got her start there, too. But as far as Curland knows, k.d. lang never set foot in the place.

Nor did she spend much time hanging out with her peers, who, more than Owen Bradley and Minnie Pearl, would have been the slew of women artists—Pam Tillis, Mary-Chapin Carpenter, Reba McEntire, and a host of others who were in the process of forging new paths for women in country music in the late 1980s. Nevertheless, most people in Nashville who gave a hoot about country music were thrilled to have k.d. among them. "She feels that country music rejected her and that was not the case," says Oermann. "This town loved her, and that's because we're music people, and we care about the art form. We care about moving it forward and we care about what she was doing as an artist. It's radio that didn't embrace her."

"I think the industry was really enthralled by her," Bill Ivey agrees. "She was one of these artists, like Lyle Lovett or Mary-Chapin Carpenter, who the real music people got really excited about. In some ways they probably worked even harder with k.d., because that's the type of music they would like to think everybody out there should hear, and that country-music radio should be playing."

"From my perspective, Nashville was very interested in seeing k.d. lang succeed," says Curland, "because one of the secrets here is that we're dying to break through some of the old ideas about Nashville. We're dying to stop being categorized as just a bunch of hats and fringe, and we're waiting for the day that we're known not only as a country-music center, but as the music center we believe that we are. I mean, we wish we were Seattle. We wish we had kids in torn flannel shirts coming out of here. And I believe that was true when k.d. was here also."

Hazel Smith is particularly incensed that k.d. could make such allegations about Nashville given the stature of the people who supported her. "For her to say that Nashville wasn't fair to her when she had the king, the man who gave birth to Music Row, produce one of her records? Well she can kiss my hillbilly ass," she says irately. "That man is papal, as far as I'm concerned. And look at the women who sang with her. We're talking about two people in the Country Music Hall of Fame, and Brenda Lee, who's sold 100 million records in her career. I mean, she needs to appreciate what all of these people did for her, and I don't want to hear no complaints. If anything, she's the one that wasn't fair."

■

These days it's hard to find anyone in Nashville who's willing to speak ill of k.d. "You won't find anyone in Nashville who has anything negative to say about anybody," laughs Janis Ian. "This is a small town." Yet there's a lingering resentment regarding some of the things k.d. said when she was still in the heat of her predicament. "It hurts our feelings to hear her say that we didn't embrace her," says Oermann earnestly, "because we liked her, and we *tried* to make her a star."

As for her statements about Christians and rednecks, Oermann is sick and tired of hearing arrogant Northerners bash country music and its people. "It's the one popular-music form that writers and intellectuals feel perfectly comfortable deriding and degrading," he observes. "They say things about country singers and country stars, about the music and the fans, that they would never dream of saying about other genres of music. Jazz has achieved an intellectual cache, the blues, soul music, even rap. But it's perfectly all right, still, to deal with country music as though it were the equivalent of 'nigger.' The prejudices are literally that strong, and just as wrong. The white working class has great elements of dignity in it."

Even in the age of Garth Brooks, country music seems stuck with its reputation of being in the ignorant backwaters of American consciousness, even if the reality doesn't bear that out. "Country music is a very fertile field for the validation of certain assumptions," Bill Ivey concurs. "It's easy to perceive it as a music for Southern, white, male, sexist Christians, and if you come to it that way, then sure enough, that's how it appears. But when you really start looking at the quirky personalities that make it up, or the wide range of lifestyles that seem to be permitted among the participants, and the kind of 'in your face' confrontation of real-life issues that folks put into song, it's sometimes hard to actually prove the assumption."

There's no doubt that Nashville exudes its own sort of homogeneity, and that many in the country-music establishment seem rather shut off from what's happening in the rest of the world. But to Oermann it's no more xenophobic than any other city in America. "There's an element here on Music Row that looks around Nashville and thinks all of America is like this," he explains. "That all of America goes to church three times a week, and has a little nose, blond hair, and blue eyes. Nashville is a very white-bread town—a landlocked, boring, petty-bourgeois, white, Southern town. And there's enough out there to reinforce the notion that yes, Nashville is a microcosm of America. But there is a lot about America that Nashville isn't, which is why the two-stepping dance phenomenon took them by surprise. Nashvillians don't dance, and wouldn't know how to do it if you gave them a map. And obviously they'd never been to Dallas or Pittsburgh, where people were getting down.

"Consequently," Oermann continues, addressing k.d.'s assertion that Nashville didn't know what to make of her, "fringe artists may not get the marketing muscle they should. The press, the publicists, and the A&R people, the people who are really in it for the music, were all like 'Yes! k.d. lang!' But maybe if you asked a marketing guy, whose vision is colored by looking around Nashville and going, 'Well, *that's* not going to work,' maybe he'd tell you that k.d. lang just wasn't going to happen. It's like the old saying goes: 'If you don't expect it to sell, of course it's not going to sell.' "

Yet k.d.'s records *did* sell, and the people at Sire didn't appreciate being lumped in with her complaints about the country-music industry. "Man, we just busted our butts to make her happen," Bill Ivey remembers someone at the Warner Brothers office protesting. "It was tough and we were really out there, and really trying to make her career work because we really believed in her. And now she just acts like we were mistreating her." Years later, when she returned to Nashville as part of a concert tour, k.d. clarified that her statements were never meant to imply a lack of support from her record company. But at the time, she wasn't so careful.

■

To the extent that people in Nashville were wary of k.d., she only made matters worse when she waltzed into town announcing her intention to "change country music," and then left when she failed to do so. "There are some people around who think that she consciously used country to launch her career," says Ivey. "That she saw it as a place to start, and never had any intention of staying."

In hindsight, it's certainly easy to find things to support that suspicion. "She called her band the reclines, and now she's changed that, so she didn't really respect Patsy the way she said she did, did she?" hisses Hazel Smith. "That was just a publicity ploy on her part, because if it were true, she wouldn't have changed from Patsy to somebody else. The way she's up there bragging on Ben Mink now, and done forgot about Patsy? Give me a break. I ain't forgot Patsy yet, honey."

Even Ivey, as much as he enjoyed k.d.'s talent, was never quite sure where she was coming from. "I met her several times and spent some time talking with her, but I never knew if she was sincere or not. I just couldn't tell if she really wanted to be a country star, or if she was just some really hip singer who had a certain take on country and was just sort of playing with it."

If anything, it was precisely the way k.d. toyed with country music that troubled people the most. "I think people were suspicious of her," says Mary Martin, who worked closely with k.d. while she was in Nashville. "There's still a lot of good ol' boys in Nashville, and if they think they are being wanked, they aren't going to like it." That people didn't enjoy her wry, irreverent humor may have taken her by surprise, growing up as she did with the cornball comedy of Minnie Pearl and the rest of the "Hee Haw" crew. But what k.d. failed to understand about country was that, by and large, most of the people in it were trying desperately to overcome the music's image as a hokey, homespun art form. The last thing they needed was some yahoo from Canada coming along to misappropriate it.

For example, k.d.'s attraction to country kitsch disturbed some of the more mainstream country-music cadre, as illustrated by an incident journalist Michael McCall remembers from one of the CMA awards shows. "k.d. had just finished rehearsing her part, and the stage was set up in hay bales, with blue skies and clouds and all," he recalls.

"Next, Rodney Crowell, who was also part of the show, came out to rehearse his part, and when he saw the hay bales, he went backstage and had a discussion with some people. Soon someone came out and said that Rodney didn't want the hay bales onstage because he felt it was the wrong image, and he didn't want to present himself as this hokey country artist. So they started to take them away, and then k.d. jumped up and yelled, 'Hey, wait. That's my album cover.' " All she had wanted was to celebrate her own rural roots and prairie upbringing. But Crowell wanted nothing to do with such an image.

The same seemed true of her humor. Historically, comedy had always been a large a part of country music, and every show had at least one comedian. The tradition goes back to the days of vaudeville, and the music's live performance roots, which often had a lot to do with the early traveling medicine shows. It was never a concert music at all, but rather a back-porch kind of music. And yet it was the back porch that, to many in the business of making country music, began to seem like its own kind of ghetto. "I think the comedy aspect began to be downplayed by professionals wanting to see the music develop a broader audience," says Ivey. "That's because it was in the comedy that you tended to see the rural, local-yokel character that Nashville was always afraid made it look unsophisticated. It's an image people feared would not travel well to an urban audience." Today "Hee Haw" is no longer on the air, and comedy at the Grand Ole Opry has all but disappeared, even though it was once a major part of both the Opry and its forerunner, the barn dance.

k.d. acknowledges that, when all was said and done, country music was less a part of her essence than it was a point in her career. "If you look at the long curve, or the whole career, I think k.d. lang and the reclines would have definitely been a project," she told Denise Donlon of MuchMusic. "It's not so cut-and-dry, but it was definitely a period in my musical life."

∎

If k.d. failed to understand why her humor rubbed some people the wrong way, at least it was an honest and forgivable mistake. What's more interesting, and perhaps a little more annoying to some, is the way she seemed to view country women. On many occasions she spoke of how she intended to "change" country music for women. But insinuated in such claims were assumptions that illustrated a lack of understanding of both of the musical genre and the women who had created their own rich history within it.

There is a widely held belief in America that rural, Southern women are weak, submissive, and ignorant—a stereotype country-music historians find repugnant. "Tammy has gotten a bad rap," says Bob Oermann angrily, referring to the woman who once was the subject of verbal attack by Hillary Clinton. Unfortunately, "Stand By Your Man" is a quick grab for anyone trying to prove country women as pathetically obsequious and unable to stand up for their rights, and even k.d. has said that she liked Patsy Cline because she "wasn't a victim like Tammy Wynette."

"Sure, you can point to 'Stand By Your Man,' " Oermann continues. "And then look at 'Your Good Girl's Gonna Go Bad,' or 'Another Chance,' where she kicks the guy out and leaves his clothes in the yard." Oermann and his wife Mary Bufwack have spent years documenting women in country music, and have gotten pretty fed up with the suggestion that Southern rural women are less feminist than their Northern, urban, and often upper-class counterparts. "The stereotypes are not true now, and never were true," he insists. "People say that all country music by women is about being a victim. That's bullshit. Go back to the Carter Family and listen to 'Hello Stranger.' Or go back to Patsy Montana. I mean, there are tons of examples, all the way through, of women who are outstanding female figures."

Strong, independent-minded music may not be the bulk of what country women have been writing over the years, but it's certainly been a persistent and significant trend. Consider the standard "I Never Will Marry (I Will Be No Man's Wife)," or the lyrics to "Single Life," recorded in 1925 by country music's first significant female performer, Roba Stanley: "Single life is a happy life, single life is lovely/I am single and no man's wife, and no man shall control me." The Carter family, too, had a song extolling the virtues of the single life for women, which landed them their first recording contract with RCA Victor around the same time.

The assumption is that country women—the so-called "white-trash wives"—don't recognize their exploitation at home and in the work force, and don't comprehend their oppressed status in society. But a glance at country music's history reveals that nothing could be further from the truth. Southern, rural, working-class women, often facing dire poverty and unbearable work conditions, are not only

acutely aware of their situations, but have long found solace and courage in songs that speak directly to these issues. What else could explain
the enormous popularity of someone like Loretta Lynn, who has written such graphically woman-oriented songs as "Fist City," "The Pill,"
and "One's on the Way"? She's not the only one who has so diligently
documented the laughter and tears of Southern women—only one of
the most well-known.

Musically speaking, it was women from country-music back-
grounds who became the only white women to experiment significantly with rock 'n' roll in the 1950s as part of the nascent rockabilly
movement. Barbara Pittman, Maggie Sue Wimberly, and the Miller
Sisters were just a few of the early rockabilly pioneers in a movement
that also led to more female instrumentalists, including the all-girl
band the Coon Creek Girls, later known as the Hoot Owl Holler Girls.
In fact, it was Coon Creek Girl Jean Chapel who went on to become
the first rockabilly woman to be distributed by a major record label
(RCA), and the first female rockabilly artist to appear on "The Tonight
Show." Such stories of strong women are often hard to find amid the
long shadows of the men who've made country-music history. Who
knew, for example, that "Heartbreak Hotel," one of Elvis Presley's
biggest hits, was written by a woman named Mae Boren Axton in
1956, or that "Hound Dog" was originally recorded by Big Mama
Thornton? Nevertheless, these and other stories are there, if only one
cares to dig for it.

In fact, very little of k.d.'s act was without historical precedent.
As for that aggressive, rebellious attitude often associated with male
performers, few embodied it more boldly than Wanda Jackson, the
woman who had a hit with "Fujiyama Mama" in the 1950s (inspiring
Pearl Harbor and the Explosions to rerecord it in the 1980s). In 1989,
k.d. inspired pundits to dub her the female Elvis Presley, but it was
Janis Martin who was first billed as "The Female Elvis" when she
performed at the Grand Ole Opry in 1957. As for k.d.'s manic stage
energy, it could have easily been derived from the hard-driving music
and crazed, anarchic stage antics of Rose Maddox, or from Charline
Arthur, a Texas wildwoman who routinely jumped from the tops of
her amps and ran circles around her band on the stages of the small
honky-tonks where she performed.

Of course, there are limits to just how threatening any of these
women were to the status quo. Photos of Janis Martin left no doubt
that, for all her "ballsiness" onstage, she was still every man's every-

woman—a full-figured girl oozing with extremely feminine sensuality. On a far more tragic note, Charline Arthur, who Oermann unequivocally calls "the k.d. lang of her day," died an alcoholic at a very young age amid rumors that she was a lesbian. Yet, had k.d. had a better understanding of these women, she might have had an easier time articulating her place in the country-music continuum. Instead, she saw herself as a maverick, and spared nothing in presenting herself as such.

■

In light of country music's recent popularity in the early 1990s, and its growing diversity with regard to both its artists and its audience, there are some who suggest that k.d. just didn't stick around long enough, and that time was the only thing standing between her and her rhinestone-studded crown. "Nashville can be a cruel mother, it really can," says Hazel Smith. "You really have to pay your dues, and it takes a long time. Just look at a man like Kris Kristofferson. Even with the talent in his pen, it took him seven years. And there are those who have taken longer." Patsy Cline, too, went a long time before she had a hit record, because, as Owen Bradley explains, they just hadn't found the right formula.

Even more significant than the amount of time she spent in Nashville was the point at which k.d. arrived. In the mid-1980s, the country-music industry was in the throes of a serious stylistic shake-up, spurred on by a loose collection of artists dubbed the "new traditionalists," who embraced a back-to-basics approach to music that rejected country's decades-long dance with pop aesthetics and the kind of crossover success synonymous with artists like Ray Price, Glen Campbell, and Olivia Newton-John. This roots revival was a continuation of the "outlaw" movement of the 1970s, when artists like George Jones, hungry for a rougher, grittier, and more authentic sound, fled Nashville for Bakersfield, Austin, and Los Angeles, predicting that if the "Nashville Sound" was allowed to continue, country music would simply be absorbed into the pop charts, disappearing as a genre altogether. It almost happened, too. Economically and critically, by 1979, country music was teetering on the brink of collapse.

k.d.'s relationship to the 1980s version of this "roots" movement, embodied by artists like Ricky Scaggs, the Judds, Rosanne Cash, and others, was odd and schizophrenic. In the beginning she was often lumped in with the "new traditionalists," since her music, her look, and in particular her attitude, all stood in direct challenge to the status quo. She would have fit right in in Bakersfield, where the music scene took great pride in its rough-and-tumble honky-tonks, and the brazenly kinetic rockabilly that came with it. The "Bakersfield sound," with its poetic combination of cornball humor and tragically lonely pathos, would have been a perfect match for the high-camp emotion of k.d.'s act. Yet her keen attachment to jazz and the blues-brushed sound Owen Bradley had created set her apart from the "new traditionalists," who denounced the polished productions created over and over again by the same handful of studio musicians.

"The 'Nashville sound' just lived too long," explains Bill Ivey. "It had become a kind of formula and had gotten pretty stale." Ironically, k.d. made *Shadowland* with Bradley at the same time the rest of country music was reaching back to an even earlier era for inspiration—back to Hank Williams, bluegrass, and the much more hard-edged, primitive styles that were there before the "Nashville sound" came along. The record was a valiant attempt to show her appreciation for country tradition by hooking up with a group of people who had a long and stable past. But in many ways, she chose the wrong tradition at the wrong time.

Country radio, too, was undergoing tumultuous change as it faced its own mortality in the mid-1980s. When Bob Oermann first suggested that country radio was in trouble in 1984, pointing to an obvious downturn in ratings caused in part by the burgeoning cable TV market and the emergence of music video on The Nashville Network, nobody wanted to listen. "When I introduced that idea I was despised." He shakes his head. "At the time, it was perceived as an act of disloyalty on my part, that I wasn't cheerleading for the industry." But in retrospect, even his critics agree that country radio had lost touch with what was happening in country music.

It only takes a quick glance at the charts to notice the changes that have taken place since then: Lyle Lovett, Nanci Griffith, Dwight Yoakam, and Mary-Chapin Carpenter are just a few of the many artists who have altered the face and sound of country music, yet all were considered renegades in the late 1980s. "k.d. could not have landed here with more talent at a worse time," says the CMA's Ed Benson. "At the time she came along, she and several other artists of a similar ilk—Lyle Lovett, Dwight Yoakam, Steve Earle—those people were ahead of their time. It wasn't her talent, or her abilities or her creativity, because those things were recognized very quickly. The problem was the structure of radio, and principally, the broadcasters and what they were willing to play."

Benson isn't the only one who regrets the fact that k.d. took such a battering. "I wish country music would have embraced these artists," Lon Helton sadly agrees, "because the Steve Earles, and the Lyle Lovetts, and the Nanci Griffiths, and the k.d. langs were the acts who could have brought younger demographics into the country format." But at the time k.d. was knocking around Nashville, country radio hadn't yet come around to the fact that it was in trouble.

Benson maintains that if k.d. would have arrived in Nashville five years later, she would have been readily embraced and accepted. But Nick Hunter, who worked hard to market k.d., doesn't think it's so simple. "It's easy to say it was timing—you're ahead of your time, you're too late," he says from his office on the edge of Music Row. "But I think when you have that much talent, you make your own time and let everybody else get on your timetable." Hunter firmly believes that k.d.'s being a trendsetter is what enabled her to weather her years in Nashville, and to eventually end up on top. "Believe me, she's more successful doing it the way she did than had she stayed in country music."

Still, it was a rough couple of years. "There's a very stiff price you pay for being a ground-breaker, and the price is paid in so many ways," says Janis Ian, remembering her own battles around "Society's Child," a song about an interracial relationship that was banned from the radio when it came out in 1964. "In my case, with 'Society's Child,' people used to spit at me when I walked past them. In k.d.'s case, I guess that whatever expectations and whatever dreams she had around country music didn't come to fruition. And I think that having been born with that voice—which is just such a staggering instrument— it's got to be unbelievably frustrating to then have doors close in your face. It's like you've got the instrument, you've got the songs, you've got the talent—what are you doing wrong?"

Oermann empathizes with how k.d. felt when country radio didn't embrace her, even if he is a little put off by her comments about the people in Nashville. "I still maintain that *Absolute Torch and Twang* was one of the finest female country albums ever cut," he says emphatically. "That was her masterpiece, unquestionably. That's when she really found her voice. And that's probably why she feels burned, because that was her finest hour as a country star, and it got such rejection. She should have been given her due for that album."

At the same time, k.d.'s brazen approach baffled even her most likely allies. "This is a small town," says Janis Ian, "and small towns have a different ethic than cities do. You have to respect that." Even Oermann, whose work often includes a well-rounded respect for feminism, confesses to having wished she would have tried a little harder to fit in. "There was a part of me that, because she was such an extraordinary talent, wished she would have played ball a little bit," he concedes. "Like 'C'mon, just put on some lipstick, honey.' "

But like many young, artistic rebels, k.d. didn't give a damn about protocol. One record company executive tells the story of a group of them attending a special Brenda Lee concert. The show culminated in a rousing rendition of "America, the Beautiful," and instinctively, everyone in the audience stood in reverence—everyone except for k.d., that is. "You'd have to be a communist not to stand up for that song," cracked the storyteller. Right or wrong, it certainly spoke to what many people around her were thinking.

"Within country music, you *can* change things, but you've got to do it from the inside," says Nick Hunter, who applauds k.d.'s ability to stand up for what she believed in, while at the same time admitting that within the strict boundaries of the country-music market, her fierce individualism was a detriment to her cause. "You've got to push the boundaries from the inside out. You can't stand on the outside and pull them." Unfortunately, k.d. was never very good at submitting to other people's rules. Her whole demeanor—the way she approached her music and, indeed, the way she approached her life— was just so contrary to the chummy, family, "you scratch my back and I'll scratch yours" atmosphere that pervades Nashville. *Shadowland* may have been engineered to signal to Nashville that k.d. was willing to immerse herself in the tradition and say, "I will be one of you," but there were clearly limits to just how much she was willing to conform.

Should an artist have to worry about placating people as part of her job? Some, like Ed Benson, think not. "I'm sure k.d. realized that there were things that she could have done to allow herself to be more easily embraced by the country-music establishment, but I don't think an artist should do that," he says. "Somebody who feels very strongly about what they're doing needs to stick to it, because that sort of compromising ultimately affects the personality and the very creative essence that makes them a talent. It's wrong to try to mutate somebody away from what they really are in order to conform to the commercial need of the time."

For people like Nick Hunter, who had to confront k.d.'s radio dilemma on a regular basis, his solace came with the deep gut feeling that in the end, true talent will always win out. "How crucial is radio to selling records?" he asks. "I think in k.d.'s case it turned out to be not that important. She has always sold an awful lot of records, and for many years, did so with a minimal amount of airplay. It's an old statement, but I think it's true: If you've got talent, and you're real good, people will find you. I hope I'm not offending anyone when I say that there aren't too many artists out there who could have done what she did, because to pull off something like that you have to be awfully good. But in her case, it ended up being not such a big deal."

As for whether or not k.d. should have tried a little harder, Hunter believes it's a moot point. "Maybe she could have done a little more radio appreciation shows, but you know what? I don't think, in the long run, it would have made any difference. I think people had their minds made up, and I just take my hat off to her. k.d. is one of those artists who, whether you agree with her or you don't, has a real good idea of who and what she is, and how to present herself. Just about every move she made was calculated, and most of them worked. And every time she wins an award I just say, 'Nashville, look how stupid you were.' It's like, 'Hey, k.d., great, you stuck it up their butts and you did it your way. More power to you.' "

12

"She's one of those personalities who are totally incomparable. It's what I call primary rock. It happens in a total experience—a mixture of innocence and slyness. Young, and at the same time wise and old. Both a woman and a man. Tough, and yet very delicate and fragile. Never, ever naive, but always innocent and vulnerable."

—PERCY ADLON

SATURN RETURNS

GERMAN filmmaker Percy Adlon was sitting with his wife in a cheap Indian restaurant in Hollywood when it hit him. He was waiting to meet k.d., after she had contacted him to ask if he would be willing to direct her video for "Red Hot & Blue," a high-profile AIDS-awareness and fund-raising project based on the music of Cole Porter. Adlon had never heard of the young singer who was so in love with his work in films like *Bagdad Cafe.* But the moment she walked into the restaurant that evening he sensed it: k.d. was one of those remarkable characters that he loved to put in front of the camera—the kind of "primary rock" upon which endless tales could be built. "I saw it all in her gait," he says, as if freezing a frame in the film that endlessly loops through his mind, "like in slow motion."

Adlon's crystallized image of k.d. suspended at the nexus of divergent character elements is a perfect metaphor for the point she was at in her life. At age twenty-nine she had reached the crossroads and was entering her "Saturn Return," an astrologically defined period of change and turmoil, a time of endings and beginnings.

If her reputation in 1982 was that of slacker supreme, by 1990 she had become an unstoppable workaholic, one whose life often seemed like one big hustle. Hardly a child when she launched the reclines at age twenty-two, her career had nevertheless forced her to do a lot of growing up in public. Furthermore, the inordinate amount of time she spent on the road with her band had left little room for anything beyond the daily grind of the entertainment business. Now it seemed that the moment had arrived for her to step back and assess her life, and to explore aspects of herself that she had been neglecting, both in terms of her art and in other, more personal aspirations.

"I've got a lot of dreams, and they don't all revolve around music," she had expressed in an interview a year earlier. "I'd like to be a farmer. I'd like to be an actress, a painter, a motorcycle mechanic. I dream every night that I play for the Edmonton Oilers."

She began this quest, coincidentally enough, even before she had quit country music, when she accepted the invitation to participate in "Red Hot & Blue." The project gave her the chance to address an issue she felt had been shrouded in prejudice and misinformation, and she wasn't at all shy about letting it be known that she wasn't happy with the way Western society was handling the crisis. "It's been mismanaged by the media from the early stages," she said, "and I think Christian society has been really irresponsible as well. When AIDS was first being publicized, the Christians jumped on it as being some sort of righteous [punishment], and I think it's very unfortunate." In addition to being a good cause, "Red Hot & Blue" also gave k.d. an opportunity to expand her musical horizons, as she pored over the Cole Porter songbook for a cut that excited her.

Her commitment to "Red Hot & Blue" included finding a well-known filmmaker to produce a video of the song she chose. A lover of French and German films, k.d. expressed interest in working with either Adlon or Werner Herzog, two of her favorite directors. Adlon, in particular, made sense, since he was already working in Hollywood and had achieved a certain level of commercial success in America. When contacted, he agreed to meet with k.d. to discuss the matter further.

A funny thing happened that cool winter evening when k.d. first sat down to discuss "Red Hot & Blue" with her new German friend. Adlon had been briefed about the project, and as soon as he saw k.d.'s face across the table from his, it all came together in his mind: he knew just what song he wanted her to do, and he could imagine the video for it clearly. But k.d. had her own ideas. "We started to talk about it, and she immediately said, 'I have a concept,' " he recalls. "She was very straightforward that *she had a concept*."

Adlon's idea was to do "So in Love," a somber piece in which he imagined k.d. crying incessantly. The funny thing was, k.d. had in mind to do a number called "I Am In Love," and although Adlon's idea didn't seem to make much sense, it wasn't until later that the two artists realized they were talking about two completely different songs. Despite the mix-up, they still managed to come to an agreement. "It was like, somehow these two trains met, although they were running on totally different tracks," says Adlon, amazed. "Once I realized what had happened, I called her and said, 'You know, k.d., I think we are talking about two different songs.' And she said, 'I know, I also realized that after I got home.' "

Eventually, Adlon convinced k.d. that "So in Love" would be a stronger piece, able to stand up against the other well-known Porter songs already selected by some of the other artists involved. They also nixed the idea of k.d. weeping throughout the song, figuring that it was too close in concept to Annie Lennox's "Every Time I Say Goodbye," another "Red Hot" selection. Instead, the final video finds k.d. toiling resignedly over a boiling pot of laundry and linens, a woman weary with grief and longing. As the song reaches climax, she breaks down momentarily and buries her head in a woman's slip she has just hung to dry. The inherent message pleased AIDS activists.

"It's important for me to let people know that women get AIDS too," she said of this enduring image. "To me, my holding the slip showed how it could be my mother, my aunt, my lover, my sister. It could be me. Women get AIDS." To lesbians and gay men, the slip further underscored what the dark, brooding tone of the piece made clear: that AIDS was impacting on people's lives in the most intimate ways possible. The general public may not have caught the subtle nuances of what was implied, but for those who picked up on it, k.d. admitted the message was there. "I actually approached the song in the light of being a lover who has lost a lover," she allowed.

■

k.d.'s involvement in "Red Hot & Blue" was almost lost in the commotion of her "Meat Stinks" campaign, which seemed by far the more
political act. Yet neither were intended to provoke. If anything, she
was just catching up with some things she had always wanted to do,
but hadn't had time for until now. No sooner had she made the decision
to take a break from recording and touring when she found herself
agreeing to all sorts of side projects, from television appearances and
short films to singing on other people's albums.

In February 1990, she participated in a Roy Orbison tribute concert and benefit for the homeless that premiered on HBO that May,
and featured a lineup that included Emmylou Harris, Chris Isaak,
Bonnie Raitt, and Iggy Pop. k.d. performed yet another knockout
rendition of "Crying," and camped it up with Raitt, Tina Weymouth,
and several other women who transformed themselves into "The
Femmes Fatales" for a goofy rendition of "Oh, Pretty Woman." While
taping the Orbison tribute, she also met Wendy Melvoin and Lisa
Coleman, otherwise known as Wendy and Lisa, a duo that was once
part of Prince's band. The two were thrilled to meet k.d., and before
they knew it, had convinced her to come into the studio and join
them on "Mother of Pearl," a song they were working on as part of
their album, *Eroica*.

There were other singing collaborations that made it to vinyl in
1990 as well. The "Sin City" duet k.d. did with Dwight Yoakam as part
of "k.d. lang's Buffalo Cafe" turned up on Yoakam's *Just Looking for
a Hit,* and "Our Day Will Come," a second collaboration with label-
mates Take 6, was released on the soundtrack for the unmemorable
movie *Shag*. Another Warner-inspired coupling had k.d. working with
fellow Canadian Jane Siberry on "Calling All Angels," a hauntingly
gorgeous song penned by Siberry and released on the soundtrack for
the Wim Wenders film *Until the End of the World,* eventually showing
up again on Siberry's 1993 album *When I Was A Boy*.

For British television's Channel Four, k.d. ventured into "Beyond
the Groove," an odd musical fantasy created by Dave Stewart, formerly
of the Eurythmics. In Los Angeles, she pitched in to help aspiring
filmmaker friend Julie Cypher make *Arduous Moon,* a half-hour short
about a restaurant, starring Lou Diamond Phillips as a janitor, k.d. lang
as an outraged customer, and Cypher's girlfriend Melissa Etheridge as
the performer in the piano bar. Both of these rekindled k.d.'s itch to

do some more acting, and at one point she talked of Broadway, going so far as to muse that it might be fun to star in *Annie Get Your Gun*. *Annie* never panned out, but she kept one ear open, hoping that some other acting project might come along.

■

Around the same time k.d. was immersing herself in the politics of AIDS and animal rights, she sat down for a lengthy interview that, when printed, angered a number of her female fans. It was a conversation that appeared in *Ms.* magazine between k.d. and former teen crooner Lesley Gore, in which the two talked about life, music, and feminism. At one point, as they were discussing political commitments, k.d. noted that her "number one protectionist energy goes toward animals, maybe even before women." This was *not* the type of thing the typical *Ms.* reader wanted to hear.

Not that people doubted k.d.'s feminism, regardless of her rhetoric. Even in the article she expressed the importance of challenging sexism on all fronts, and extolled the virtues of women supporting each other's work. Yet for some this wasn't enough. k.d.'s status as a celebrity brought with it a lot of pressure to conform to the needs of the people who loved her, and in the case of the women's movement in particular, a lot of feminists were angered by k.d.'s unwillingness to toe the party line and set her priorities as *they* saw fit.

She loves to tell the story, for example, of the angry letters generated by a song like "Johnny Get Angry," in which she portrays a woman getting beaten by her man. Apparently, women have often been shocked by the song, confused as to how k.d. could be so sarcastic about what essentially boils down to spouse abuse. "I try to deliver a song like 'Johnny Get Angry' with layers, so that a member of the audience who has been abused can go 'Wow, she's talking to me,' or a guy who's sitting there dreaming about slapping his wife can also feel something from it," she explained, acknowledging that the ambiguity of her stance left her wide-open to criticism. "I received a letter just the other day from a feminist saying, 'I'm really upset by you doing "Johnny Get Angry" because I can't figure out whether you're condemning or condoning it.' I would assume that a woman who looks and acts like me, well, it would be pretty obvious what I felt about it. But you know, that's fans." Complicating matters on the feminist front was the rumor that k.d. was a lesbian, leading some to conclude, based on her "Meat Stinks" campaign, that while she wasn't

willing to jeopardize her career by coming out, she was willing to
risk it for a cow.

■

For years, k.d.'s overwhelmingly female fan base had fascinated journalists, but scant few ever dared to say so in writing. Then in September
1989, Stephen Rae took note of the phenomenon in the seminal downtown Manhattan weekly 7 *Days*. "A fanatical cult following of mostly
female devotees known as k.d. heads travel hundreds of miles for her
concerts, ape her haircuts, fund her fan club, and swap videos of her
performances," he observed when k.d.'s *Torch and Twang* tour
stopped off at New York's Beacon Theater. "To step out of the subway
station at Broadway and 72nd Street a half hour before curtain time
at the Beacon is to enter a pandemonium of k.d. heads stretching clear
to 74th Street. Gigantic women in plaid shirts and Stetsons jostle punks
with 3-inch spiked hair in leotards; manicured women in Paul Stuart
pinstripes embrace motorcyclists in chains." He then goes on to note
that "though k.d. has never publicly called herself a lesbian, most fans
assume she is."

Not long after the 7 *Days* article appeared, Connie Chung had
America on the edge of their couches as she too addressed the dreaded
question—or at least hinted at it. While millions of viewers gaped
over their popcorn bowls, Chung plowed her way through a coded
and highly comic set of exchanges no doubt designed to address the
rumors of k.d.'s sexual orientation. She started with an open-ended
comment, offering k.d. the chance to shape the discussion. "I'm trying
to figure out what this androgynous thing is with you," she mused.
"Because I know that *I* kind of like saying, 'Here babe, have a cherries
jubilee on me,' you know?"

"No, what's a cherries jubilee?" k.d. laughed, forcing Chung to be
more specific.

"What I'm getting at is that I like being macho," Chung shrugged,
confessing a predilection for man-tailored suits. The conversation
trailed off toward issues of female assertiveness, but a few minutes
later, she tried the question again, as k.d. playfully presented her with
an opening.

"Has fame changed you?" she asked innocently enough.

"Of course I've changed," k.d. responded. "But I think I'm still
'normal.' I mean, I still go to the bathroom, I still feel insecure, and I
still fall in love."

176

There it was—the topic of love—handed to Chung almost as a challenge.

"Are you in love now?" the journalist asked, testing the waters.

"Yeah," k.d. responded with a grin.

"Somebody back home?"

"Yeah."

"I want to ask, marriage?" Chung pushed, nudging closer to the issue.

"No." k.d. said, still not giving in.

"Why not?"

"It's just not important. A piece of paper doesn't mean anything to me. Let's change the subject."

As the show's closing credits rolled across the screen, the nation's phone lines lit up with legions of lesbians eager to swap gossip about how smoothly k.d. had handled the line of questioning. She hadn't come out, the logic went, but at least she didn't lie, and in fact, she seemed to be amused by the way in which nervous reporters pranced around the topic.

This straddling the fence—coyly letting people think that *maybe* she had a twinkle in her eyes for women, while refusing to say so flat-out—seemed to be a game for k.d. Increasingly, women who attended her shows dared her to embrace them, draping banners, throwing roses, and calling out adoringly during breaks between songs. k.d. loved to flirt back, and, during the *Torch and Twang* tour, introduced one of her more popular songs by teasing her lovesick fans. "This next song is for all the women in the audience . . ." she would say, pausing as squeals of delight rose from the crowd, ". . . who consider them-selves . . ."—more commotion, as all of the lesbians in the audience gasped—". . . Big-Boned Gals!" she bellowed, bursting into song as hundreds of women poured into the aisles to dance.

Then there was the video for her 1989 single "Trail of Broken Hearts," which could not have been more lesbian if it tried. The clip opens with k.d. walking through a vast Albertan wheat field, looking forlorn and forsaken. Soon, a beautiful blond woman begins to weave in and out of the frame. The song, of course, is of love gone bad, and one can only assume that blondie is the one who broke k.d.'s heart.

When the *Ms.* piece emerged in July 1990, there were rumors in some corners of the publishing world that k.d. and Lesley Gore were each supposed to have revealed a hidden secret about themselves. But the closest k.d. ever got to the topic on everybody's mind was a discussion of men in the music industry. While asking k.d. if she thought she intimidated the men she worked with, Gore speculates, "You've felt the extra pressures on a female star who chooses to remain unmarried."

"Oh yeah," k.d. agreed. "Sure there's *that* question." And *that* question wasn't going to go away. In fact, it was about to arrive front and center in k.d.'s life, as she had accepted an offer by Percy Adlon to play a lesbian in his feature film, *Salmonberries.*

The Percy Adlon–k.d. collaboration for "Red Hot & Blue" had left a lasting impression on the filmmaker, and as the months progressed, he found that he couldn't get her out of his mind. He was intrigued with what he saw to be her innocence around the camera and her eagerness to embrace the visual medium. "Film was very new for her, especially with a director," he explains, "so she opened up and just experienced what came from me. She was very curious, and very shy, and had an attitude of waiting to see what would happen instead of just pushing forward." It certainly wasn't the k.d. that most people in the music industry knew. Then again, k.d. was getting older, and starting to show signs of a new maturity.

Adlon was dying to "discover" her on film much the same way he had done with Marianne Sagebrecht, another thoroughly unique but underrated actress who had become a radiant star in Adlon's celluloid world, most notably as the blond protagonist in *Bagdad Cafe.* But he didn't really have anything concrete to offer k.d. in terms of a role. Then, one day, in a plane high above the frozen Canadian tundra, it came to him. "I was scheduled to go to Alaska to visit a place called Kotzebue, because I wanted to write something about this place and make a picture," he said, referring to a tiny Eskimo village perched 26 miles above the Arctic Circle, the setting where he planned to tell the story of the coming of age of a teenage Eskimo boy. "I was on the plane, and all of a sudden I saw k.d. as an Eskimo."

Picturing it so clearly in his mind, Adlon immediately picked up the phone and contacted the singer, telling her he wanted to write a script for her. She was stunned and thrilled. Then he said, "You know, it's strange, but I see something in you that you could play an Eskimo."

"Well, it's not that strange," she told him. "I have Sioux blood." Then he asked her if she thought she would be able to learn to ride a Ski-Doo, at which point she laughed. "I don't have to learn it. I did it all the time as a kid."

Soon k.d. was dusting off her parka and heading for the Arctic

Circle, where she would transform herself into a native teen named Kotz, who, orphaned at birth, was searching to discover her identity. Her co-star was German actress Rosel Zech, in the role of a Holocaust survivor who had migrated to North America and was working at the local library. As the story unfolds, the two women become enmeshed a turbulent emotional relationship that is part maternal, part romantic, and entirely predicated on their status as loners. The title of the film, *Salmonberries,* refers to a type of berries that the librarian preserved in jars, and which, when aged, become intoxicating. In k.d.'s mind the berries were a symbol of the passion that hung precariously between the two women. "It also may be a symbol for both of them," Adlon chuckles. "That maybe they were both too long in the jar."

It didn't matter to Adlon that k.d. had very little in the way of an acting technique, and in fact, he was adamantly against it. His was a craft rooted in the documentary style, and he preferred that his actors retain as much of their natural temperament as possible. "I do what they call 'character casting,'" he explains, noting that he usually chooses his cast based not so much on their acting ability, but on how much personality they have. He often used people who had no professional acting experience at all, which suited k.d. just fine.

She did, however, spend considerable time studying the culture that informed the film. "We didn't have to find the character," Adlon emphasizes again. "The character was there." What they did instead was try to absorb and appreciate the environment in which k.d.'s character was to live. "We watched young men up there, and we knew when we saw them: here was a piece of Kotz, there was a piece of Kotz. We would just look at each other, because we saw this young man everywhere. And anyway, she knew instinctually who this person was."

Regardless of her intuition regarding the character she was playing, it took a few days on the set for k.d. to warm up to her role as an actress. The first time the camera pointed on her she started to giggle nervously, at which point Adlon encouraged her to just relax and be herself. "I don't know how much she understood what I meant when I said that," he says, thinking back, "but all of what she was expressing to the camera was fine. I didn't want to design things. Instead I wanted to discover something, to open up something and let the water come out. And k.d. was so right for that."

In the beginning k.d.'s co-star was a little annoyed by Adlon's lackadaisical approach to k.d.'s acting. After all, Rosel Zech was a classically trained actress, known in the States primarily for her role as the protagonist of Fassbinder's *Veronika Voss*. As Adlon recalls, she wasn't at all amused with k.d.'s lack of craft. It probably didn't help, either, that k.d. had never heard of her before, and for a while kept getting her confused with Fassbinder's *other* star, Hanna Schygulla. But in the end, Zech proved to be an incredible inspiration for k.d., and the two became quite close—so close, in fact, that Zech showed up later as a guest on one of k.d.'s albums. "She's an experienced actress and she just kept hammering me with 'Vulnerability! Innocence! Subtlety!' " she recalls. Over and over and over again, she repeated those words, until finally k.d. had to face the question of whether to grow as an artist or take the easy way out. And as anyone who knew k.d. knows, she never, ever, takes the easy route.

■

Hosting the crew of *Salmonberries* was no easy task for a town with one hotel, and while they must have been intrigued by the hubbub, and happy to see the flow of revenues, the people of Kotzebue seemed a little taken aback by this slice of the American entertainment industry that descended upon them one morning. "The locals were, on the surface, very amenable to everything," notes a journalist who spent a few days on the set. "But, there was sort of an underlying resentment that Hollywood had come out there and disrupted their lives."

It was an inevitable culture clash, but one that Adlon, whose budget was reported to be only $3 million, felt needed to be endured in order to get the proper feel for the film. All but a few scenes were shot there in the harsh Alaskan winter, which provided the perfect backdrop for k.d.'s character—a rough-and-tumble dock worker whose love of the outdoors was enough to put any actor to the test. "Sometimes the role demanded a lot of physical energy," explained Adlon, noting that even k.d.'s enthusiasm wasn't always enough to override the rugged temperatures and strenuous nature of many of the outdoor scenes. "In one scene, for example, she had to pull this sled with Rosel on it, and we had to do it over and over again. It was shot on a day when k.d. had her period, and she was crying, but she wanted to do it. It was so physical, and it was so stressful, that it was almost unbearable for her. But she went through it until she broke down, and we got just what we wanted."

As the film progressed, Adlon became more and more amazed with k.d.'s herculean determination. "Once, she was on the sled and she was being pulled by another vehicle on the ice," he says, delighting in the stories he recalls. "We were filming and filming, until suddenly I noticed this white-yellow spot on the tip of her nose. I said, 'Quick, k.d., we have to do something. Your nose is in danger.' " Adlon realized that k.d. was on the verge of getting frostbite, but he couldn't get her to stop what she was doing. "You know, k.d. is vain in a certain way, but at that moment she was not at all. She was so much into the character, that she would have said, 'So what about my nose. Chop it off!' "

It wasn't until later, when everyone had returned to the hotel, that k.d. looked in the mirror and was struck with the fear that she might have permanently damaged her face. "We were very, very lucky that nothing bad happened," Adlon reports. "It was just the surface of her nose that changed color, and left a spot for months afterwards. Then, after a long time, it finally went back to her normal skin tone. But it was pretty terrifying."

There's one more story that Adlon tells as a testament to k.d.'s will. It's the story of a scene that was supposed to fall at the end of the film, when k.d.'s character presents a speech to the local villagers about how she finally found her father and her mother. The scene was later cut, but the story behind it resonates in the filmmaker's mind. "Unfortunately, that day it was about 55 below zero," he says, pointing out the technical challenges facing the cast and crew. "We were filming on this huge ice field out in the ocean, and it was a fantastic landscape, but there was also a wind blowing. The windchill factor made it so bad that even the Eskimos were hidden in their huge furs, and women were crying because it was so cold. Nobody could take it, and everyone was wrapped in thousands of blankets, our eyes just little slivers showing."

k.d.'s parka had a giant hood, but it wasn't going to do her any good, since she didn't want to deliver the speech wearing it. Instead, she wanted her face to be seen, her hair blowing in the wind. "She took her hood off," Adlon says incredulously. "It was 55 below, and because of the extreme cold, the cameras kept dying, so she had to keep starting over. She must have read this speech ten or twelve times, I don't know how often. And this is really when I saw how strong she was. I mean, she's like a bear. It's incredible."

■

As anxious as k.d.'s fans were to see her sapphic film debut—especially the rumored nude scene in the early part of the story—most would have to wait, since *Salmonberries* bombed when it hit the big screen at a couple of film festivals. At its American debut in June 1991, at New York's Lesbian and Gay Film Festival, only a handful of people in an audience of several hundred admitted to liking anything more than the movie's theme song, a piece called "Barefoot," written by Bob Telson and k.d. Curiously, *Salmonberries* won an award for "Best Film" at the Montreal film festival later that year, but aside from that it was thumbs-down from nearly every critic who reviewed it. "Percy Adlon has friends in town. So does k.d. lang. After *Salmonberries,* they're going to need them," wrote John Griffin in the *Montreal Gazette,* calling the film "ponderous and pretentious." "The story is at once simplistic and helplessly convoluted, with confusing editing, often inaudible sound and an atmosphere of repressed lesbian sexuality that was old-fashioned in the fifties."

There was gossip that even k.d. was disappointed with the film, and that she refused to promote it, which was untrue, although she did later confess that, had it been her film, she might have done a few things differently. "I would have explored their relationship more," she said of the two main characters. At the same time, she defended the frustrating climax, which finds the women paralyzed with sexual tension and fear as they huddle in a hotel room in Berlin. "I think it was a very real way of dealing with it, because I think that's exactly how the librarian would have reacted," k.d. said of the aborted sex scene. "I know that one of the first times I ever had someone come on to me, I sort of went, 'No.' Then, 'Well...' " Unfortunately, the "Well..." never occurred in the film, leaving an eager audience high and dry.

"*Salmonberries* had some lovers," notes Adlon, "but it was not a successful film, and k.d. was not successful in it." What he means is that it wasn't a performance that audiences responded to. "For most people, staged acting is much more readable," he continues by way of explanation. "They didn't get from k.d. what they expected, so they said 'Well, she's doing nothing.' " It was true. As far as the audience was concerned, k.d. was just playing a depressing version of herself.

It would take three years for *Salmonberries* to find distribution in North America, and in the meantime, few had the chance to see the film at all. But k.d. didn't really mind, since her motive for participating in the project was not to become a big screen star. "Things ferment in a good way," she said, using an old farm analogy to speculate that perhaps the film would someday become a cult classic. "It's like silage. You put it in the ground for a while, bring it back out, and it tastes better."

Regardless of the critical response, working on the film was a life-altering experience, both because of the process itself, and because of what it gave to her development as an artist. "It was a big undertaking, because it was a lead role, I had a nude scene, and it was a love story between women," she explained. "It was a giant step for me as an artist, going, 'Look. Art knows no prejudice, art knows no boundaries, art doesn't really have judgment in its purest form. So just go, just go.' "

Go she did, both metaphorically and literally, venturing not only into the Alaskan wilderness but to Poland and Germany to shoot portions of the film and, in the following year, to promote it. While in Europe she spent her 30th birthday alone in Paris, where she checked into a cheap hotel, bought an expensive bottle of wine and some bread, and went down to the bank of the river to feed the pigeons and toast her life. "Traveling renews you," she remarked to Liza Minnelli in a conversation in *Interview* magazine. "In fact, my trip to Poland made me feel born again. Not that fame has been an overwhelming thing in my life, but it was great just going someplace where no one cares who the hell you are and you don't care who the hell you are. Going where people just live their lives. There was no pretense."

Working as an actress in *Salmonberries* taught her things that would impact on her work for a long time to come, and which immediately began showing up in her music. It was as if, after all these years of projecting herself as bigger-than-life on the stage, acting gave her the key to take a look inside, and inside herself seemed exactly where k.d. needed to go as she entered the fourth decade of her life. "This character she played gave her the last push into this new world that she was ready for," remarks Adlon of the changes k.d. was going through at the time. "She was waiting for this to happen, and this is why she chose me. This is why she found me."

It was as if everything that needed to happen was unfolding neatly around her, giving further credence to her heartfelt belief that there was no arguing with destiny. "I think I was a singer before I came out of the womb," she states matter-of-factly. "I also think that the way you live your life, and the choices you make parallel what doors open up for you." It was time for her to launch the next phase of her career, and while she didn't exactly know where she was going, she seemed to know instinctively how to get there. As always, it was one of the magical mysteries of k.d.'s phenomenal success.

"This is always k.d.," says Adlon, paying homage to her psychic presence. "She is a strong force, who designs everything. At the same time things happen to her, she lets them happen, and this is her personality. She has impeccable taste, she knows how to do things, and she waits until she's ready to do them. She suffers, and she goes through her defeats, like all of us do. But her secret is that she doesn't give up."

As her time working with Adlon was drawing to a close, k.d. was given the opportunity to return something to the director who'd given her so much. "We were at the wrap party," he recalls with delight, "and this nice music came up. We said to each other at exactly the same time, 'Let's dance.' My left arm reached out, and her left arm reached out, and then she took my right arm and said, 'I lead.' At that moment I found myself in that position of being a woman, and I loved it."

13

"Love makes you do things that you wouldn't normally think you were capable of. That's a powerful thing—and I hate it."

IT was raining buckets—a rare, torrential Los Angeleno storm—the day Terry David Mulligan checked into the Chateau Marmont and began to set up for his MuchMusic interview with k.d. He had inter-

R A I N

viewed her five times over the last decade, with varying degrees of success. But when he saw that they were working in room 44, he knew Providence was about to shine down on him. Four is his lucky number.

It was March 1992, and finally, after what had seemed to fans like an unbearable three years, k.d. had released a new album. Not that there hadn't been numerous opportunities to see and hear her while she was on hiatus. Her activities with PETA and the debut of *Salmonberries* had kept the media fires stoked, and her name had continued to pop up in articles throughout Canada, the United States, and England. In the winter of 1991 she interviewed Liza Minnelli for *Interview* magazine, and at the end of the year she joined Jacqueline Onassis and five other women inducted into *Glamour* magazine's first "*Glamour* Do Hall of Fame," a celebration of the 25th-anniversary of *Glamour*'s annual "Dos and Don'ts," and an ironic turning of the tide for the singer, whose career had often been portrayed as one big fashion faux pas. k.d. had also been turning up frequently in gossip columns, spotted with Madonna at one or another AIDS benefit, or simply out to lunch with friends at one of the many hipster hangouts around Hollywood. In case that wasn't enough, Sire Records released *Harvest of Seven Years: Cropped and Chronicled,* a video retrospective of k.d.'s life.

None of this could have prepared people for *Ingénue,* the body of work that emerged in 1992, after k.d.'s long break.

■

Stylistically, *Ingénue* shouldn't have surprised anyone. "Jazz" was the word circulating before the album was unveiled, hinting that maybe k.d. had finally gotten back to her original dream of becoming a jazz singer. Country music had turned her into a power vocalist, belting and crooning until her clothes were drenched with sweat. But as she grew older, and fell in love with artists like Peggy Lee and Julie London, she yearned to explore the more subtle aspects of her voice. "I think people always knew that I was able to, and probably going to, make a right turn at any second," she explained to her old friend Peter Gzowski in an interview that winter. "I just feel that there's another aspect of my personality that wants to come out now, and I'm going to let her."

As it turns out, *Ingénue* wasn't so much a jazz album as jazz ballad meets pop cabaret, couching the softer elements of k.d.'s voice in a lush, sultry ambiance again reminiscent of *Shadowland,* and in particular, the song "Western Stars." She perfected this sound for Cole Porter's "So in Love," and in the work she did with Bob Telson on "Barefoot." With the album, she incorporated the influences of a long list of favorite artists and musical genres, ranging from Julie London and Mahalia Jackson to Middle Eastern, North African, and Asian music.

Ingénue was easy listening, pure and simple, and it suited k.d.'s voice well. But the story behind the music was hardly the "pop lite" associated with elevators and dentist offices. The lyrical content of the album was painful—enough to make a person weep, as it pondered dark thoughts of passion and betrayal. The raw ache, the melancholy, and the hopelessness revealed surprised everyone who heard *Ingénue* in the context of k.d.'s previous work. For an artist whose entire career had been built on camp and artifice—from the wild histrionics of "Johnny Get Angry," to the manipulative props of "Three Cigarettes in an Ashtray" and the tethered country metaphors in songs like "Pullin' Back the Reins" and "Trail of Broken Hearts"—*Ingénue* presented the woman behind the mask: Kathryn Dawn Lang, standing wounded and naked, save for perhaps a shred of sanity.

Dripping with romantic angst that bordered on the suicidal, *Ingénue* possessed a tragic beauty rarely found in pop music. "Nothing about k.d. lang seems easy or simple anymore, if it ever was," wrote Peter Goddard in the *Toronto Star* on February 29, 1992. "For starters, there's the throb of loss and pain felt through each of the ten songs on the new album. Without having her tell you, you know: someone had got to her—deeply. The recurring image is of love in her veins. She became a love junkie, and *Ingénue* is her attempt to kick." Clearly, rain was the theme that winter, and k.d.'s heart was the eye of the storm, as she confessed to the world that she was trying desperately to recover from unrequited love.

■

Although k.d. didn't write any songs in Alaska, the barren landscape served as a perfect metaphor for what was obviously going on in her life. "When I listen to that album, I always hear *Salmonberries,*" says Percy Adlon. "This loneliness, and the yearning, and the 'Constant Craving'—all of that which she experienced in Alaska." It seems that k.d.'s time spent sequestered far from the sun and glam of Hollywood, or the string of hotel rooms that marked the first six years of her career, had given her the space she needed for introspection. She needed the solitude, in part because of her growing fame, which she continued to distrust even as she accepted the nature of the beast. But it was also the experience of acting that taught her to mine her own soul, and she dug deep, discovering a place that had heretofore remained fairly removed from her work.

When k.d. returned to Vancouver after wrapping *Salmonberries* in the winter of '91, she telephoned Ben Mink, eager to resume their musical partnership. To her delight, the two of them were able to pick up almost exactly where they had left off. "When I called him up about working on this new record," she marveled, "we hadn't talked, literally, for a year. But he was right with me, and we were totally parallel in our thoughts about where the music should be going."

Mink had an even clearer picture of what needed to happen in the studio once he caught a glimpse of the journey his partner's lyrics revealed. Somewhere between Nashville and their reunification, k.d. had fallen in love, and her heart had been broken in the process. Now Mink's job was to help k.d. create a space to explore that experience, no matter how difficult it might be. "I knew when we started writing that it was raining in k.d.'s life," he said. "We just went with the rain."

Making *Ingénue* became a form of catharsis for k.d., allowing her to purge herself of the pain she was going through by wallowing in it. "Save me, save me from you/But pave me, the way to you," she wrote, obsessed by something that seemed to lie frustratingly beyond her reach. As she moved through the ten-song cycle, tear-stained phrases fell like petals from a wilted rose; *Ingénue* became the physical incarnation of her emotional turmoil. Eventually, she arrived on the other side, taking solace only in the knowledge that "fate must have a reason."

"To me it's about simplicity and adolescence," she told Mulligan that rainy March afternoon at the Chateau Marmont when he asked about the title. Artless, unworldly, innocent, naive—that's what love made her feel. But in a sense, she also felt free. "The title fit for two reasons," she explained. "One, because I took the challenge of going from a successful place in terms of my genre, and saying, 'That's fine, but I really need to explore another side of myself.' I was going back to square zero and back to naiveté in terms of what I was doing. The other reason I wrote this record is that I fell in love and was experiencing emotions that I'd never felt before. Love makes you feel like an ingénue sometimes."

Aside from "Outside Myself," which she wrote while filming a segment of *Salmonberries* in Berlin, and "Mind of Love," written in Los Angeles, most of *Ingénue* was conceived in her Chinatown apartment in Vancouver, and fed to Mink as winter turned to spring. To capture the mood of the songs, Mink originally imagined the new material designed for a jazz trio: himself, Teddy Borowiecki on piano, and David Piltch of the Holly Cole trio on bass. But eventually, as he and k.d. tinkered in the studio, *Ingénue* took on a much bigger sound. "Even during the middle of the writing process we didn't know exactly what was happening," she says. "We'd get glimpses of what we were doing, but it was never a full focus, and we'd just keep creating these sounds and these pieces." Part of the process involved going to the store, buying hundreds of CDs and sorting through them in search of new sound ideas. "Sometimes we'd take something like Hawaiian music and put it over Kurt Weill and see what it sounded like, and then put them on two different channels and mix them together," she recalled.

Indian film soundtracks, tangos, the Bulgarian State Choir, Mink's Hasidic heritage—all of it ended up in a collage that included marimbas, clarinets, accordions, and vibraphones alongside Mink's violin,

Greg Leisz's pedal steel guitar, and the usual array of drums, guitars, and keys. "We're like two monkeys in a room," Mink explained, calling their studio a "trapeze of instruments." "Whatever our subconscious or conscious minds throw out, we'll grab and turn into a song. Maybe it's a joke or a phrase, or maybe a pot will fall on the floor and make a musical note. Anything can go into the mix."

The production responsibilities were nicely divided, with Ben in charge of the more technical aspects of the creation and k.d. in charge of song ideas. "I'm more into things like walking through Stanley Park in Vancouver and getting ideas," she says, explaining how "Season of Hollow Soul," for example, came to her when she stopped to ponder a dead tree trunk. It was indicative of how she let her natural sur-roundings inspire her work. She also likens this approach to "walking down a long, dark corridor, myopically focused on what I'm doing, yet seeing glimpses, audio-glimpses of what I want to do musically, groove-wise or with instrumentation. My internal banks either store it or edit it out. I never use a tape machine." Ben is completely the opposite, constantly recording and mixing different sounds, or playing instruments and cataloging them on tape.

On the other hand, the two are very similar in the way they hear music, which in turn informs how they write. While working on a profile for *Vanity Fair,* Leslie Bennetts observed the way the two of them operate, making note of a particular rehearsal. "As the percus-sionist worked on the drum pattern for one of the songs, lang lounged out in front of the auditorium, talking to me while Ben fiddled around onstage with sound equipment," she reports. "She didn't even appear to be listening to the drummer, but suddenly she jumped out of her seat. She and Ben converged on him simultaneously: they had inde-pendently arrived at the same conclusion about a specific but minute change in the drum pattern."

"It's like a comma in the wrong place in an entire novel," Mink later explained. "When you pay attention to detail like that, it's really rare. I think we have similar sensitivities."

They certainly have similarly eclectic tastes in music, and working the various styles into a seamless musical package took special care. The general flow and mood of *Ingénue* took only a couple of weeks to sort out, but they spent quite a bit longer agonizing over the ar-rangements. "k.d. can sing a line and accompany herself on guitar, but she won't be able to finesse it," notes Greg Penny, who, after working on *Absolute Torch and Twang,* cemented his standing as the third pillar of a wildly successful production triumvirate on *Ingénue.* "Ben can pick it up and develop it."

As with *Absolute,* k.d. built on her previous experiences to guide her work. Much of *Ingénue,* for example, incorporated the use of first takes, a trick she had learned from Dave Edmunds when working on *Angel With A Lariat.* Her songwriting, meanwhile, was done with Roy Orbison in mind. "It's hard to define his influence on me exactly," she tried to explain. "Definitely the orchestral grandeur, the contemporary opera feel. Ben and I were really aware of Roy's unusual song forms. That's one of the things we study strongly and try very hard to make work in our own writing."

In a way *Ingénue* was as much Ben Mink's masterpiece as it was k.d's, leaving no doubt that the key to her success was in the collab- orations between the two. Mink seemed even more pleased than she was to get away from country music, and once out of earshot of Nashville, he confessed that the music on *Ingénue* was probably the type of material they should have been doing all along. Now that she had dumped the reclines—and decided to let Ben get back to being a violinist instead of a second-rate fiddler—the possibilities seemed endless.

■

Any relief k.d. might have felt in not having to deal with the country- music scene was tempered by the fact that she was now jumping into the great abyss of the unknown, and once the record was finished, it was anybody's guess as to what the reaction to it would be. "Larry Wanagas was very worried about this record," Bill Ivey recalls of a discussion he had with k.d.'s manager before *Ingénue* came out. "I remember him saying something like, 'She sold 325,000 records at country without any radio play. Maybe she's only going to sell 125,000 without any radio at pop.' " But it wasn't Wanagas's job to tell k.d. what to do. As her manager, his job was to help her do what *she* wanted to do, and from all reports, it's a job he does well.

For many listeners, the first taste of *Ingénue* was a little hard to swallow. "If we're going to get all français about it, *ennuyeuse* ('boring') might be more apt," wrote Ralph Novak in a review in *People.* "Next time Ben and Greg come by peddling song ideas, k.d., bar the door." For those who were counting on more of k.d.'s bold spirit, *Ingénue was* a big snore. The lyrics were trite and self-absorbed, like embarrassing doodles on a teenage girl's notebook. And the music? It may as well have been Percy Faith or Neil Diamond, as far as the hipsters were concerned. The album found particular resistance in England, where k.d.'s country kitsch had always been in perfect keeping with the way the British viewed Americana. *Ingénue,* it seemed, was simply *too* earnest to be taken seriously. Nevertheless, there was something about the album that beckoned a second listen, and after four, five, maybe six times around, even the most jaded pop critics were hooked. In the process, the most personal work of art k.d. had ever created became her most commercially viable one as well.

It was a remarkable change to hear k.d. being so open and honest about her life, not only in her music, but in the dozens of interviews she gave over the next few months. Here, before her adoring public sat a softer, gentler, more accessible k.d., and everyone, it seemed, was smitten. Even Mulligan himself confessed that listening to *Ingénue* had caused him to fall in love with her. "That's cool, because I certainly fall in love with artists," she told him. "I think that's probably the aspiration of an artist, to make a listener empathize so deeply that they do fall in love with you."

Far more interesting than the music itself was the revelation k.d. made in light of *Ingénue*'s tormented splendor: that not only had she fallen in love, but that it had been the most significantly heartrending experience of her adult life, since the object of her affection was someone who could not return her passion. "Have you ever been in love with somebody who's in love with someone else, and you've had really queer, hateful thoughts about this other person?" she asked one journalist rhetorically. "Like wishing they would just vanish from the face of the earth or die or something? And then you go, 'I am sick, man. I am totally sick,' and you feel completely guilty about it."

Being in pain didn't make k.d.'s writing process any easier; it only made her words seem more ripe when they finally came. "I go into such a funk when I write lyrics," she confessed to Mulligan. "I have to be completely alone, and I usually get really weird. It's like a storm comes over me, like in L.A. when there's an earthquake, when everything just sort of stops and there's this really weird void, or vacuum. That's sort of what happens in my head when the lyrics come."

Her heart did give her a whole new world to write about, and though it wasn't easy terrain to cross, it certainly was rich. It was a tremendous discovery when k.d. realized that love was as much about pain as pleasure, and one that she claims gave her the kind of fuel necessary to go on as an artist. Sounding very much the *Ingénue* as she dredged up clichés like "Pain creates great art," and "There's nothing like a good heartbreak to get a good song," she seemed absolutely amazed by how the experience affected her music. "There's only one subject to ever talk about, really," she said, sounding hopelessly romantic. "It's certainly the only thing to write about."

■

By now, of course, the big question on everybody's mind was: *Who had k.d. fallen so in love with?* To this day, she has given few clues, except to say that the person was "married."

Was she engulfed in the flames of passion while in Alaska filming *Salmonberries*? If she was, she certainly kept it to herself. "All I know is that she was always longing, always waiting, and I think she felt very alone," says Adlon in retrospect. "I don't know, because we never got into it. I mean, I was always asking her if she had somebody, and that sort of thing. But I never realized that there was something that could break her heart. I rather had the feeling that she hadn't yet found her real partner."

Was the sadness Adlon thought he saw in k.d.'s eyes the result of having fallen in love, or was it simply a more general melancholy that others had also noticed over the years? Being an artist himself, the filmmaker doesn't see any difference. "You cannot distinguish between private and creative pain," he argues. "It's the same thing. And it's such a natural thing, that I never wondered, in the case of k.d., why she was that way. It's something that's often there with artists, and before or during a major work, it's even stronger." Perhaps this is why when Ben and k.d. wrote "Season of Hollow Soul" they both got physically sick from it.

■

Performance-wise *Ingénue* was a sleeper, and although it entered the pop charts on April 4, 1992—eventually peaking at No. 44—it was two more months before the first single, "Constant Craving," attracted much attention. Nevertheless, even before the record was climbing the charts, Sire knew that k.d.'s day had finally arrived. "She's delivered an album that allows Warner Brothers to bring out all their artillery," Wanagas bragged, and it was true. Sire had been patient with k.d., carefully nurturing her throughout her years in country music, with the faith that sooner or later, their hard work and commitment would pay off.

With *Ingénue,* the marketing staff at Sire was convinced they finally had an album that even the most hardheaded radio programmers would find impossible to ignore. And for the first time, they didn't have to split their energy between the seemingly disparate tastes of country and pop. Instead, they sent the material out to the wide variety of Top 40 stations, and watched as *Ingénue* took root on both the pop-music charts, and, following artists like Annie Lennox, Anita Baker, and Elton John, in the growing popularity of "Adult Contemporary."

"I feel grown-up now, so maybe it's good that I go into that," k.d. joked as she and Jay Leno discussed her leap to the AC charts. "You know, it's Adult Contemporary, and now I'm a contemporary adult." On June 20, "Constant Craving" debuted at No. 39 on *Billboard*'s Top AC Singles chart, rising to No. 2 before ending its run 27 weeks later. Six weeks later, with the song blasting from radios, car stereos, and even through the speakers at Tower Records, where the album was clocking heavy sales, "Constant Craving" leapt over to *Billboard*'s Top Pop Singles chart, eventually making it into the Top 40 when it peaked at No. 38, and proving once and for all that her music appealed to no one single audience. She had become the queen of crossover, picking up an entirely new audience for *Ingénue* while losing little, if any, of her previous fan base.

Seymour Stein always knew that k.d. had the potential for universal greatness. "k.d. defies categorization even in an era in America when categorization is king," he told *Billboard,* discussing the marketing of *Ingénue.* "But I think that people here all saw that she had the potential for pop, for jazz, for AC, for every market." This time around, she had settled on a sound she called "post-nucular [sic] cabaret."

Amazingly enough, k.d.'s biggest hit almost didn't happen. She and Mink spent days reworking the most minor details of "Constant Craving," the headaches starting, as usual, with the lyrics. "I hated it," she said, obviously surprised by the song's success. Part of the problem was her inability to be objective about the material. "I was just too emotional about it. I had a hard time finishing the lyrics and I had a hard time coming up with the way I wanted to sing it. I didn't want to sing it with pathos, but at the same time I wanted to sing it right on the border of being hungry and full, which is just exactly what the song is about. And that was very difficult."

Her inability to distance herself from the material affected the whole album, and there was a point during the recording of *Ingénue* when she feared the entire project was in jeopardy. Panic set in as she, Mink, and Penny began to lay down the vocal tracks, and she suddenly realized that she couldn't hit the notes. "I would try to sing and my pitch was flat," she says, reliving the horror. "To lose your pitch at thirty years old—I'm going like, 'Please God, don't take it away.' " She tried everything to get her voice and ear back—massages, homeopathic remedies, consultations with her vocal coach—but nowhere could she discover the source of the problem. As a last resort, she went to her dentist, who found an infected tooth in need of a root canal. "The infection was pushing on my Eustachian tube, so my higher frequency was cut down a little bit in my right ear," she explained. "It was taking me out of tune."

There was something else hindering k.d.'s singing, and it wasn't until she took a break from the studio to do some promotions for *Salmonberries* that she realized what was happening. "Because this record was so painful in the writing process, I found that when I approached the vocals in the studio, I was singing from a very painful and introspective place," she recalled. Like the saying goes, you can't be blue to sing the blues, so throughout the ordeal Mink and Penny stayed on top of k.d., pushing her to work through the problems she was having, and refusing to let her get by with a track that was less than her best. They also gave her the support she needed to let herself go. "I think the older I get and the more comfortable I get with myself, the more I realize that art is about relinquishing control of your emotions and being vulnerable and innocent," she remarked. In other words, she didn't always have to supply an escape valve with her music; the props and posturing she had used to present those country ballads were no longer needed.

■

It was 1989 when k.d. met Henry Duarte on her search for something to wear to the Grammy Awards. At the time he was an up-and-coming Hollywood fashion designer, known for his bold use of color, and for clothing such entertainment mavericks as Axl Rose, Lenny Kravitz, and Tom Jones. k.d. was looking for something that could match the splendor of the award she was about to receive, and since Nudie Cohen was gone, she had to find someone who could replicate his look. Henry Duarte was her man.

Duarte's first k.d. creation was a beautiful rhinestone-studded suit that took him over a week to make it. She loved it, and called to tell him so just hours after walking away with the Grammy. "She timed it just right," he recalls. "I think she'd gone to a party or two, but then right home, and she was sitting in her hotel room when she called me. I was sitting in bed watching the awards, and she called and said, 'Oh, I just want to thank you so much. I looked so great.' Then, the minute she hung up it came on, and she won. It was just really exciting to know that you made somebody happy on such a big night."

Three years later, when it was time for k.d. to tour with *Ingénue*, she called on Duarte again, bringing around a tape of her newly finished masterpiece and some skeins of fabric she had picked up at a flea market. "She was going for a very opulent look, so we used a lot of tapestries and things," he explains, referring to the fabric as "old catholic material." He made her a total of six or seven jackets, with prices ranging from $600–$1,000 per item, his favorite being an olive green coat with a black velvet print. It was a new, more glamorous look for k.d., befitting of the ingénue she had become.

That spring, as k.d. prepared to embark on a vigorous tour of *Ingénue*, a sojourn that would eventually draw in excess of 300,000 fans to 94 shows in 6 countries, the dreaded question of her sexual orientation was popping up all over again. On May 2, 1992, the *Vancouver Sun* ran a review of an exhibit by local artist Brian Lynch that was captioned "Sexual Images, Both Gay and Light-hearted." Describing the show as "a local perspective on the gay sensibility," critic Ann Rosenberg roamed through images of bare-chested youths until she came to Lynch's portraits of k.d., which she described as "frontier allusions that suggest that sexual frontiers are also expanding to include new expressions of androgyny."

On May 8, *New Statesman & Society* referred to k.d. as a "lesbian icon." And on May 10, Wendy Leigh asked readers of London's *Mail on Sunday* to consider "the enormous attraction to the homosexual community of a particular kind of female performer." She began by referencing Judy Garland and Liz Taylor, whose appeal to gay men is legendary. She then goes on to add that "the eclectic Canadian cabaret singer k.d. lang has another kind of audience . . . she must now be ranked as a world-class lesbian cult hero."

Finally, on May 27, *New York Newsday* columnist Liz Smith, whose own relationship to the gay community has caused much consternation, announced that k.d. would soon put an end to speculation around her sexuality. "Next week, when the June 2 issue of *The Advocate* hits the stands, Warner Records may still be grinding its teeth," she wrote, "because k.d. lang, one of the company's brightest stars, says toward the end of her interview that she has 'come out' to her mother."

14

*"When I interviewed her for that article, we discussed
her sexuality, and at that point it was off the record.
But she said to me then that she would come out
when the time was right."*
—Jay Scott,
on *Chatelaine*'s 1988
k.d. lang cover story

T E L L   M E   A   S E C R E T

THE trick would be knowing when the time was right.

Like just about anywhere else in life, show business has never
been a pleasant place for queers—lesbian, gay, or otherwise. "The first
time I went to L.A., I was fifteen years old, and I was there to do the
Smothers Brothers' show," recalls Janis Ian of her first Hollywood
experience in the early sixties. "I had a friend of my parents as my
chaperone. I was waiting around on the set of the show, and at one
point I sort of fell asleep in her lap. And for three years after that, all
I heard was that I couldn't get work because I was a dyke."

Things have changed quite a bit in the quarter century since the
Stonewall Riots, that infamous summer night in 1969 when a motley
crew of New York drag queens and butch lesbians took to the streets
in protest of police harassment, sparking a movement that had heretofore been merely a twinkle in a few civil-rights activists' eyes. The
message written in blood that night reverberated across the nation:
lesbians and gay men weren't going to remain passive and silent any
longer. Since then, as America has slowly begun to understand the

indignity of the closet, the entertainment industry has begun to reflect these changes in consciousness.

Yet twenty years later, positive images of gay men and lesbians were still nearly impossible to find in American pop culture. When "Red Hot & Blue" presented its beautifully packaged program to ABC television in 1990, large chunks of the original show ended up on the cutting-room floor, failing to pass the scrutiny of ABC's Department of Standards and Practices, which deemed videos like Jimmy Somerville's, with two men embracing, too hot to handle. How k.d.'s video slipped by is anyone's guess; most likely, the people at ABC simply didn't recognize the lesbian subtext. But overall, it was still easier to find violently homophobic rap and rock groups on MTV than it was to buy records by openly gay artists, and gay representation in the movies was still limited to the usual parade of pedophiles, serial killers, and pathetic creatures on the brink of suicide.

"The entertainment industry likes to pride itself on the fact that it's progressive and liberal, and to a large extent it is," says Jehan Agrama, media outreach coordinator for the Los Angeles chapter of the Gay and Lesbian Alliance Against Defamation (GLAAD). "But within that progressiveness, its reputation far outreaches the reality. Homophobia exists, and people in the industry become very offended and defensive when you even say that, because it's a dichotomy they can't live with. But the jokes still continue to happen, and the truth in Hollywood is that people are still fearful for their jobs."

In the case of "Red Hot & Blue," not even Cole Porter was a convincing-enough Trojan Horse to allow ABC to present an honest and compassionate message about AIDS to late-night television viewers. Agrama, whose own family has long worked in and around Hollywood, gives a sober assessment of the situation. "The thing is that it's a business," she says, alluding to everything from corporate sponsorships and TV advertising to the seemingly simple act of selling a good record. "Yes, Hollywood is the creative vanguard, perhaps. But this is a very big business, and what happens on the creative side is just a small part of it. When you go in the back room and see how the deals are made, those are the people you're really dealing with."

Those people, many of them self-loathing gay men and lesbians themselves, have their own ideas of how queers should be portrayed and accepted in popular culture. And while there's been some improvement over the years, stereotypes still abound. "For men, it's okay to be queer as long as you're a cute kind of queer," Agrama points out. "If you're an effeminate man, and especially if you're an agent or a publicist and you can play the dandy and serve as the escort for the female star, then you're okay. But you're still a faggot, deep down."

Women, on the other hand, have an entirely different problem, as sexism and homophobia dovetail to become a complex web of oppression. For most women, the problems that arise have much more to do with visibility and perceptions than who the person chooses as a romantic partner. After all, lesbianism itself has always titillated straight men, provided the women involved are what society considers attractive and feminine. But if a woman is a little too competent or powerful, she'll probably be branded a dyke regardless of her sexual orientation. Women who don't rely on men are usually seen as an incredible threat, and this is especially true for women who are too chummy with other women, or who—God forbid—openly embrace any sort of feminism.

Then there are the publicists, many of whom, again, are lesbians or gay men suffering severe cases of internalized homophobia. "Publicists are some of the most conservative and homophobic people I've ever encountered," says Richard Jennings, executive director of Hollywood Supports, an organization designed specifically to address homophobia and AIDS-phobia in the entertainment industry. "These are people whose job it is to help their stars—the people they represent—to communicate to the public, and to talk about who they are in a way that people understand. Yet very few seem at all inclined to challenge the notion that being open about your sexual orientation will kill your career. Madonna has done a good job of talking about sex and sexual orientation, and so has Garth Brooks. But these are straight people, who don't have a lot to lose."

Things aren't any better on the country-music front. In October 1992, as Bill Clinton was campaigning hard for the gay vote and most of gay America was planning the biggest civil-rights march in U.S. history—an event that would draw nearly a million people to Washington the following spring—a lesbian and gay organization in Washington, D.C., threw country-music station WMZQ into a tailspin when they attempted to purchase air time for a public-service announcement addressing anti-gay discrimination. The PSA included the tag line, "Hatred and intolerance are not what America stands for." As reported in the national gay magazine *The Advocate,* WMZQ VP and general manager Charlie Ochs allegedly refused to run the ad on the premise that listeners didn't want to hear about such controversial topics. Eventually Ochs acquiesced, ostensibly to avoid media attention that would brand his station anti-gay. Yet he maintains that WMZQ received complaints from its listeners after the ad was aired.

At the same time, back in Nashville, the Country Music Association had its own scandal brewing, this time around AIDS. It began with an article in the entertainment trade *Daily Variety,* which reported that the board of the CMA had rejected a proposal to have participants wear red ribbons during its annual awards ceremony—a symbol that had become a universally recognized reminder of the AIDS crisis, and which had been worn by participants at the Academy Awards, the Emmys, the Tonys, the Grammys, the Essence Awards, and other nationally televised events. Instead, the article reported, the CMA offered attendees green ribbons, in recognition of the environment.

As the CMA scrambled to deny the charges, Kathy Mattea took the stage the night of the event wearing not one, but *three* red ribbons—for three friends who had died of AIDS. Afterward, a Nashville record company executive approached Mattea and told her, "Next year you'll probably be wearing a fourth ribbon—for me."

Homophobia and AIDS-phobia aren't synonymous, but one surely fuels the other. As for queers in Music City, Mattea told the gay paper *Southern Voice,* "There's an unspoken thing here in Nashville that if you're gay and in country music, then you better keep your mouth shut."

■

Not everyone interested in the business of making music has been willing to keep quiet about gay issues. In the annals of music history, 1973 stands out as a watershed year for lesbians in the recording industry. It was the year that a lesbian folk artist by the name of Alix Dobkin released *Lavender Jane Loves Women,* the first nationally distributed album to openly celebrate "the love that dares not speak its name." From there, and with the support of the burgeoning women's movement, an entire cottage industry was born, as dozens of artists and hundreds of business-minded women learned the art of production, distribution, and concert booking, discovering an enormous, untapped market of women eager to get their hands on lesbian-identified music. In 1975, openly gay singer/songwriter Chris Williamson released her landmark *The Changer and the Changed,* an album that went on to sell over a quarter of a million copies, proving the economic viability of both its lesbian-owned label, Olivia Records, and a musical genre that came to be known as "women's music."

Although she was of a younger generation, k.d. was fully aware of "women's music," and in particular, its network of summer music festivals that took place each year throughout North America. But it was a scene she wanted no part of. She recoiled at the suggestion, made by a lesbian musician who opened for the reclines during one of their early tours, that she consider spending a summer on the "women's music" circuit, which regularly attracted thousands of women from all over the world. "I'm not interested in that," she said bluntly.

Instead, k.d. seemed almost to go out of her way to distance herself from "women's music." Jim Fouratt, a former New York club promoter and free-lance journalist, remembers meeting k.d. after a show in 1988 when she opened for Lyle Lovett at the Ritz in New York City. "At the time, I was working with the openly gay Austin band Two Nice Girls, and I knew that some of these women probably knew each other," he explains. "So I went into the VIP room to say hi to k.d., but the moment I said something about Two Nice Girls, she was whisked away. 'Whisked' is not even the right word, because it was clear, *she wanted out of there*. It was as though she didn't want to be seen talking to me about Two Nice Girls in front of anybody else."

If k.d. was terrified to be associated with "women's music" it's not hard to understand why. After all, few artists want to be pigeon-holed in ways that might impinge on their ability to reach a broad audience, especially when it involves a label that bears no reflection of the music they make. "Women's music," in particular, was defined not so much by the art that represented it, but by the audience for whom the art was made. In the 1970s, it became synonymous with unabashed feminism and proud lesbianism, and while there were plenty of records and concert tickets sold under the "women's music" banner, by the 1980s, it had become an artistic ghetto, restricted not so much by the talent of the people involved, but by the larger entertainment industry's inability to see past the politics of the movement in order to judge the material on its own merit. "None of the 'women's music' records ever crossed over," Fouratt observes, "even when they were commercially viable on rock radio. Just look at someone like [singer/songwriter] Ferron. No matter how many good reviews she got, she was hindered by the fact that everyone thought she was gay."

Whether this is true or not, k.d. was certainly aware of the ways in which artists could be categorized and stereotyped. "In this society Ferron gets called a woman's musician because she sings from a woman's perspective," she commented to a journalist in 1989. "But when Bruce Springsteen sings from a very obvious male perspective, he's seen as a great artist by men and women." She could have also guessed, given the paucity of openly gay artists in the entertainment industry, that coming out as a lesbian would have invited all sorts of trouble, giving radio programmers one more excuse not to play her music.

Despite k.d.'s apparent desire to be all things to all people, there are some things a girl just can't hide, and in her case, her sexuality was one of them. "I kinda suspected it from the way she looked, and the way she wore her hair and the way she dressed," says Buddy Harmon, one of the session musicians on *Shadowland,* when asked if he had known k.d. was a lesbian. "She just didn't seem like the regular, normal everyday person."

On the other hand, people will believe what they want to believe, and as long as k.d. didn't make an issue of her sexual orientation, it left people the option of ignoring it. Instead of presenting herself as a lesbian, she had become America's most beloved androgyne, fashioning a persona that allowed her to become a rather unusual sex symbol. It also allowed her to keep a safe distance between herself and her audience. "I think k.d. was always terrified of letting her personal life show through her art," Fouratt speculates, looking back to her early years. "In terms of her performance—and don't forget she comes from a performance art background—I think she was always playing with people's reality of who she was. That's why a lot of queers go into performance art. To play with reality, because they don't like the roles they've been given."

How convenient, it seems in retrospect, that the record company to finally sign k.d. following the bidding wars of 1984 was Sire Records, a company that Fouratt feels has almost single-handedly mastered the art of marketing homoeroticism in music. "We're talking about a record company that's headed by a gay man, and which had many bands in the eighties that made good use of what we might call the homoerotic image," he says, dropping names like Depeche Mode, Echo and the Bunnymen, Soft Cell, and Blanc Mange. These bands may or may not have been gay, but it didn't matter. "Almost all of the British bands that got signed to Sire in the early eighties had cute young boys, and what the company did was market these bands in a way that took the shirts off of them in a very different way than any other record company had ever done."

Fouratt applauds the label for its ability to embrace the gay community. "It's brilliant," he says simply. "Seymour Stein has an incredible ear for talent, and he didn't sign Madonna or k.d. lang purely on their homoerotic quality. But he had the ability not only to see talent, but to image it in a way that was coded to appeal to a wide variety of people, so that it did not threaten heterosexuals, but at the same time it gave a message that was very clear to gay and lesbian people—that there was a possibility that this person was a fag or a dyke. It was great, because it gave us a chance to see ourselves up there. And it's very different from the Geffen bands, like Guns N' Roses or Poison, who also wore lipstick and tight clothes, but who made it so clear that they were voraciously heterosexual.

"In terms of k.d.," he continues, "you can say that the record company sat on the fact that she was gay, or that they didn't really do anything in particular with that information. But hey, we all knew it, didn't we? I don't think it's an accident that the one major record company headed by a gay man is the one who signed her."

That's not to say that Sire Records was gunning for k.d. to come out of the closet, or that they had any say at all in how she dealt with such personal issues. One company insider swears that her sexual orientation was never even discussed within the company. Yet it's hard to imagine that the issue didn't cross people's minds. k.d. is the first to admit that much of what she has learned in terms of presenting herself to the media and the public has come under the careful guidance of a small group of record company advisers—people like Liz Rosenberg and Carl Scott, who, while not officially her publicists, are renowned for their talent at image creation and spin control. "I listen to the people I trust at the record company," she acknowledges. "I think of them as artists at what they do."

There's no doubt that these people were open-minded enough to accept k.d.'s lesbianism. But at the same time, it's hard to imagine, given the breadth and depth of homophobia in this society, that they didn't chafe at the potential problems her sexual orientation could have caused. If they were surprised by the tempest that arose in response to k.d.'s "Meat Stinks" campaign, they couldn't have possibly been so naive regarding the issue of homosexuality, which is still considered by much of the general public to be the single most transgressive act an artist could be associated with. Guns, adultery, violence, drugs—none seem to push people's buttons the way homosexuality does. Nor does the issue stop with the artist, her representatives, or even her fans. "Don't forget," warns Fouratt, "there's not a single artist who owns a major radio station, a television network, or a distribution company, and these are all things an artist is dependent on to have a successful career."

The potential of alienating so many people is still something that few record companies care to risk, and to that extent, Fouratt finds it hard to believe that nobody at Sire had an opinion on the subject. "I don't think the record company wanted her to come out. I think they wanted her to continue to be imaged the way she was, in a way that appealed to everybody, because that's how they sell records," he says frankly. "Sire is not an activist record company. It's a business."

■

If lesbians and gay men were thrilled to see even a *hint* of themselves on the stage, on album covers, and on MTV in the 1980s, by the end of the decade, it wasn't enough. By 1990, with the AIDS virus choking the life out of so many in the gay community, duplicity came to be seen as homophobia's genocidal handmaiden, as more and more people embraced the notion that silence does indeed equal death. It was in an effort to fight such perceived complicity that the concept of "outing" arose, as a new breed of gay activists and journalists, hell-bent on destroying the closet once and for all, took it upon themselves to force the hand of many who still kept their sexual orientation under wraps.

Ultimately, many in the gay rights movement rejected outing as a tactic, not only because it was coercive, but because, as Jehan Agrama expressed, "I'm really not interested in having a bunch of wounded queers as role models. If they aren't going to be able to get it together enough to be out, then we don't really need them." Yet, rather than being a strategy of coercion, outing's real intent was to raise issues of disclosure, begging the question, "What constitutes privacy?" It was, more than anything, a question aimed directly at the press.

Journalists have long respected the sanctity of the closet, ostensibly in deference to the subject's right to privacy. But as anyone who reads the gossip columns knows, love and sex are always considered hot topics when it comes to reporting on the lives of famous people. Who a person is married to, living with, or dating is almost always discussed in celebrity profiles, even in the most respected magazines.

In this context, to ignore such things when it involves same-sex couplings can be seen as nothing less than homophobia, since it reinforces the notion that lesbian and gay love affairs are just too perverse to expose. It's what some proponents of "outing" call "inning."

"What blows me away is that the mainstream press can interview someone like k.d. lang and *not* ask her if she's gay," says Jeff Yarbrough, editor in chief of *The Advocate,* a national lesbian and gay magazine based in Los Angeles. "I mean, you can say, 'It's been rumored that you're a lesbian. How do you respond to that?' And it's perfectly fine for her to say, 'I don't want to discuss my personal life.' But I just couldn't believe that nobody ever said, 'Are you a lesbian like everybody says you are?' When *Vanity Fair* does a story on Warren Beatty, they're going to talk about this big macho guy and how he's screwed around with all these women. Here are their names, and in fact, let's include pictures of all twelve of the famous women he's slept with. That's fine, and that's accepted. But it becomes a real double standard that homosexuality is something that can't be talked about. We can't print the pictures of ex-lovers, and we can't go and interview them and ask them how this person was to deal with."

The idea that gay relationships should be celebrated rather than covered up is such a foreign concept in our culture, that even some of the most liberal-minded people have trouble grasping it. Take, for example, the furor that was caused by Connie Chung's 1989 interview of k.d., in which she asked what some people thought were too many personal questions. "I was very angry watching it," confesses Brendon Lemon, an openly gay editor at *The New Yorker,* who would later have to make his own decisions on how to handle the topic when he interviewed k.d. for *The Advocate.* For Lemon, it wasn't that Chung had asked k.d. about her love life—he just felt she had gone overboard in pursuing it. "k.d. says she wasn't angry with that interview because she knew that Connie's questions were approximating those of middle America," he notes. "But I, as a viewer, was very annoyed. It seemed pretty clear to me that certain boundaries were probably established before the interview took place. If not then, certainly once the tape was rolling and k.d. made it clear that she wasn't going to give any of the details about her personal life. I think Connie pushed her one step beyond where a good, probing journalist would have stopped. It's like, okay, you gotta ask the question, but there's a point beyond which it becomes almost insulting to the subject."

June Cross, who produced the Connie Chung interview, denies

that they were given any conditions or restrictions regarding what could be discussed, and says that considering the way k.d. used her sexuality onstage, it was a topic that was important to explore. "It was kind of obvious that she was really playing up to her fans who were gay women, which I realized as soon as I started looking at the old footage," she says. "It's not like we were trying to out her. If we had captured a shot of her and her girlfriend kissing, and put it on the air without her consent, we would have been outing her. But we didn't do that. All we did was raise the issue that she herself had been raising more or less obliquely throughout the shoot. I mean, you can't be with the woman and not know she's gay. It's like trying not to look at the white elephant."

Canadians had a particularly hard time grasping Chung's approach, due perhaps to cultural differences. "In the States, if Bill Clinton slugged Hillary, or vice versa, we know damn well it would be front-page news," journalist Alan Hustak explains, drawing analogies with an incident that occurred between a certain Canadian politician and his wife. "But there's a subtle belief in Canada that it's nobody's damn business what you do in your private life until the point where it affects how you do your job." Even Hustak received the wrath of angry k.d. fans when, in a profile of k.d. he reported that her father had referred to her as his "boy-girl." "People thought I went too far with that one," he recalls, "because it was too easy to read between the lines."

Responding to accusations that Chung went overboard with her line of questioning, Cross emphasizes that k.d. encouraged it. "I think that if k.d. had decided she didn't want to answer the question, she was perfectly capable of shutting it down all together," she insists. "But she didn't. She played with it, and that section of the tape actually goes on for about a good twenty minutes while the two of them kind of play footsy with the issue. k.d. could have just said, 'Look, I don't want to talk about this anymore.' But instead she kind of flirted with Connie, and Connie was kind of flirting with her, and it went on like that for a while."

On issues of sexuality and disclosure, many people also fail to differentiate between sexual orientation and sex. "In terms of k.d.'s sex life, a lot of people just felt that it was none of Connie Chung's fucking business," says Hustak. "You didn't hear k.d. asking Connie what kind of a lay her husband is." But it's an argument many gay people feel misses the point entirely.

"We don't talk about what someone does in bed," says Yarbrough, clearly tired of responding to what he sees as a bunch of nonsense. "That's where we get into a lot of trouble with the mainstream press, and it's something people give me a really hard time about. Everyone wants to know why we're so obsessed with the issue, but it's not that we're obsessed with it. It's just that part of our mission is to have it be known that—you know the old cliché—*we are everywhere.* The only way to do that is to get people to come out. And we really get a jump on it when famous people do it."

Janis Ian, who recently put an end to speculation about her own sexuality by coming out, also has a hard time buying the old chestnut that who someone sleeps with is their own business. "I think it's hard, as a performer, to distinguish between what is a privacy issue and what simply makes you nervous to talk about," she says slowly. "It takes a long time for an artist to sort out what areas of your life you need to keep private to have a private life, and what parts of your life you won't talk about simply because you're scared. And that's something gay people have to figure out almost every day."

Ian agrees that the name, occupation, and other personal details of her romantic partner isn't necessarily something that should appear in the press, since her lover has no desire to lead the life of a public figure. But in terms of the more general issue of her sexual orientation, she's clear. "It would be nice if who we slept with was a private issue," she says. "But since the straight world has made it a civil-rights issue by denying us our rights—by arresting us or excluding us from society in many ways—it becomes everyone's business."

The Advocate, one of America's oldest and most widely distributed lesbian and gay magazines, has long been eager to talk with celebrities who are rumored to be lesbian and gay, and with good reason. "In the gay media, it's rare that we have the star power to look up to that the straight media has," says Yarbrough. "When you look at *Vanity Fair*'s covers, you see a sort of parade of heterosexuality there. We don't have the equivalent in the gay media. We have a lot of straight people that we sort of emulate, like Elizabeth Taylor and Ann-Margret. But when someone comes along who's gay or lesbian, and who's a media star, I think we tend to get overly excited about it."

The editors of *The Advocate* were definitely excited about k.d. lang. For years they had been trying to get to the bottom of the music industry's worst-kept secret, and for years k.d. had managed to avoid speaking to the magazine. It wasn't that the publication lacked prestige, or that it didn't have a large enough circulation to merit granting them an interview; profiles on k.d. had appeared in such offbeat publications as the *Quakertown Free Press* and *Vegetarian Times*. Yet she knew that once she agreed to sit with someone from *The Advocate,* it would be difficult for her to sidestep discussions of her personal life the way she had with Connie Chung.

"When *The Advocate* calls, people know why we're calling," says Yarbrough matter-of-factly. "Do we call and say, 'We know you're gay and would like to talk to you about it?' Certainly not. But I guess in a way it's said but not said. If the interview is with someone like Tom Arnold, or Sarah Jessica Parker, these people are secure enough in their own sexuality to know that we don't think they're gay. But when someone *is* gay, or has been, or whatever, they know that when we call, that's probably why."

The way a magazine goes about getting celebrity interviews is always a convoluted process, and even for the most popular and high-profile publications, timing is usually the key, since most artists only want to talk to the press when they have a product to sell. Following this rule of thumb, *The Advocate*'s editors had always kept abreast of what k.d. was doing, renewing their interview requests whenever a new album or a project like *Salmonberries* came along. Their efforts included repeated requests to Larry Wanagas and various people at Sire, as well as some behind-the-scenes maneuvering which involved people who had personal contact with the artist. Each time, they came up empty-handed.

By the spring of 1992, in an effort to remain a leader in a burgeoning gay magazine market, the publishers of *The Advocate* decided to give the magazine a face-lift, redesigning it into a slick, four-color glossy. In doing so they hoped to reposition the publication at the top of the gay media pack. It was also an attempt to make it appear more mainstream in order to attract more national advertisers. To celebrate their new look and to launch the first issue, the editors needed to find a cover story that would really grab people's attention. What could be better, they thought, than to put k.d. lang on the cover?

Since the timing coincided perfectly with the release of k.d.'s new album, they again contacted the people at Sire and told them what they had in mind. This time, the label's publicity department expressed interest in the idea, especially when Yarbrough told them that he would be willing to postpone the launch of the new format for a couple of weeks in order to work within the confines of k.d.'s schedule. Still, the editor wasn't entirely confident that Sire could deliver the interview, and as the weeks dragged on, he began to worry. "We'd call over there to find out where things were," he recalls, "and they would just basically tell us to hurry up and wait. Apparently k.d. was very aware of the request, and her manager was always very polite on the phone. But he always kept us at a distance."

Finally, when *The Advocate*'s editors saw k.d. in a couple of other publications, they asked again why they hadn't been included on the interview list. Again they got excuses. "We were told that they needed to give exclusives to some of the big mainstream magazines," Yarbrough scoffs. Things, it seemed, were going nowhere.

In early May, Yarbrough got the call he'd been waiting for. k.d. was ready to do the interview, provided *The Advocate* could send a writer to England, where the first leg of her tour was about to kick off. The article would be late, since most of the press for the album had already died down. But, Sire reasoned, by the time it appeared on the newsstands a few weeks later, her tour of the U.S. and Canada would be well under way, and the renewed media exposure would hopefully help sell some concert tickets.

It was now up to Yarbrough and Richard Rouilard, who was then the editor in chief, to figure out who would be the most appropriate person to interview k.d. According to Yarbrough, their hope was to get a well-known, mainstream, profile writer, preferably a woman. "It's not that I'm that gender-specific about interviews, but I do have opinions about certain subjects, and who can get the most out of them. For example, I wouldn't have wanted a woman to interview Madonna," Yarbrough explains, referring to a two-part story *The Advocate* did with her, "because it's very obvious that she basically relates to gay men. But with someone like k.d., I figured she might be more willing to open up to a woman."

He asked a couple of different lesbian writers to do the piece, but the ones he called were too busy to drop what they were doing and fly to London. So was Hal Rubenstein, a well-known profile writer who had expressed interest in k.d., but again, was too busy to squeeze it in on such short notice. "The problem was that k.d. gave us a real hassle about scheduling the interview," Yarbrough explains. "I basically had to put the writer on a plane with six hours' notice." Eventually, Yarbrough tapped Brendon Lemon, who flew to London on Saturday, May 9, checked into the Holiday Inn where k.d. was staying, attended her show, caught up on his sleep, and began preparing questions for his interview the following day. Finally, the k.d. story was happening.

If Lemon was at all nervous about interviewing k.d., his anxiety disappeared as soon as he met her. "I liked her immediately," he recalls, detailing how she had arrived at his hotel room door with her assistant, Darlene Blazer. He was impressed that she had taken the initiative to fetch him from his room, giving him the immediate sense that here was somebody incredibly down-to-earth. The impression was reinforced as k.d. wandered into Lemon's room. "For some reason, they had put me in a family-sized room with a crib in it," he explains, "and she walked into the room and, seeing this crib, turned to me and said, 'So, are you a pedophile?' " Lemon bursts out laughing at the memory. "It was great, because she had that one quality that I look for in somebody if I'm going to get along with them, and that is a sense of humor. She had a mocking, sharp sense of humor that was slightly political and slightly naughty, all in one. And I instinctively felt that she was not going to be a diva in that horrible sense." Instead, there seemed to be chemistry between them.

After this brief icebreaker, Lemon and k.d. left Darlene at the hotel and set out on foot, casing the Kensington area for a quiet place to sit and talk. Eventually they came upon a small, forlorn cafe and wandered in, choosing a table away from the hustle and bustle of the regular lunch crowd. It was perfect timing, since no sooner had they ordered salad and tea when another omen came to shed its blessings on the interview, this time in the shape of a young Peggy Lee crooning over the restaurant's sound system. "Oh, it's Miss Peggy," k.d. cooed. "I want to be Miss Peggy. She's one of my people." Throughout the rest of the afternoon, as the two sat talking, a hodgepodge of canned easy-listening music—one of k.d.'s quiet pleasures—served as conversational guideposts, touching off memories, desires, and emotions that k.d. would then share with Lemon.

"The dynamic of the interview was interesting, because I think we immediately liked each other, but at the same time the big question mark for me, if not for her, was, 'Is she going to talk much about her private life?' " Lemon recalls, thinking back on that remarkable lunch. It was a question that remained unclear until well into the interview.

Lemon began by asking k.d. about the inspiration behind *Ingénue,* and in particular, about the reports that it was the result of an unrequited love affair. His hope was that by poking around at the issue a little further, he could get k.d. to reveal more about herself. But as he recalls, her response was a classic case of someone talking about a lover without giving even the slightest clue as to the gender of the person being discussed—a trick gay men and lesbians have crafted to perfection.

From there the discussion proceeded naturally from questions about *Ingénue* to more personal issues of childhood crushes, the animal rights controversy, and k.d.'s relationship with her audience. He hinted at the gay thing by asking her about the overwhelming number of women at her concerts, to which she rhetorically shot back, "Nobody ever says, 'Why, at football games, is it 90 percent men?' It's another example of how women are constantly scrutinized for having any sort of bond. I mean, who cares if they're lesbians? There's a lot of straight women at my shows too." The issue of lesbians came up again when Lemon asked her about *Salmonberries,* but *not,* as the printed piece reveals, during the more detailed discussion of the types of people that she was sexually attracted to. Eventually the discourse wound its way back to the far safer subject of her music.

Then, just as *Advocate* readers were starting to suspect that Brendon Lemon had struck out, k.d. let the ball drop. It was all very sudden, as Lemon, propelled by the same issue that had moved Connie Chung to broach the question, asked her to talk about the way she presented her sexuality onstage. She responded by saying that she used her sexuality in performance because it was easier than having to talk about it, suddenly adding, "I don't want to be out."

At that point everyone reading the interview must have fallen off their chairs.

"There's a big difference between not denying it and finally just saying, 'I'm a lesbian,' " Lemon replied, moving in for the kill. "I think the danger for you is that there's going to be a point at which you just don't want to hedge anymore and you say, 'Let me come out and then go on with my life as an artist.' "

"Well, I think I'm at that point," she said calmly. The feeling of relief was so palpable it practically rose from the pages of the magazine. Finally, the charade was over.

■

Back in Los Angeles, Yarbrough and Rouilard were delighted with the job Lemon had done in getting k.d. to talk. "It really is one of the best interviews I've ever seen," says Yarbrough, who comes from a main-

stream publishing background. "The things she gets into in the interview—it's just very rare that you have someone who decides to open
up that much."

"She was very generous in the interview," Lemon agrees. "And
it was one of those situations where, when we got around to the
subject of her personal life, it pretty much came up organically. In
other words, there was no point at which I said, 'k.d., are you a lesbian?'
And I was glad about that, because, as in life, it's always more comfortable, when you're with people who aren't family or friends, if this
arises naturally in the course of a conversation, rather than in a con-
frontational way. I was lucky, because when you see it on the page,
you realize that she really didn't have to say, 'Yes, I'm a lesbian.' By
that point it was so obvious between us that it just came out in very
sweet, familiar terms."

Apparently, though, the people at the Warner Brothers offices
didn't see it that way. "She called me up and said, 'I think I just came
out to *The Advocate*,' " Carl Scott told Leslie Bennetts in *Vanity Fair*
a year later. His response, as he recalls, was "Oh, shit."

It's a dramatic reaction, considering Scott was one of the people
involved in arranging the interview. "They know *The Advocate* very
well, and they've had a lot of experience with us, including the article
on Madonna," says Yarbrough. "They know what kind of interviews
we do." What's more, the editor remembers discussing the issue in
great detail with k.d.'s publicist, Melanie Caldwell. "It was strange,
because when we were arranging the interview, we kept asking the
people at Warner, 'Will she talk about being a lesbian?' " he recalls.
"And they said, 'Well, if you ask her, be careful.' And we kept thinking,
what does 'be careful' mean? Is she prone to violent rages? What's
going to happen?"

Yarbrough had basically assumed that "Be careful" meant yes, k.d.
might talk about her sexuality, but that it needed to be handled prop-
erly. He also knew that there was a risk she wouldn't talk at all, which
made him even more nervous. "We weren't sure what we were going
to get," he confesses, "and with our reputation as a magazine that does
a sort of no-holds-barred kind of questioning, if she *didn't* answer the
question, we would have looked really bad, and we probably would
have had to kill the story."

There have been times, as in the case of a potential interview
with Melissa Etheridge in 1991, that *The Advocate* has refused to
interview celebrities who were unwilling to talk about their personal

lives. "She didn't want to be asked about her relationship with her girlfriend," Yarbrough recalls of the cancelled Etheridge interview. "And we just said, 'You know, an *Advocate* interview is about sexuality, it's about privacy, and it's about issues of disclosure. All of those things play into every interview we do.' So we just sort of said, 'No, we're not going to interview you,'" Yet with k.d., they felt it was worth the risk.

Rather than make k.d.'s coming-out a requirement of the interview, *The Advocate* actually did the reverse, making every effort to put the artist at ease. Rouilard even went so far as promising Sire's PR department that the interviewer assigned to the piece would not try to *force* k.d. to come out, backing up his promise by offering to let them see the finished piece before it went to press. Rouilard acknowledges that making such deals with publicists was not exactly the kind of journalism his magazine was striving for, but apparently the people at Warner were nervous after seeing another *Advocate* article, in which a journalist had been extremely pushy with the subject.

"I had sent Donna Minkowitz to interview Lily Tomlin," Rouilard explains, "and it was essentially 'Forty Ways to Ask if You're a Lesbian or Not.'" Tomlin, naturally, responded with forty ways to sidestep the question, and while it was a fascinating study on the art of deflection, it had a faint smell of harassment to it. Warner was afraid that the same type of thing would happen to k.d., who hadn't really made up her mind about what she was and wasn't going to say to *The Advocate*. So Rouilard appeased them by saying, "Look, I'll let you see the interview, and if we 'out' her—as opposed to her coming out—we'll let you have a chance to make changes."

■

In the end, the gamble paid off, and k.d. came out on her own free will. In fact, she came out all over the place, talking in extremely personal terms about her decision to do so. But in the days following the interview, Yarbrough was dismayed to find that Sire still wanted to make changes to the story. "Once the piece was laid out, and all set to go to press, we sent a copy over to them, just so they could see it and get excited about it," he says. "And then I got this frantic call from Carl Scott. So I picked up the phone and I said, 'How are you?' And he said, 'I'm gonna kill myself.'"

According to Yarbrough, Scott wasn't happy with the interview. When the phone call came in, it was too late to consider drastic copy changes, since the magazine was already laid out and about to be sent to the printer. Nevertheless, Yarbrough listened as Scott voiced his concerns. "He said, 'I need to edit a few things out,' and I thought, well, it's probably worth preserving our relationship with Warner Brothers to edit a couple of things out, not thinking that it would be the lesbian stuff," the editor explains. "So he started going through the interview line by line, and just cutting and slashing, to where it would have come down from eight pages to four and a half. And at the end of it I said to him, 'You know, unfortunately we can't do this. I don't know what you thought this was going to be, but what you're asking for is a four-and-a-half page diatribe on her music, and nothing personal.' "

Rouilard, who is no longer with the magazine, disagrees with Yarbrough's allegations that Scott tried to sanitize the piece. "The changes they wanted to make were out of the best of motives," he says, although he concedes that perhaps they misunderstood how much control they would have over the process. "I think they thought they had more editing possibilities than they did," he speculates, "and that's probably why Jeff felt that they overstepped their bounds."

As Rouilard remembers it, nobody had any problems with k.d.'s coming-out, although they may have been shocked by the degree to which she had detailed certain things. "I'm sure they were surprised by the candid nature of that interview," he says. "I mean, she did not just come out of the closet. She didn't just casually mention that she was bisexual, or that she had a lover. *She kicked that closet door wide open.* And I think it probably surprised a couple of people at Warner Brothers."

The real problem came up around the fact that k.d. had mentioned other people in the article. One was her mom, who she worried about in light of the "Meat Stinks" controversy. But the major issue had to do with some things that k.d. supposedly said regarding the love object of *Ingénue,* whom she had described as a married woman. In the days following the interview, she was apparently concerned that she had given a little too much information. Rouilard agreed that it was a problem. "*The Advocate*'s policy is to not out anyone without certain journalistic standards being applied. In other words, I would have had to find this woman, ask her about it, and so on. And given the way certain tabloids investigate things like this, they could have used our interview to find that woman, had they been willing to do the work."

Even if they hadn't, Rouilard just didn't think it was appropriate for k.d. to be talking about someone else's private life to the press. "Take the Madonna interview, for example," he says, referring to the lurid piece the magazine did with the siren in 1991. "In that interview she outed her brother. Then, while we were printing, she had second thoughts about it and asked me to remove it, which I couldn't do, because the magazine was already in print. But it was not a fair thing to do, and I think that's what k.d. thought about this. You know, when people are giving these sorts of interviews, they get very emotional, and they sometimes go over the edge. That can hurt other people, and I just think that k.d. did not want to do that."

Yarbrough maintains that they did not back down, partly because it would have been too costly to make changes at that point in the process, and partly because it would have set a bad precedent by giving an interview subject too much control over the finished article. Yet nowhere in the finished piece is there the slightest hint as to the identity of the married woman that k.d. was so obsessed with. On that subject, at least, her adoring public would be left to their own wild fantasies.

15

"Maybe a great magnet pulls all souls toward truth."

"K. D. lang is the type of politically radical vegetarian lesbian defender of wildlife you'd want to bring home to mother," wrote Michael Specter in the *New York Times* on July 23, 1992.

It had been a little over seven weeks since k.d. had come out as a lesbian in the pages of *The Advocate,* and it was still quite a shock

to see it there, bold as could be, in print. The shock wasn't in the revelation that k.d. was gay; anyone who ever wondered had long ago figured it out. But to see it written so freely and easily on the front page of the *New York Times* arts section—in the first sentence, even! It was more than even the most zealous gay rights activists would have expected a year earlier.

By coming out, k.d. suddenly became one of the world's most well-known living lesbians. Second only to Martina Navratilova in terms of her widespread appeal, she stood alone in the world of pop entertainment as the first out lesbian ever to have been nominated for a Grammy. The irony is that k.d. had never wanted to become a lesbian icon. She never imagined herself a lesbian role model, and certainly never wanted to be a professional dyke. And while her feminist approach to country music may have seemed like a radical gesture at the time, it was motivated more by a personal desire to remain true to herself than by any real plan to change the world. "I don't want to be a political artist," she insists. "My issues are based from my spirituality and are things that I happen to have spoken out on. But I don't want to become a political rallyist. I want to be a musician who speaks out about a couple of her beliefs."

By the same token, she's never been one to deny what's in her heart. She may not sit around debating the state of the union, but she did what she thought needed to be done, like the day she was late for an interview because she stopped to rescue a rain-drenched beagle puppy that had been abandoned on a busy Los Angeles street. "I always knew her as an animal rights person, and she had very strong ideas about it," says Loraine Segato, a Canadian musician and acquaintance of k.d.'s. "We used to have discussions where we'd talk about the politics of vegetarianism, and she'd be like, 'Oh, you're talking about too many things.' But then she went and did something that was way more political."

Now k.d. had unwittingly become a lesbian folk hero. Funny, since it wasn't that long ago that she had been a favorite target of the more strident gay rights activists, who admonished her and other closeted celebrities for supposedly selling out. But k.d. never did care much what other people thought, gay or otherwise. "I don't think it was calculated at all," says Segato when asked if she felt k.d.'s coming-out fit into some sort of political game plan. "I just think it was something important enough that she said, 'I can go to the line with this one. I don't know what it's gonna look like, but I'm gonna ride the wave on it.'"

Whatever the reason, k.d. suddenly found herself removed from Queer Nation's shit list, and catapulted to the top of the list of people who'd made monumental contributions to the gay rights movement.

Looking back, it seems clear that for most of her adult life, k.d. didn't feel any great need to get up onstage and proclaim her lesbianism. She had always been out to her family, breaking the news to her mother and siblings almost as soon as she knew it herself. And among the people she ran with in Edmonton, it just never seemed to be something that people cared too much about. "There was no reason for her to hide it from us, because that was sort of our scene," recalls Gordie Matthews of the early years of the reclines. "In the beginning, the band was kind of alternative anyway. We weren't doing the country clubs, and maybe if we were we would have run into a problem. But it was all just pretty casual, really, and I don't think it ever caused much of a problem with anyone in our group."

Perhaps it's indicative of a country like Canada—where the men are polite, the women are rugged, and concepts like "Unity through diversity" stand in place of "Rally 'round the flag, boys"—that the campaign for gay rights just doesn't resonate the way it does in the United States. "In terms of English-speaking Canada, because our major influence was and remains Britain, and not the United States," explains Canadian journalist Jay Scott, "in a lot of subtle cultural ways, it's a much less overtly macho society, and that makes it easier for gay people." The tangible proof of these cultural differences can be found in the Canadian legislature, which did away with laws prohibiting homosexual acts in the late 1960s. Such "sodomy laws," as they're called in the U.S., are still on the books in many American states.

This is not to say that homophobia doesn't exist in Canada. "In some ways Canada is more homophobic, simply because the gay community doesn't have nearly the size and the scope and the power that you have in America," says journalist Peter Goddard. "I mean, there's no real gay vote here." However, he does believe that Canadians as a whole tend to be more open-minded and liberal. "Try as you might to be right-wing," he says, "there's really no such thing as a hawk in Canada."

In this context, the concept of gay rights in Canadia has met with very little fanfare, making it harder for Canadians to view the issue with any sort of urgency. It might also explain why someone like k.d. would be prone to say, "If you go around screaming, 'I'm a lesbian!' what good is it?" It's not that she had anything to hide; she just didn't see any reason to make her sexuality an issue. "I always thought I was out," she insists. "I presented myself as myself. I didn't try to dispel lesbian rumors. I sang songs like 'Bopalena,' which was about my girlfriend. I didn't take boyfriends to the Grammys. I didn't do anything to cover it up."

Even before she officially came out, k.d. had always presented herself with a lot more honesty than most celebrities can muster, and for that she can be commended. "There's no way that k.d. could have gone onstage looking that androgynous, even masculine, without people asking the question," says Jehan Agrama. "She was already pushing the envelope, by going against the standards of beauty for a female country singer—she was a male country singer, you know? She said, 'I'm gonna swagger, and I'm gonna have fun up here, and I'm gonna be sexy, and I don't have to look like Dolly Parton to do it.' "

Or as one Los Angeles restaurant owner put it, "It wasn't such a

219

big deal for me when k.d. came out, because how could anybody think otherwise. I mean, she's the biggest dyke that's ever stepped foot on MTV."

■

In the spring of 1992, just a couple of short months before the *Advocate* interview came out, k.d. was slated to be on the cover of *Chatelaine* magazine once again, partly at the urging of journalist Peter Goddard, who was thoroughly fascinated with *Ingénue*. "I heard the album, and it was so . . ." He pauses, searching for the right words. "It outed her, I thought, emotionally."

Chatelaine agreed to have Goddard do the piece, which he anchored around yet another exploration of how k.d. presented herself sexually. "My take was actually a question," he says recalling the months between the time *Ingénue* came out and the day k.d. did. "I mean, she was pushing it right to the edge. She was teasing, so that those who knew, knew, and those who didn't know would never know. That was her game." But in his article, Goddard came to the conclusion that, sooner or later, k.d. would have to come out. "You just can't go on like that," he figured. "I mean, on the phone she's very open about her gayness, but it was still like, 'I'm not going to say for the record that I'm gay. I'll say everything else, but I won't say that.' " It was simple enough to see it: k.d. was sitting on a fence, and it seemed only a matter of time before she would lose her balance. The question was simply "When?"

It's true that for those who cared to look closely, k.d. *was* already out. If the subtext of her "Red Hot & Blue" video weren't enough, a comment she made about the undertaking during an interview for a small Los Angeles paper should have clinched it. The journalist, Alex Demyanenko, asked, "With your participation in this project, there's a chance you'll be looked upon as a spokesperson for the gay community. Do you accept the role?" Her response was casual and free-flowing. "Yeah, sure I do."

For a brief moment, the gay press seized the quote as proof of k.d.'s gay identity. But the way Demyanenko remembers it, it wasn't really all that clear what k.d. had meant by the remark. "She didn't say 'Yeah, sure I do,' in a really enthusiastic manner like, 'Yes, I'm coming out,' " he explains. "She was just saying 'Sure,' like 'Yeah, whatever.' " Demyanenko was a little annoyed that people would take such a simple sentence to mean that k.d. was confirming her lesbianism. "I think it was a bit exaggerated, although I have no way of knowing whether, at the time, she wanted to express her sexuality or not," he says. "It's just that I certainly didn't take it as such."

Yet her ambivalence on the subject was constantly showing. Even as the *Advocate* interview was rolling off the presses and onto the trucks, k.d. was ribbing audiences who turned out for the *Ingénue* tour with oblique references to it. "Now you all know the rumors that have been circulating in the press," she prodded. "And I have to say it's true. It's true, I am a L-L-L-Lawrence Welk fan."

■

What was it in k.d.'s personal and career evolution that finally brought her to the point where she felt she had to take this next step? What was it that finally made her come out? For one thing, it seemed pretty clear from her six years on the country-music circuit that staying in the closet hadn't helped her one iota. Even with her set of pipes, she realized that those who wanted to mess with her would do so whether she called herself a lesbian or not. To that extent, it made sense that she should just face the issue head-on, since she worried that the speculation, controversy, and novelty that had dogged her career for so long was starting to once again overshadow her singing.

Even more important was all the commotion around "outing," which undoubtedly pushed a number of prominent gay men and lesbians to think seriously about their own situations. If k.d. hadn't come out when she did, chances were that sooner or later someone would do it for her. Or worse, that the rumors would just continue, a nagging distraction in her life. In either case, k.d. wasn't about to let others commandeer the course of her career. Instead, she decided to grab the ball. "In a world that is increasingly homophobic, I think it's important for people who feel strong enough and ready to come out," she told the CBC shortly after her *Advocate* article appeared on the stands. "I think as a responsibility to the gay community and to myself, it's important to display confidence, because I'm certainly not ashamed of it."

Perhaps the strength of *Ingénue* gave her added courage, as it became hard to imagine anyone rejecting such a stunning piece of work. "She went through a lot of soul-searching," says Los Angeles friend and fellow musician Melissa Etheridge. "I actually told her, 'Look, you're a personality, you're unique. People are gonna go, 'Yeah, we knew, we're fine with that.' " You're beyond that." Etheridge knew that, given k.d.'s penchant for being fiercely independent, there was a good chance that her coming-out would be interpreted as one more victory, further proof that yes, it *was* possible to be successful without compromising one's integrity.

Some might have expected k.d. to be less outspoken after all the trouble "Meat Stinks" had caused. But she had learned a lot from living through that struggle, and had derived a great sense of satisfaction from standing up for what she believed in. She pondered this in an interview with Peter Gzowski just a few short months before her interview with *The Advocate*, when she said, "Volunteering information is a scary process, and I think I've maybe been a little too overzealous in that area. No, I take that back. No I haven't, but it's a scary process to voice your opinion voluntarily, and you have to be pretty strong to be able to do it. I don't . . . yes I do, actually, recommend it." Her life had been changed by suffering through real controversy, but in the end, it only made her stronger.

Her family, on the other hand, hadn't found it so wonderful, and that, more than anything, was the crux of k.d.'s dilemma. In the wake of "Meat Stinks," and the effect it had on her mother and the community back in Consort, k.d. had been asked by her family not to be so outspoken. It was hard, since she tended to be the kind of person who blurted things out. Yet she had to consider that her mom wasn't keen on becoming embroiled in another one of her daughter's controversies. "I don't want to hurt my mother by coming out in the press," she confided to Brendon Lemon, obviously conflicted as to what should be done. "At the same time, I don't want to hurt my culture, and it's like—what do you do? It's taken me a long time to say yes to an interview with *The Advocate*, because I know what the repercussions are gonna be. It's like, I want to be out. I want to be out! Man, if I didn't worry about my mother, I'd be the biggest parader in the whole world."

"Has your mother ever said to you, 'Please, k.d., don't come out.'?" Lemon asked.

"Yes."

"Still?"

"Yes."

"Recently?"

"Yes."

"And what did you say to her?"
"I go, 'Mum, if they ask me, I'm not gonna lie to them.' "

■

The issue of families, and the typical parental concern of "What will the neighbors think?" weighs heavy on the minds of nearly all lesbians and gay men when they grapple with the idea of coming out. For people who live in small towns, or, conversely, have large reputations, such issues become even more amplified. "I'm sure k.d. always knew that she wasn't going to spend the rest of her life in Consort," says Alan Hustak, who, having grown up in a small town in Saskatchewan, is all too familiar with the codes of conduct that are part and parcel of rural life. "But at the same time, and this is true for all of us, there are great family ties, which perhaps in Alberta are particularly strong. She has said, and it's true when you grow up in any small town, that everybody knows everybody on the street. But it's sort of like, nobody cares what you do, as long as you don't acknowledge what you do. In a small town like Consort, for example, you may have a Baptist who is forbidden by his religion from drinking, but you know very well that he gets crocked every Saturday night before going to work on Sunday. You just don't say anything about it. You know that the local druggist is teaching his daughter to shoot in the store in the evenings, because you hear the guns going off. But you don't say anything. And maybe you know that the skater down the street is sleeping with the church organist, but you *just don't say anything*. It's just none of your business, and it only becomes your business when somebody rubs your nose in it."

When k.d. rubbed people's noses in the fact that she wanted the beef industry put out of business, all hell broke loose, and lots of people in Alberta who had previously been content to look the other way regarding k.d.'s "alternative lifestyle" found themselves suddenly forced to take a stand. Years later she could joke about it, as she did in the *Advocate* interview when she smirked, "You know the beef commission. As soon as they get this, they're gonna say, 'Lesbians don't eat meat.' " Yet she didn't have to live with these people the way her mom did.

On the other hand, k.d. also felt a tremendous responsibility to her fans, and she knew the opportunities her fame afforded her were not something she could take lightly. Her willingness to show courage and strong convictions had always been part of what made her popular, and she hesitantly accepted that her status as a celebrity gave her the power to shed light on things that might otherwise be ignored. In 1992, the gay rights movement is the one that got her attention.

Destiny, too, ultimately left her no choice in the matter, as her Saturn Return seemed to be teaching her. "You reach a point where you realize that you have to live with yourself for the rest of your life and that you're not in control of anything," she told Terry David Mulligan that rainy spring day at the Chateau Marmont, when he asked about the impact these astrological forces had had on her life. "The more you relinquish control, the better off it is. That's what I've found."

In relinquishing control she found Percy Adlon, the man who envisioned her, naked and in love, as the lesbian protagonist in *Salmonberries*. The film made her realize she would have to resolve the conflict between her art, her sexuality, and her mom, since once she agreed to portray a lesbian on film, it would be ridiculously impossible to deny the real-life connection. "I said, 'Okay, what am I gonna do here?' " she recalls, looking back. "I don't want to lie. And yet you go, 'Is your job as an artist more important than the love between a mother and daughter? Or is lying to "protect" your mother the biggest sin of all?' "

It's also possible that 1992 was simply the year that brought answers to a lot of k.d.'s questions, as changes in her own life converged with the tumultuous transformations taking place regarding lesbians and gay men in North American society. "Timing is everything," says Loraine Segato thoughtfully. "If you believe in the hundredth-monkey theory, then you have to assume you'll be the hundredth monkey who will tip the scales in terms of being in synchronicity with what other people are thinking. And one of the things I think about Kathy is that she has really good timing. Even when she does things that appear to be controversial, I think she has a good internal sense of timing about what's right for her." Call it the year of living honestly.

■

"You know how many others are running around out there like that?" grins Nashville's Ted Lawrence when talk turns to k.d.'s sexual orientation. It doesn't bother him what k.d. does in the privacy of her own bedroom, because, as he says quite earnestly, "There's no reason for it to. It shouldn't matter to nobody." But he knows the kind of people to whom it *does* matter. "It's the ones who're like that themselves that get all bothered about it and make such a fuss."

If there was one thing k.d. learned in 1992, it was that coming out didn't hurt her career at all. In September, *Ingénue* became her first certified gold record in the U.S., selling over half a million copies in only six months, and nearly one million worldwide. In November, she won a *Billboard* Music Video award for Best Female Artist and, in December, she was nominated for her first American Music Award as the Best New Female Artist in the Adult Contemporary category, based on calculations of year-end sales and, believe it or not, radio play. On December 16, she flew to New York to tape a segment for "MTV Unplugged," after having just finished a similar performance for VH-1's "Center Stage." And in January she was nominated for five Grammy Awards, including Best Album and Best Female Vocalist. It was more than even she had hoped for.

"There's so many different ways to look at it," she said when asked how she felt about the surge in popularity her Grammy nominations represented. "There's a part of me that thinks it's totally overwhelming and a bit scary, because whenever you achieve really high goals you wonder what's next—if it's over, or if you even deserve it. And then there's a part of me that goes, 'Sure I deserve it, what am I talking about?' "

When she was announced as having won the award for Best Female Vocal Performance, she was ecstatic. "What could I possibly do to top this?" she chided a group of reporters backstage at the Grammy ceremonies. "Best Male Vocalist?" Her Grammy win caused *Ingénue* to jump from No. 56 to No. 18 on the *Billboard 200* album chart, representing an increase in American sales—over 100,000 copies in the four weeks that followed—that pushed the album past the million mark, making it her first platinum record.

In some ways, though, it was the American Music Award that was most significant of all, since, unlike the peer-based Grammy Awards, it represented the vote of the general public. When k.d. strode to the podium to accept her award on January 25, looking for all the world like Lenny Kravitz's white stepbrother in her ruffled blouse, luxuriously textured suit, and red-tinted granny glasses, she told an electrified crowd of curious onlookers, many who had never heard of her before, "I've had eight years to practice for this."

When a neighbor back home at her rented L.A. apartment asked her how it felt to be receiving so many awards, she stretched her arms wide and took a deep breath. He took the gesture to mean "mission accomplished" when he saw the "Entertainment Tonight" van pull up outside of the house. At last, k.d. was becoming a household name.

Her award for "Best New Artist" seemed strange to long-time k.d. fans, but the title had more to do with her debut in a new genre of music—not that she had been mistaken as new to the industry. Still, Jay Leno couldn't resist yucking it up about the odd designation when k.d. joined him on his show a few days later. "Congratulations," he said slyly. "You're one of the new faces. How long have you been in business now, six or eight weeks?"

"Yep, it's funny, that overnight success," k.d. snorted back. "It can really throw you for a jilt."

What really threw people for a jilt were the several hundred thousand new fans who were digging k.d.'s music, seemingly unconcerned with anything other than the fact she had possibly the best singing voice of her generation. All of those fans who were snapping up her records and dragging their friends and families to her shows not only meant that she would finally make a superstar's salary, but that somehow people had managed to sidestep common bigotry. "So what if she is a lesbian?" they seemed to say. "More power to her."

"The really, really big thing I experienced this year was the intimacy between me and the audience," she said looking back on a gap she had never noticed until she bridged it. "Not just because of the number of women, although that's part of it. It's that I feel comfortable knowing that they came there knowing. I don't have to worry that if they finally figured it out, they would get up and leave. Being out is just great. I recommend it to people who are ready to do it. Just do it." It wasn't the kind of advice anyone in the music business was used to hearing, and it wasn't advice that many were likely to follow. Still, for k.d. at least, a storybook fantasy had come true: with little more in her corner than talent, hard work, and faith, she had succeeded in becoming a superstar.

In March, she won yet another Juno, performed on England's "Top of the Pops," and participated in the Brit Awards, the British version of the Grammys, where she was nominated for Best International Solo Artist, and joined Erasure's Andy Bell in a duet of the old Barbra Streisand–Donna Summer classic, "Enough is Enough." In Canada, Toronto's "new country" station CISS-FM was playing several of k.d.'s old country tunes, while a number of different pop and "lite rock" stations continued to play "Constant Craving," and the new single, "Miss Chatelaine." American Vice President Al Gore was given *Ingénue* for his birthday, and Gloria Estefan told *USA Today* it was one of her most frequently listened-to CDs. In short, k.d.-mania was everywhere.

Far from hindering her career, there are indications that k.d.'s coming-out actually helped her—if not directly, then indirectly. "I don't know if Jeff Yarbrough told you," says Brendon Lemon, "but I believe the label told him that they tracked their numbers from the sales of the album, and that they got a nice bump in their figures about the time the *Advocate* piece came out. Which is nice, because it suggests that coming out can be positive, and lays to rest, at least in her case, the canard that coming out will hurt your record sales or hurt your career." That bump may have meant that k.d.'s coming-out drew more attention to her music, or it could have been merely coincidental, since a lot of people probably bought *Ingénue* after seeing her summer concerts.

But even back in Consort, few had anything negative to say about k.d.'s latest political musings. Margaret Mitchell, a retired school secretary, admitted that she had always suspected Kathy was gay, but hadn't really been too concerned. "Because of her masculine dress she was sometimes the subject of rumors," she explained. "But I think she's an incredible talent and her personal life won't make any difference in how I enjoy her creativeness and her music."

The mayor of Consort, Marlene Arp, assured the press that k.d. would remain a strong ambassador for the town, noting that everyone was proud of her. "She's done more to put us on the map than anybody, and we are extremely pleased with her. She's still personable and very approachable, and her preferred lifestyle is insignificant to me."

There was a small handful of people who jumped at the chance to lash out at k.d. once it was proven she was gay, but most of them were ranchers still licking their wounds from the beef blowout. On June 19, 1992, a concert in Owen Sound, Ontario, had to be canceled after local beef farmers threatened to protest, and a few months later, a slightly bigger backlash occurred when Albertan politician William Roberts proposed that the provincial legislature send a formal congratulations to k.d. for her American Music Award. The motion, which needed a consensus in order to pass in the Conservative-led government, was rejected when Agriculture Minister Ernie Isley said he was against it because "she is anti-agriculture and because she's a lesbian."

Most Canadians just shook their heads at the childishness of Isley's grudge. "It would be funny if it weren't so sad," read an editorial in the *Ottawa Citizen* on January 30, 1993. "The government's decision to snub its most famous daughter for not conforming to its idea of what a good ol' country girl should be is just plain cruel. k.d. lang is a vegetarian, she did make a 'Meat Stinks' commercial, and she openly says she is a lesbian. None of this makes her a criminal or has anything to do with her artistic achievements. k.d. has style, which is more than can be said for her backbench critics in Alberta."

k.d. got the last laugh again when Canada's national government agreed to do what Alberta's provincial government would not: they sent her a proclamation commending her for being such an fine example of what Canada has to offer. Back at Consort High School, Larry Kjearsgaard also seized the controversy as an essay-writing topic, sparking a lively debate among his students. "I have to say, I was a little surprised at the range of opinions," he says. "At that age a lot of what the kids say are still things they get from their parents, and one kid did say something like, 'She crapped in her nest, now she'll have to sit in it.' But others said, 'No, that award was for her singing, and it shouldn't have any bearing on her lifestyle.' "

Kjearsgaard was pleased that the kids didn't seem overly concerned about her lesbianism. "I'm not sure to what extent she inspires young people," he says, "but I know that here in Consort people are very proud. I, for one, constantly remind everyone that k.d. is an example of what they can achieve. We'll be going off to some volleyball tournament, for example, and I'll be trying to pump them up. And sometimes, when we play teams from some of the bigger towns, the attitude will be like, 'Oh, but we're just from Consort.' That's when I remind them that Kathy Lang was from Consort too."

Even her father, who never really knew this side of his daughter, was content in knowing that k.d. was comfortable in her own skin. "She never made any bones about anything she wanted to be or do," he says. "Now she says she's a lesbian, and that's okay with her dad. As long as she's happy, it's fine with me, however she wants to live her life."

"I think people are more liberal than they realize." k.d. said philosophically when it became clear that her coming-out had brought no backlash at all. "I think people have surprised themselves by saying, 'Wow. This doesn't bother me the way I thought it would!' " Still, she couldn't help but be relieved.

■

Does k.d.'s overwhelming success mean the entertainment business—and more specifically the music industry—is undergoing a metamorphosis? Most say yes, and see the momentum reflected in everything from *The Crying Game* to RuPaul and lesbian chic. "People know what homophobia is now, thank you very much, and they don't say 'avowed homosexual' anymore—they say lesbian or gay," says GLAAD's Jehan Agrama. "We are now part of the consciousness, good or bad, and people have to deal with us." She's cautious in her assessment, pointing out the fact that one of the biggest flourishes of out gay culture in the Western world occurred in Germany just before Hitler came to power. "We don't know what will happen down the line," she says, "but these people can't go back in the closet. Kids that are coming up have more role models now, and they'll be coming out earlier, feeling good about themselves. Hopefully, that means that we're creating something that will continue and sustain itself."

Brendon Lemon is a little more hesitant. "I think the great hope is that what k.d. has done will give courage to others, by showing them that coming out won't necessarily ruin their careers," he says. "But then again, it's hard to tell, because very few people in the music business have a natural gift as great as hers."

It's a sentiment that Jim Fouratt agrees with wholeheartedly. "k.d. lang has the best voice of her generation," he notes. "She can sing the shit out of any song, and on that level, it doesn't read 'dyke.' It just reads great singer." Fouratt is skeptical that the success of people like k.d. and Elton John can be so easily transferred to up-and-coming artists, who don't already have a proven track record. "It takes an enormous investment to launch an artist in this country, and I think record companies are very worried about narrowing their market in any way, sexual orientation being one way," he says. "But it does signify a change, and certainly once k.d. lang and Elton John are on the radio, it's going to be much harder for the programmers to say they won't play artists because they're gay."

In the final analysis, most agree that an artist's ability to sell records will be what ultimately determines lesbian and gay survival in the music business. "It's not that the industry is changing," says Melissa Etheridge. "Things are changing in the country which affect the entertainment industry. It's all about money, and as soon as someone proves that a gay artist can be accepted and make money and win Grammys—that they can turn it into dollars and it's not gonna hurt them, then people will say, 'Okay, I'm gonna go home. That's no problem.'"

In Janis Ian's opinion, the success of k.d. and others may even spark a trend in which artists are specifically targeted at a newly recognized lesbian and gay market. "I think in about two years the entire straight world is gonna realize that the gay market is huge, and it's going to be very funny to watch people just shoot themselves in the foot," she predicts.

■

"k.d. lang is so butch that her concept of cross-dressing involves putting on makeup and a dress," teased a gossip columnist, marveling at the character k.d. unleashed for the video for her second *Ingénue* single. Finally, after all the drama surrounding broken hearts and closet doors, the witty, irreverent k.d. lang was back in full effect.

It began on a hot July 4th weekend in a nondescript warehouse on the edge of Manhattan's meat-packing district. A sign at the top of the first flight of stairs read "Miss Chatelaine," indicating the studio where a video crew prepared for their next shoot. Perhaps it was too soon for the mostly transexual streetwalkers who strutted along the hot, gritty sidewalk below to recognize the moniker. Perhaps they just didn't care. But had they wandered upstairs, they surely would have treasured the sight of k.d., draped dramatically across a slowly turning divan, wearing a yellow chiffon gown and the most gorgeous heap of borrowed curls a working girl could hope for. It was a drag performance—k.d. as a femme.

She'd been there since 8:00 A.M., her face uncharacteristically caked with makeup, yet she was friendly, even cheerful, as the crew, many of them other lesbians, bustled around her, stoking the bubble machine or adjusting the lights. Every few minutes they would stop, the cameras would roll, and the magic of k.d.'s voice would fill the room. "She's like cotton candy," the director cooed, pleased with her easygoing enthusiasm. Everyone in the room was enchanted. "Miss Chatelaine" had arrived.

Eight months later, on February 2, 1993, k.d.'s fans swooned and screamed as she walked the length of a makeshift runway, flanked by Lady Bunny and a royal lineup of New York's finest female interpreters. It was PETA's annual "Fur is a Drag" party at Manhattan's Hard Rock Cafe, and the place was packed with hundreds of New Yorkers who pushed and shoved to get a glimpse of the year's most glorious photo opportunity.

"Growing up in a small town, Lord knows I've seen cruelty," k.d. half smirked and half sighed, affecting her best bitch-queen attitude as she alluded to the matter at hand. Then, with the opening strains of "Miss Chatelaine" rising up behind her, a smile spread across her face. The crowd roared as she burst into song, drag queens twirling and sashaying around her.

The most memorable part of the evening was witnessing the natural chaos that came from having too many divas occupying such a small stage, all typically vying for the spotlight. Halfway through the number, it looked as though a couple of them might be headed for a stiletto-induced collision, as an unforeseen error in choreography caused pandemonium onstage. "It was kind of funny," Bunny purrs in her trademark Southern drawl, settling in for some post-party dish. "Ebony Jet and Mistress Formika were supposed to choreograph something to do behind her as she performed 'Miss Chatelaine.' Everything was cool. We got together at my place and rehearsed the number to my cassette, and when it was time for the show, we felt pretty confident that the choreography was ready." They hadn't knocked themselves out over it, because it was meant to be silly. But still, they had it down.

Yet when it came to the actual performance, something in the routine went awry. "The song had this one part in it where—are you familiar with it?—she sort of sings 'Ahhhh.'" Lady Bunny warbles into the phone. "At that point we were supposed to all flit in front of her like in that classic old, queeny, steal-the-spotlight kind of thing. And we actually asked Dan Mathews of PETA to check with her to make sure that it was all right, and it got back to us that she said yes, that was fine. Well, we had picked a part of the song where she wasn't singing, but we had choreographed it to the album, and she used a different version of the song." The Lady laughs at how flustered the girls got as they tried to regain their composure after diving in front of k.d. just as she hit the climax to the song. But k.d. didn't mind. In fact, she appeared to be having the time of her life.

"What is this world coming to, when dykes are dressing up like fags who dress up like women?" snickered *Out* magazine editor Sarah Pettit as she leaned over the second-floor railing. It was a quintessential moment—a sublime irony. It was the "Gay Nineties" in a nutshell.

16

*"Coming out was totally positive—
like an emotional veil had been lifted
and taken away."*

BETWEEN falling in love and coming out, k.d.'s journey had stripped her clean, leaving nothing to stand between her and her audience but pure, guileless emotion. The reward was that it enabled her to express

herself more honestly and openly than she ever had before. The flip side was that it made her more vulnerable.

"When she announced her sexuality last year, that was a very, very courageous thing for her to do," notes MuchMusic's Denise Donlon, commenting not only on the risk k.d. took in the face of homophobia, but also in terms of how it would affect her audience. "We discussed it at one point and I said, 'k.d., you've completely stripped away your mystique. Now people know exactly who and what you are. There's now no difference between the entertainer, the public person, and the private person. You are one and the same thing, and that's very difficult to live with.'"

If k.d.'s fans were fervent before, it was nothing compared to what lay in store for her now that she had come out. In early 1993, as she was frolicking Stateside in femme drag, upward of 300 women were convening in England for the first-of-its-kind "k.d. lang convention." Committed fans, mostly lesbians, flocked to Wesley House, home of the London Women's Centre, to share their passions, aspirations, and sisterly concern for one of their most beloved heroines. Organizers of the convention reported a sell-out crowd of women who came to cavort and try their luck at a k.d. look-alike contest, square dancing, and k.d. karaoke, and to peruse the many stalls selling k.d. memorabilia.

"The atmosphere was a mixture of frivolity and reverence, underwritten by serious fan-ness," wrote Rosa Ainley and Sarah Cooper in *Shebang,* a London-based lesbian magazine that seems to have been the only media outlet admitted into the event. "Devotion and concern, not unfounded, about her situation as a lesbian in a heterosexual and homophobic music business, were expressed by fans overjoyed at the success of an out mainstream performer."

As with many pop idols, overzealous fans have long been a trademark of k.d.'s success—particularly fans of the female variety. In 1989, while she was still in her country period, journalist Stephen Rea decided to check out the crowd waiting for k.d. after a show. He found that "the scene at the stage door is like something out of *A Hard Day's Night,* with fans shrieking at movements in the windows above. Then, as it begins to pour, it turns into Woodstock. The star emerges and in the rain gracefully signs photos, album covers, jean jackets, and anything else thrust at her." Crazy Nanny's, a Manhattan lesbian bar and favorite watering hole for many k.d. heads, knows this culture well: once, minutes after a David Letterman interview with k.d., a breathless patron raced to the bar with a videotape of the show, just for the thrill of an instant group replay. Even today, a giant print of k.d.'s Gap ad—which was "liberated" from a bus stop by an anonymous collector—hangs framed above the bar, guarded by the staff against offers of up to $1,000 from love-struck patrons wanting to buy it.

The psychology behind such hard-core fans is hard to ever fully explain. One thing, however, is universally true: it's not just lesbians who swoon after her. Terri Horak, a twenty-something woman who works in the music industry and has a thing for country music, discovered k.d. when a friend gave her a copy of *Angel With A Lariat* in 1987. She was immediately transfixed. "The first time I heard the album I was completely hooked," she recalls. "I called my friend in Chicago who was a complete country-music fan, and I played it for him over the phone. I mean, that's how excited I was." Horak's enthusiasm for k.d.'s music made her an instant fan, and she soon found herself sending k.d. tapes to friends, and traveling great distances to hear the singer perform. It wasn't long before her interest in k.d. blossomed into an obsession.

"There's no doubt in my mind that I'm in love with her," she says matter-of-factly. "And, of course, that has caused me to think a lot about my sexuality. But when all is said and done, it really doesn't matter. Maybe if she were really in your face about being gay, I would feel excluded, like, 'Gee, I don't fit in with that world.' But the same might be true if she were married and had four children, because that's not my world either." Horak's attraction to k.d., along with the fantasies and obsessions of thousands of other heterosexual men and women who've fallen for the singer over the years, raises a plethora of fascinating questions about the nature of sexual desire and its ability to transgress boundaries when presented in a way that is safely beyond reach. But on a simpler level, it also speaks to the universal impulses that k.d. touches in everyone. "One of the things that's so appealing about her is that she's like the champion of the individual," Horak explains. "If she's gay, so be it. That's just one more facet of her life that makes her interesting."

Lesbian fans, on the other hand, are much more direct in their desire for k.d.—a desire which has only crescendoed since her coming-out. "God, those eyes, those cheekbones, that smile," wrote one woman after seeing k.d. on the cover of *Interview* magazine at the end of 1992. "A human aphrodisiac, to say the least. Hey k.d., will you marry me?"

This unabashed love fest has spawned at least two k.d. lang "fanzines" since *Ingénue* was released: the London-based *Angel With An Attitude,* and *Highway Twelve,* produced by a couple of women in Aberdeen, Scotland. Like most celebrity-driven fanzines, these do-it-yourself projects, created with little more than typewriters, xerox machines, and a sturdy stapler, are replete with historical trivia, reprinted quotes, concert reviews, and the occasional poem or letter written by an adoring fan. *Highway Twelve* is particularly witty, with items like "Canada for Beginners" (map included); a vocabulary list of words k.d. has been known to utter ("to facilitate audience understanding," it explains, giving definitions of words like "deleterious," "matutinal," and "sapiential"); "The Cookery Corner," featuring "exciting, cow-friendly recipes"; and a page entitled "Dress You Up," with a k.d. cutout doll and full winter wardrobe.

The other thing that *Highway Twelve* does quite well is to act as a conduit for gossip. In its premier issue, a whole page was devoted to the question of *Ingénue*'s mystery girl—the "married woman" who had scorned k.d.'s love. Entitled "Place Your Bets," the piece is a screamingly funny summation of the potential contenders vying for k.d.'s heart, offering names, explanations, and a rating system that guesses at the odds for each being "the lucky sod." The list is rife with comic detail, suggesting people as far-reaching and unlikely as Ben Mink and River Phoenix (both at 800–1 odds before the latter's death), and Rosel Zech (900–1). Anne Murray ranks a little better at 250–1, in part because of k.d.'s childhood crush, and because she had once been photographed with her arms around k.d. The editors place more serious bids on Madonna (8–1), Martina (25–1), and Liza Minnelli (10–1), all three of whom have, at one time or another, been photographed with their arms around k.d.

The most curious entry was the one weighing in at second place: Wendy Melvoin, of Wendy and Lisa, at 6–1 odds. According to the magazine, Melvoin had been spotted with k.d. at the U.S. opening of *In Bed With Madonna,* where the two of them were—you guessed it—also photographed with their arms around each other. Why the Melvoin-k.d. connection was afforded more weight than the others is a mystery, suggesting that maybe *Highway Twelve*'s editors are privvy to more substantial gossip than they're letting on. Then again, they pegged the first-place winner as Jodie Foster, with 4–1 odds, even though she had not only never been photographed with k.d., but had probably never even been seen in the same room with the singer. Perhaps it was meant simply to underscore the ridiculousness of it all. "We phoned her agent," the accompanying caption teased. "She told us 'no comment' and we all know what that means!"

■

The best way to kill a good piece of gossip is for someone to simply admit that it's true. After all, it's no fun to spread stories if everyone else has already heard them. k.d. knew this, and hoped that her coming-out would put an end to the whispers about her personal life, logic being that if she just admitted she was a lesbian, people would quickly tire of the subject. But, in an age where people live vicariously through hours of weekly television, and media hype invades our every thought, k.d.'s coming-out instigated a strange turn of events, and unleashed a different sort of gossip altogether.

If rumors of k.d.'s lesbianism dogged her for most of her career, nobody had ever dared to make such a claim out loud. For years she had been the subject of gossip and innuendo, but as far as journalists were concerned, if she wasn't going to talk about her sexual orientation, neither were they. Now, however, it was as if her coming-out had liberated the gossip columnists also. Suddenly they were free to poke around in her private affairs with the same gusto they used to write about heterosexual celebrities. Almost overnight, a feeding frenzy began, with everybody scrambling to dig up dirt. *"Who is k.d. sleeping with?"* came the curious refrain. Not surprisingly, all eyes turned unimaginatively toward Madonna.

k.d. first met Madonna in 1989 when the brassy blonde popped backstage following a reclines concert at the Wiltern Theater in Los Angeles. Stargazing columns would have us believe that the two became fast friends, and were often seen at the same parties. No big deal, since the two were on the same record label, and it is even less interesting given Madonna's penchant for being seen in the company of lesbians. But it was enough to get curious minds moving in all sorts of wild directions.

k.d. laughed at the rumors that she and Madonna were close, joking that Madonna probably liked her because she looked like Sean Penn. She shrugged it off by saying that the media had made a bigger thing out of it than it was, and when asked by Peter Goddard in early 1992 if it was true that the two were hanging out together, all she had to say was, "Hanging out? Really?" Still the rumors persisted, coming to a head around a party Madonna threw for k.d. when she arrived in New York to promote *Ingénue* later that summer.

As the story goes, Madonna and a crowd of assorted celebrities and paparazzi had gathered at Manhattan's Remi Restaurant to fete k.d. following her opening night at Radio City Music Hall. Tony Bennett, Martina Navratilova, and a 72-year-old Peggy Lee were just a few of the many entertainment dignitaries on hand, wining and dining as they waited for the guest of honor to arrive. But it seems that k.d. had been detained back at the Hall, presumably engulfed by a throng of fans that awaited her at the venue's back door. As the evening wore on, Madonna finally announced that she couldn't stick around any longer, spinning on her heels and heading for the door, the glue on her gold tooth cap barely dry from her own album/book pre-publicity blitz.

The next morning, the gossip columns were fairly subdued, taking note that k.d. had missed her host, but presenting it as a nonevent in which the two divas were just too busy to get their schedules in synch.

Madonna, as everyone understood, had rushed back to the studio. Liz Smith offered her own excuse for k.d. "Listen, when you've just spent two hours onstage, giving a brilliant performance and having 5,000 people screaming their love, a compliment from Madonna maybe isn't quite the thrill it would be to you and me," she wrote in *Newsday* the next morning. "No big whoop."

But the buzz among industry insiders who had attended the event was much more sensational. People seemed thoroughly titillated by the idea that k.d. had blown Madonna off, and soon the story had all the makings of a lover's tiff. "Listen, Madonna was still there when k.d. walked in, and they definitely exchanged some harsh words," insists one anonymous MTV staffer. Others felt sure that Madonna was mad because k.d. had been flirting with Ingrid Caseras, whose primary claim to fame was being pegged as Madonna's girlfriend—or as the media now likes to call lesbian paramours, "gal pal"—after Madonna supposedly stole her from Sandra Bernhardt. Before long the story snowballed, as behind-the-scenes accounts from Los Angeles had k.d., spotted variously with Madonna on the back of her motorcycle; grocery shopping with Ingrid at Erewon; arriving at Madonna's house in a convertible to whisk the girls off to a secluded beach; and, buying Ingrid a BMW.

It wasn't until six months later that these rumors got a brief respite (although new rumors about Ingrid later reappeared), when Liz Smith announced that k.d. was actually having an affair with Martina Navratilova. On March 10, 1993, an item in her daily column read: "A lot of people noted that k.d. lang's date on the night she won the Grammy was none other than the celebrated tennis ace Martina Navratilova. Inquiries reveal that about a month ago, Martina's liaison with Cindy Nelson, an Aspen ski instructor, had ended. . . . Anyway, to settle all questions that could still arise—yes, now it's k.d. and Martina."

Such a bold assertion appearing in print was enough to put k.d. lang fans over the edge—those who swallowed it, that is. "Did you hear about k.d. and Martina?" rang the refrain through offices, restaurants, bars, and Ma Bell the day Smith's column first appeared. It was news that turned the lesbian nation on its head.

■

As in any crowd, comparing notes on "who's sleeping with who" is an endless source of entertainment for lesbians and gay men, whether the talk is of celebrities or a more parochial survey of the local population. That the gay community revels in such frivolity regarding other people's sex lives makes it no different than any other group of people bound by neighborhood, workplace, or other social activities. But the stories take on an even greater urgency when they reveal gay liaisons involving people not "known" to be gay, and the juice really flows when the world inhabited by celebrities collides with the world of the common queer—which it always inevitably does, since no matter how big the numbers get, the lesbian and gay world is a small world indeed.

Of course, there's always a gap between what people *really* know and what they merely *think* they know. Take, for instance, the rumors that sprung from the admission that *Ingénue* was written for a "married woman." "Married," as the gay community knew, didn't really mean married to a *man*—it only meant unavailable. That assumption agreed upon, the most commonly heard votes were split three ways: In New York, gossip queens were convinced that k.d. had been rejected by Liza Minnelli. In Toronto, people just assumed it was Anne Murray. And in Los Angeles, everyone beyond k.d.'s innermost circle of friends swore that the woman in question had to be Melissa Etheridge.

Being a lesbian wasn't a prerequisite for a part in this particular rumor, given that k.d.'s affection was not returned. Each of these women had been seen in the company of k.d. during the year preceding *Ingénue*'s release. In Liza's case, the two were good friends, which seemed enough for some people to make the love leap. "I have the real scoop about who Liza Minnelli is seeing these days," a muffled voice reportedly told a Toronto-based gossip columnist in 1991. "It's not Billy Stritch, it's k.d. lang. They've been seen everywhere together."

As for Anne Murray, her duet with k.d. for the Canadian TV special "Country Gold" was enough to cause lesbian tongues to wag as the couple crooned "I Want To Sing You a Love Song" to each other before collapsing into silly schoolgirl giggles. And let's not forget the much-publicized childhood crush k.d. had once had on the former gym teacher.

And Melissa Etheridge? Who knows, except that again, she and k.d. were friends, and were known to hang out from time to time.

Supported by such elliptical associations as being in the same place at the same time, and supplemented by other vague and unsubstantiated gossip, these stories and others took on a life of their own within the gay community. On a more personal level, everybody who's anybody seems to carry around at least one torrid k.d. lang story to share over cocktails, whether it involves a lawyer in New Orleans, a married woman in London, a jewelry-maker in New York, or a makeup artist who travels the globe. Some accounts tell of k.d. picking up fans who have then gone on to become her lifelong friends. Others are stories of k.d. striking out, as she did with the woman she purportedly tried to woo by serenading her in a bar one night.

In every case, the stories themselves are vividly detailed, while the proof is nearly nonexistent. But it doesn't matter, since whether the stories are true or not is completely beside the point. The real story is in the telling, and like the old children's game "Telephone," as the information gets passed from one person to the next, it changes shape, hue, and context, until the original incident is nowhere to be recognized. Who k.d. has slept with really doesn't matter. What matters is that by telling and retelling stories of gay love, lesbians and gay men are reminded of its existence.

■

As much as Kathryn Dawn Lang is inclined to live her life honestly, she's also made it clear that she'd prefer to do so without much fanfare. She's not keen on the fact that everyone wants to know her personal business, and even more dismayed that her sexuality has become a political issue. "There are things I don't want the public to know, because they're special," she explains earnestly. "Just like if you slept with someone, you wouldn't call your mother up and go, 'Hey, I just boinked somebody.' There are things you want to covet, to cherish, for yourself. That's a human instinct, not because I'm a star."

It's a problem nearly all celebrities are forced to grapple with, but in k.d.'s case, her particularly close relationship to her fans makes it all the more difficult. A lot of successful artists find balance in constructing enough walls around their private selves that when they need to retreat, they've created another personna who can be there, acting in their stead. Yet k.d.'s gift to her public has been to destroy most of those barriers, leaving her open to the whims and fancies of everyone who claims her as their own. It might not be so bad if our society weren't so star-struck. But alas, hungry fans are rarely satisfied, and the gay community is particularly hard on its heroes, demanding that a tiny handful of individuals represent a broad and fragile coalition of people in ways that are often unrealistic.

To a certain extent k.d. has acquiesced, becoming, rather be-grudgingly, the universal lesbian spokeswoman. Appearing as the drag diva Miss Chatelaine on "Arsenio Hall" the winter following *Ingénue*'s release, she batted her eyelashes and smoothed her gown as the late-night host quizzed her on homophobia, Bill Clinton, and the anti-gay law that had passed in Colorado. "I'm appalled," she said, as if scolding a child. "I can't believe it's 1993 and people are still squabbling about whether gays should have rights. It's ridiculous."

It's an ironic turn of events that k.d.'s coming-out, which was meant to put an end to discussions of her sexuality, has cost her so much time talking about being a lesbian. "I don't think she thought of coming out as being political," her friend Loraine Segato emphasizes. "I think she thought of it as being true to herself, and in a way, that's the bravest thing of all. Because I'm sure she recognizes that in any community, whether it's a political community, the arts community, the gay community, or whatever, there's a whole rhetoric and dogma that is not unlike the dogma and rhetoric that exists in patriarchal society. You begin to get these rules and laws about how you have to behave, and it becomes very difficult to live with."

That is exactly what k.d. lashed out against when, in the *Advocate* interview, she snapped, "I don't want to be out like Phranc is out . . . I'm sorry to disappoint you hardcores." Yet while she often hates being the one to have to speak for the gay community, she understands why people are so hell-bent on making her a lesbian poster girl. She realizes that when lesbians look to her, they are looking for themselves—to see images of lesbians in popular culture that are just as fully developed and life-affirming as those of heterosexuals. She also knows that there are many people out there who derive courage from the way she lives her life.

"There's this amazing assumption that if somebody is famous, they actually know something, and that they're actually worth something," says Janis Ian with just a hint of bewilderment. "I've always found that to be just a horrifying responsibility myself, but I think for gay people, especially when we are adolescents, we're looking for anybody who's like us." Ian isn't joking when she says that she made *her* decision to come out after listening to the fiery lesbian activist and speaker Urvashi Vaid quote staggering statistics on the prevalence of teen suicide among gay and lesbian youth, reminding her of her own painful child-hood.

Unfortunately, there's no training school to teach celebrities how to be good role models, and even if there were, most artists would probably refuse to enroll. "Here's the paradox about being a per-former," says Segato. "A lot of performers love to go onstage because they love to make people happy. They like to be able to help people relax after a hard day, or to help people think about things they never thought about before." But what they don't like is being told how to act, what to do and how to think, whether it's by the industry or by the fans. "A lot of us go up there because we want to be loved and adored. But while we want to be loved and adored, we also want to be accepted for everything we are, just as if it were a relationship. We don't want to be owned by anybody."

k.d. knows well the tension that occurs when the fans start to feel that they own their favorite artists. Time and time again she has been chastised for not being willing to participate in political events, and even in her personal life, she is constantly being taken to task for snubbing fans who descend on her in public places like restaurants or on the street. Again, this isn't any different from the way fans relate to heterosexual stars; a fan is a fan, and nobody likes being snubbed. But it's also true that because there are so few role models for lesbians and gay men, those celebrities who do come out often find that they have to be all things to all people.

Sometimes this responsibility can be almost too much for an artist to bear. Just ask Sandra Bernhardt, who has suffered an incredible beating at the hands of the lesbian and gay community. For years, everybody wanted her to say she was a lesbian, and when she did, everyone rejoiced. But when she later clarified that she was actually bisexual, people in the gay community were outraged, insisting that she was a sellout trying to mimic Madonna's game playing. Bernhardt, of course, antagonized matters, since that's the kind of girl she is. But it was sad to see the gay community invest so much energy in trying to make her a hero against her will, and even sadder to see her sexuality being reduced to a matter of political expediency.

For better or worse, when an artist makes an impact on the world, there will always be people who have expectations of them. Does this mean an artist should just buck up and deal with the responsibility foisted upon them? It's an age-old question that has taken on a far greater sense of urgency in the 1990s, as pop culture tends more and more toward leading society rather than reflecting it. "I have a real question as to whether artists, in general, are qualified to be spokespeople," Ian says thoughtfully. "I mean, I'm certainly not, and I think it's scary sometimes, the hold we have over people. But I accept the reality of the phenomenon. I mean, it would have been great for people like us, when we were twelve, if we could have turned on the TV and seen some openly gay people on 'Johnny Carson.' Just to see them talking about their life partners, or whatever word they came up with to call them, and think nothing of it. So now I figure, if I could be on 'Oprah' or some show like that, and one kid would be saved because of it, as cliché as that sounds, it's worthy."

■

Life goes on, and in the heterosexual world, the press still seems happy to perpetuate the myth that there are only three lesbians in the world: k.d. lang, Martina Navratilova, and, more recently, Melissa Etheridge. Not only are the three of them expected to speak for the entire lesbian nation, but occasionally, with enough misguided reporting, one might be led to believe that somehow these three women just continue to trade romantic partners with Madonna. Thankfully, most regular folks know better.

"I would be surprised if Madonna and k.d. are good friends," says Brendon Lemon. "They're very different, you know. k.d.'s a nature girl, and Madonna's not. Madonna, surprisingly, likes to read a lot, and k.d. says she doesn't." Madonna loves the nightlife, k.d. does not. Madonna is a loudmouth, k.d. is not. The list goes on and on.

As for Martina, all most dykes can say is, "Two butches together? No way." Besides, one would think these gossip columnists could at least be a little more creative. "That was really the epitome of how ridiculous it all is," k.d. scoffs, referring to Liz Smith's supposed revelation. "It's like all celebrity lesbians must date each other. It's kind of an insult."

Not even a week after the k.d.-Martina item appeared in Smith's column, she was compelled to print a retraction: "Representatives for k.d. lang and Martina Navratilova insist that our item last week, linking the Grammy-winning chanteuse and the tennis great, was inaccurate," she wrote. "The two women are *not* an item, say they. Martina and k.d. do know each other, and Martina did stop by k.d.'s table to congratulate her at the Warner Records party after the show (one of several Grammy bashes Martina attended). But that, according to these reps, is as far as it goes. As one irked person remarked, 'Just because two gay women happen to be in the same massive auditorium at the same event, doesn't mean they are involved romantically.' Hmmm, perhaps my impeccable source on this story was 'peccable' after all."

17

*"Sometimes I think I'll never be granted a lover. That
I've got one—it's my voice."*

BACK at PETA's "Fur is a Drag" party at the Hard Rock Cafe, k.d.
listened attentively as her co-star, Lahoma Van Zandt, told the story
of her trip to the ladies' room. While she was there, she met a group
of girls who insisted that the drag queen introduce them to k.d. "Oh,

you've got to take us back to meet her," they pleaded. "We've got to
meet her. We love her." Lahoma promised to do her best, and was
now dutifully delivering the message to its intended recipient.

"Well, what do they look like?" k.d. asked with just a hint of
curiosity.

"Oh, they're young and cute and sexy," Lahoma replied.

"Go check out the bathroom." k.d. directed her assistant, Darlene,
and the drag queens teased her the rest of the night. So *that's* what
big stars have assistants for, they laughed.

■

It's hard to imagine k.d. lang having trouble getting dates. She spends
a lot of time in the company of women, and over the years her friends,
band members, business associates, and even a few journalists have
been introduced to a few who were probably her lovers, although
they were rarely presented as such. But since the heartbreaking journey through her Saturn Return and into *Ingénue,* k.d. seems to have

245

spent a lot more time dealing with the philosophical aspects of love, rather than the act itself. "When people say, 'Oh, *Ingénue* is so much more vulnerable, so much more honest,' it's just that I'm more pathetic now," she jokes, confessing that one of her two greatest fears in life is that she will never be truly in love.

Coming out and falling in love caused k.d. to examine some of the most fundamental aspects of her personal life. It also brought to the fore issues she'd been trying to ignore for quite some time. "If you think coming out was a big step in her life, I think there's more to come," said one friend who's watched k.d.'s struggle over the last couple of years. "A lot of people noticed a change with *Ingénue*. But I believe that her *real* change has yet to happen, both musically and personally." He pauses, and then adds cryptically, "Ask her about therapy."

Several months after that comment was made, when Leslie Bennetts went knocking on k.d.'s door on behalf of *Vanity Fair,* she didn't even have to ask. As the profile revealed, k.d. was ready to talk—and talk and talk and talk—not only about love, but about a *particular* love, one that had been haunting her for more than twenty years. As she confessed to Leslie Bennetts, k.d. *was* in therapy, and one of the things it was helping her to do was to finally confront her feelings toward her father.

"I loved both my parents very, very much, and I went into shock when my father left," she told Bennetts, recalling the pain she had felt when Fred Lang walked out on the family two decades earlier. It was a pain she tried for a long, long time to claim did not exist, and in her younger years, she rarely spoke of her father, except to insist, when asked, that his departure from her life had been more or less insignificant. There was a song called "Nowhere to Stand" on her album *Absolute Torch and Twang* that dealt with the subject of child abuse, and for a time many critics thought the song might have been auto-biographical. But k.d. denied the allegations, and given her unusually strong self-esteem and her almost arrogant sense of self-worth, it does seem a little unlikely that she would have been abused as a child. Still, she now admits that her shattered relationship with her dad has affected her in ways she never realized.

Today Fred Lang lives on a farm outside of Edmonton, driving into the city for his daily shift at another IDA pharmacy. He's getting on in years, and hasn't seen his daughter face-to-face in quite some time. "She came to visit me a couple of times when I was up in Slave

Lake," he says, remembering back to the beginning of Kathy's career, when she was performing on the barroom circuit. "She stayed with me for a couple of days. You know, borrowed the car, had a few meals with us, that sort of thing."

k.d. remembers seeing her father only two or three times since she was twelve years old, and says that she doesn't keep in touch with him at all. He did show up at one of her concerts in Edmonton once, and as her manager Larry Wanagas remembers, tears flowed down his cheeks as he stood in the back of the hall and watched his "boy-girl" perform. "I ran into him a couple of times after about eight years," k.d. notes, but adds, "It just didn't seem necessary to work it up into some kind of forced relationship with him again. He didn't put any effort into it, so I just thought, well, I'll carry on."

Fred Lang accepts this as his fate. "Sometimes people's paths just take different directions," he says wistfully. "She's gone down one path, and has probably become a millionaire by now. And me, I'm just a pharmacist." Yet he sometimes wonders if things could have been different between the two of them. "You know, you see these programs on TV where the families have drifted apart, and sometimes you think you ought to try to get back in touch with them," he says softly, his eyes beginning to grow moist. "I don't know why we lost touch the way we did. Sometimes I just think, I gave twenty-six years of my life to them, and it should be up to them to keep in touch. But I suppose that's not the right way to look at it. And I don't know why I haven't made more of an effort to look them up. I guess I just don't want to make any waves. We've all readjusted our lives, and you just don't know how people feel. I guess I just don't want to make things difficult for anyone."

In the wake of *Ingénue,* k.d.'s journey into therapy was ostensibly to come to terms with a difficulty she was having in dealing with intimate relationships. In the midst of it, it seems, she also found herself trying to reconcile what had happened in her father's life that could have caused him to abandon his favorite daughter. "I don't think my father didn't love me," she says carefully. "I just think he felt like he couldn't deal with what was happening in his own life. I knew there were troubles, but him leaving the way he did was a shock, and very hard for me to watch my mother go through."

Over the years, she's had plenty of time to consider how her childhood has shaped her adult life. For the most part she views it all with romantic stoicism, pointing out that most adults harbor some sort of deep childhood wounds. "A wound is just a highway to a new and enlightened kind of confidence," she said optimistically when the issue came up again in an interview for *Rolling Stone*. "Damage is one of the things in emotional aesthetics that makes something great, like all the scars on a tree or a banged-up coffee cup or whatever. Everything you go through is marking your soul."

Yet she allows that this damage hasn't been without its toll. "I think there's a deep pool of pain, a deep hurt that I manifest in different ways in my life," she explains. "That is not why I'm gay; it has nothing to do with that. But there is difficulty trusting, and it's exacerbated by being famous." Which brings her back to affairs of the heart.

k.d. fears she will never fall in love with someone who is able to love her back. "I think I sabotage relationships because I'm afraid of being left again," she says, slipping comfortably into a sort of shrink-ese that for most people never goes beyond the therapist's office door. Her theory is that her fear causes her to tamper with her relationships in ways that keep the escape hatch within easy reach. When that isn't enough, she loses herself in her work.

Such distress over issues of intimacy is something that her sister Keltie, also a lesbian, shares. "Sometimes you just don't know how something like that affects you." she says, echoing k.d. "There's always that fear of things not working out, a fear of being abandoned again, and also a difficulty with commitment." Instead of going out and getting wives to grow old with, the two joke that they will probably end up sitting in their rocking chairs on a farm together somewhere, shooting traps, calling the dogs, and wondering why they never got girlfriends. "That's what we do now," Keltie laughs.

Perhaps it's a scenario that seems both safer and more sane than the one k.d. had to live through the last time her heart strings were tugged. "I was definitely a stalker," she says looking back on the near-fatal attraction that had her spinning out of control. She was a woman obsessed, and not enjoying it one bit. And yet it allowed her to create such an amazing album, thereby regaining her control. "*Ingénue* was this great work of art, this great gift, this great gesture," she agrees. And although it was designed as if to say to her beloved, "You see, I'm so in love with you, look what I've done," once it was over she was ready to claim the music as something wholly her own.

Following that trauma, k.d. has decided that, at least for the time being, she's going to lighten up. "I'm not monogamous anymore," she says of her present state, noting that her constant traveling inspires a rather hefty long-distance phone bill. But lest women think this means k.d. will be an easy fish to catch, be forewarned that the competition is tremendous. "Women send me their 8-by-10s and their measurements," she boasts to Mim Udovitch in *Rolling Stone,* "but the last thing I want to do is sleep with a fan. Because k.d. lang the performer is so much cooler than me. Not that there's really a difference, but as a lover, I'm not as self-assured and cocky and invincible as she is."

Sometimes dreams *do* come true, as in the case of the woman in Philadelphia who once wrote an essay detailing her desire to meet her favorite singer, and how that fantasy became a reality. Recalling the first time she ever bought tickets to a k.d. lang concert, Anne Meredith confessed, "I couldn't sleep the night before the show, I was so excited; I arrived at the Fillmore hours before the doors even opened. In the middle of the show, I said to the person standing next to me, 'I'm going to play pool with her someday.' 'Yeah,' he replied, 'dream on.'" Today, Meredith is a screenwriter in Los Angeles, and has become one of k.d.'s best friends, having met the star through one of k.d.'s old girlfriends.

As for romance, k.d. wonders what remains for a self-proclaimed loner who doesn't like sharing a bed. She hasn't lost hope, but for the time being, she isn't holding her breath. Instead, it's all she can do to pray that when Ms. Right finally comes waltzing along, she'll have the sense to recognize her.

■

Today, k.d. has reached what some might consider the pinnacle of her career, and while her success has pleased her, it has also stoked her other biggest fear: that someday she will wake up to find that her creative juices have completely disappeared, the well from which they flow dried up. With that thought in mind, her goals, which once ran along the lines of selling a million records, have changed. Now, rather than focusing on her material wealth and well-being, she is concentrating on maintaining a career of artistic longevity. "I want to feed the muses," she says poetically, "to sustain the reciprocity between me and what makes me an artist."

Few doubt that she will do it, either. "It's very interesting," says Alan Hustak, recalling an interview he did with k.d. back in 1983. "At the time, she was very matter-of-fact about the direction of her career. She said she was going to do A, B, C, and D, and sure enough, if you look back at it now, she *did* do A, B, C, and D. She said to me then,

'Just give me ten years and we'll see who's still around.' At the time, she was referring to her peers in the music business, and it's true that many of them are nowhere to be found today. But k.d. has gone to the top."

Acting—the profession that helped launch her career with *Country Chorale* and her introduction to Patsy Cline, and which served as a catalyst for the changes that took place after she left country music and starred in *Salmonberries*—is also something she would like to do more of. If that's not enough, she still loves to paint. All of this she juggles while commuting between Los Angeles, where she once said she would "never in my wildest dreams" want to live, and Vancouver's Fraser Valley, where she has settled into the farm of her dreams with her sister Keltie and her pets.

In L.A. she maintains a tiny, mustard-colored bungalow that she rents from a local artist and his wife in the quiet, unobtrusive area known as Hollywood Heights, just a couple of short blocks from Sunset Boulevard. Sitting atop a winding stone staircase, the cabin is protected by a mezuzah nailed to the door. It is here that k.d. spends roughly three months of each year, hidden in a verdant oasis replete with the incessant chatter of finches, doves, and woodpeckers, who dance around the carefully stocked bird feeders, or flit above the wooden trolls standing guard around the stone patio dotted with rickety lounge chairs and wild vines. Her hut is sparsely decorated, save for a Formica kitchen table, a portable plastic fan, a TV, and a few scattered photos of friends. In her cupboard sits a handful of secondhand mason jars, and a few scattered knickknacks clutter the living room. Yet aside from that, little effort has gone into home furnishing here, not because the cabin sits empty so much, but because k.d. doesn't put much stock in such material distractions.

Pinehurst, as this neighborhood was once called, has seen a number of celebrities move in and off the block, Marlo Thomas among them. But these days k.d. seems to be the biggest thing happening, and it's not unusual, when she's in town, to catch a glimpse of her coming around the corner on her pea green Harley Springer, which she used to park on the street in front of her landlord's house until a neighbor offered to let her park it in his garage. Occasionally, for those who are really lucky, her sweet, sweet voice can also be heard wafting in the breeze, prompting her landlady to invite a neighbor or two over to "help in the garden," while they enjoy a private aural glimpse of k.d. in motion.

There are ways in which Hollywood is starting to show its influence on k.d. Her wardrobe is becoming an envious collection of up-and-coming designer styles—gifts from friends who know that she can lend a high profile to their sartorial creations. She's been showing a new face in photographs, too, wearing makeup, which she jokingly says she does just to make people mad. "Well, not really," she laughs again. "It's because I'm working with better photographers." That, and the fact that she's had a lot of fun showing off a softer side of herself that she says is more in keeping with her newer style of music. Yet she still maintains a natural approach to hygiene, rarely washing her hair, and using nothing on her face but a mixture of rose water and geranium oil.

k.d. has plenty of friends in L.A., many of them part of the closeted jet set known as the "Hollywood Power Dykes." When she's not out on her motorbike, she joins these women for a game of pool or volleyball at the Hollywood Athletic Club, or she heads out on her own for a hike in the hills. She does lunch at Orso and dinner at 442, and has been known to go out for a beer or a nip of tequila just often enough to make her feel like she's letting her hair down. But mostly, she remains pretty low-key. "My life may seem complicated to someone unfamiliar with the business," she says, "but I do keep things simple compared to the way some entertainers live. Once or twice a year, I dress up and do something glamorous, but generally, I don't like nightlife. I'd rather stay home and cook and then go for a walk."

When she's not in Los Angeles, much of her time is spent on the road, which is where k.d. nourishes her life as an entertainer. But there's another side to the artist as well, and that is the Western Canadian country girl.

Vancouver, with its storybook winters and cool, rain-drenched summers, is where k.d. now calls home. Hardly a city slicker, in 1991 she moved out of her downtown Chinatown apartment and bought a 12-acre farm in the Fraser Valley just an hour outside of the city. Surrounded by cedars, with a nearby pond and the snow-capped Cascade Mountains in the distance, k.d. lives with Keltie Rae, now a horse trainer, and a pet menagerie that includes a 350-pound pink pig named Grace, two goats named Hannah and Arthur, three horses named Mariah, Cory, and Jasmine, and three dogs (Troy, Rhina, and Clem), two of which are purebred greyhounds rescued from doggy death camps after four years of racing. (Stinkerton, who had been with k.d. for many, many years, sadly went missing one morning, presumably making a tasty lunch for some of k.d.'s more grizzly animal neighbors.) In addition to all that, her robin's-egg blue '64 Mercury Meteor still sits out in the garage.

When she finds herself with extended periods of time to spend on the farm, k.d. doesn't do a whole lot other than hike, swim, and play with her animals, ignoring outside turbulence from the TV and the newspaper as she knocks about in her jeans and T-shirts, the shoes always optional. She's also known for her culinary talents, which she uses to woo her friends to vegetarianism. Overall, it's a laid-back life, beginning at seven or eight in the morning with a steaming cup of organic coffee and a couple of pats on the head of each pup.

Her typical farm day involves an hour or two spent with her sister doing chores, like feeding the animals or sweeping the barn Keltie uses to train the three horses. After that she engages in an hour-long workout in the gym she has built in her basement, followed by a shower, lunch, and an afternoon spent with her manager or Ben Mink, taking care of business. In the evenings she joins friends in the city for a beer or a film, trying to avoid having too much to eat after six or seven at night. When she returns home she'll usually phone a friend or lover before fading off to sleep.

Throughout all of this, k.d.'s main objective is to remain relaxed and in touch with her spiritual center. She spends as much time as possible outside, even in the cold of winter, meditating as she absorbs the sights, sounds, and smells of her natural surroundings. Indoors, she creates a soothing environment through the use of a complicated assortment of fragrances and oils that serve as a sort of aromatherapy. Some days she sets the mood by burning sandalwood, myrrh, and frankincense to keep her in touch with the earth. Other days, when she's feeling particularly spiritual, she enjoys the scent of eucalyptus or angel lily to fill the house. And when she writes, she often burns a lot of sage, which she says is "like getting stoned without having to smoke a joint. It kind of sets you into an alternative pattern."

She also keeps one eye on the sky. "I'm very into omens," she confides. "A lot of decisions are made by flipping a coin, and I don't fuck with it—when I flip a coin, that's the way it is. The coin doesn't lie. And if I see a crow somewhere where a crow wouldn't usually be, it's some sort of a sign."

All of these things, of course, are meant to feed the muse who led her from the small town of Consort, Alberta, to the top of the pop music charts. It's a divine gift, this voice the gods have given her, and she takes it very seriously. "I don't think of it as something that I own," she says when asked how it feels to have one of the most magnificent voices in the world today. "I just happen to be using it, and so I treat it with a great deal of respect."

Aside from her spectacular career as an artist, which has taken her around the globe many times, how much has really changed since the days Kathy Lang spent scrambling around the wheat fields of eastern Alberta? Probably not as much as it might seem. "Sometimes when I'm out on my Harley, or out running around on my farm," she assures, "I'm definitely that geeky farm boy—totally. It will never go away. I am a five-foot-nine, 150-pound collection of molecules that will never change. They're still in there, and they just kind of reshape and restructure at different times." As they do she will continue to seek out olive oil, creativity, and love—the three things in life she says she craves . . . constantly.

a truly western experience (Homestead, 1984)
Angel With A Lariat (Sire, 1987)
Shadowland (Sire, 1988)
Absolute Torch and Twang (Sire, 1989)

DISCOGRAPHY

Ingénue (Sire, 1992)
Even Cowgirls Get the Blues (Sire, 1993)

COLLABORATIONS

Loretta Lynn, Kitty Wells, and Brenda Lee, "Honky Tonk Angels Medley," *Shadowland* (Sire, 1988)
Dion, *Yo, Frankie* (Arista, 1989)
Dwight Yoakam, "Sin City," *Just Looking for a Hit* (Reprise, 1989)
Wendy & Lisa, "Mother of Pearl," *Eroica* (Virgin, 1990)
Mrs. Fun, "Lulu's Lament," *They Are Not a Trio* (Mrs. Fun, 1991)
Roy Orbison, "Crying," *King of Hearts* (Virgin, 1992)
Bob Telson, "Barefoot," *Calling You* (Warner Brothers, 1992)
Andy Bell, "No More Tears (Enough Is Enough)," *Coneheads* (Warner Brothers, 1993)
Jane Siberry, "Calling All Angels," *When I Was a Boy* (Sire, 1993)

COMPILATIONS

Take 6, "Our Day Will Come," *Shag* (Sire, 1989)
Take 6, "Riding the Rails," *Dick Tracy* (Sire, 1990)
Red Hot & Blue (Chrysalis, 1990)
Tame Yourself (Rhino, 1991)
Until the End of the World (Warner Brothers, 1991)

ABC television
  "Red Hot & Blue," broadcast of,
    198
  Absolute Torch and Twang (lang
    album), 120–123, 167
  Billboard Top Country Albums
    chart, 126, 133, 138

AIDS benefits
  k.d. lang's support for, 172, 173,
    185
  "Red Hot & Blue", 171, 174,
    198
AIDS-phobia, 200
Ainley, Rosa, 234

tour, 125–126, 138, 176, 177
Academy Awards, wearing red ribbons
  at, 200
Acuff, Roy, 87, 93
Adams, Bryan, *xv,* 47, 153
Adlon, Percy, 140
  Bagdad Cafe, 171, 178
  and k.d. lang, 65, 171, 184, 187,
    192, 224
  Salmonberries, 178–183
  "So in Love" (video), 172–173
Adult Contemporary, 193
Advocate news magazine, 196, 199
  k.d. lang interview, 207–213,
    222
  Madonna interview, 212, 215
  and outing, 205, 212–213
Agrama, Jehan, 198, 219, 229
  on outing, 204
AIDS
  Country Music Association and,
    200
  and the entertainment industry,
    198–200
  red ribbons, 200

Alberta Report (magazine), 34
  and k.d. lang's appearance, 115
Albert's Hall (Toronto blues bar), 40,
  44–45, 51–52
Allman Brothers, 5
"Amazing Grace," 39
"America, the Beautiful," 168
American Music Award, 225–226
Amnesty International Tour, 104
Anderson, Lyn, 73
Andrews, Derek, 40
androgyny, 195
  of k.d. lang, 110–117, 133–135
Angel With An Attitude (lang fan-
  zine), 235
Angel With a Lariat (lang album), 81,
  83, 84, 87, 94, 121
  Billboard Top Country Albums
    chart, 73, 133
  marketing, 72–73
  recording, 69–72
  reviews, 72, 73–74
Animal Liberation (PETA album),
  142
animal rights, *xi,* 2, 141–152

257

lang, k.d., relationships
Audrey Lang (mother), 9–10, 14, 34, 215, 222–223, 224
Ben Mink, 68–69, 121–123, 125, 126, 161, 187–190, 236
Drifter Elgar, 14–19, 35–38, 42
Fred Lang (father), 3–4, 9–11, 246–247
Keltie Rae Lang (sister), 6, 10, 141, 248, 250, 251
personal, 236, 237, 239–240, 246
Verna (Edmonton friend), 19–20
lang, k.d., relationships (Patsy Cline)
album cover, photo on, 42
balloons, releasing, 85–86
falling out of an airplane, 30–31
influence of, 23, 69, 73, 82, 83, 86, 161, 250
as reincarnation of, 24, 56, 66–67, 100–102
songs of, 30, 39, 84, 94
lang, k.d., songs and poems of
"Barefoot" (with Telson), 182
Ben Mink, song writing with, 121–123, 126, 161, 187–190
"Big-Boned Gals!," 177
"Bopalena" (lang), 219
"Constant Craving" (with Mink), 192, 193, 226
"End of our Beginning, The," 12
"Friday Dance Promenade," 35
"Hoping My Dreams Will Come True," 5
"Mind of Love," 188
"Miss Chatelaine," 107, 226
"Nowhere to Stand," 151, 246
"Outside Myself," 188
"Pine and Stew," 43, 71, 97
"Pulling Back the Reins," 126, 186
"Season of Hollow Soul," 189, 192
"Trail of Broken Hearts," 126, 186
Lang, Keltie (sister), 2, 3, 6, 10, 141, 147, 248, 250, 251
"Langmas," 2
"Late Night with David Letterman," 61
Lauper, Cyndi, 55, 73
Lavender Jane Loves Women (Dobkin album), 200
Lawrence, Ted, 110–111, 114, 224
Lawrence Brothers' Record Shop (Nashville), 110–111
Laycraft, Dennis, 143
Laye, Mark, 149–150
Lee, Brenda, 49, 93, 98–100, 104, 159, 168
Lee, Peggy, 32, 95, 118, 186, 210, 237

Leisz, Greg, 120
Lemon, Brendon, 205, 209–212, 222, 227, 229
Lennox, Annie, 113, 173, 193
Leno, Jay, 6, 226
Lesbian and Gay Film Festival, 182
lesbians
coming out, xi-xii, xiii-xiv, 196, 200, 202, 211, 213–215, 217–222, 224–225, 227–230
families and, 222–223
and gossip, 239
heros, demands made on, 240, 242
"Hollywood Power Dykes," 251
homophobia and, 197, 198–199, 200, 202, 221
and k.d. lang, 176, 177, 195, 217–220
k.d. lang as role model, 217–220, 233–235
lesbian chic, xiv, 229
lesbian market, 229–230
life style, 18, 19–20, 21
outing, 204–205, 212–213, 221
Stonewall Riots, 197
Triangle Ball, xi-xii
Washington, D.C., march on, 199
women's music, 200–201
See also Crazy Nanny; gays; Shebang
Letterman, David, 38, 88, 234
Lewis, Mark, 134
Lightfoot, Gordon, xv, 11
"Lock, Stock and Teardrops" (Miller), 95, 104
London, Julie, 186
Longhorn Saloon (Calgary), 111
Loveless, Patty, 110
Loverboy, 47
Lovett, Lyle, 103, 132, 133, 158, 166, 167, 201
Lydon, Johnny, 118
Lynch, Brian, 195
Lynn, Loretta, 73, 87, 94, 98–100, 104, 127, 164

McCall, Michael, 84, 116, 161
McCartney, Paul, 144, 146, 149
McClaren, Malcolm, 74
McDougall, Stewart "Stu," 29, 48, 95
McEntire, Reba, 158
MacGonigill, Neil, 49
McGrath, Paul, 64–65, 67, 68, 119
MacInnis, Craig, 146, 153
MacLaine, Shirley, 67
McLauchlan, Murray, 11
McRae, Carman, 95

Maddox, Rose, 164
Madonna, *xiii*, 56, 58, 72, 151
  Advocate interview, 212, 215
  and k.d. lang, 100, 114, 118, 185
  k.d. lang, alleged relationship with,
    236, 237–238, 243
  and sexuality, 199
Mail on Sunday (London), 195
Manley, Elizabeth, 107
Marcenko, Dennis, 49, 120
Martin, Janis, 164–165
Martin, Mary, 82–83, 94, 161
Mathews, Dan, 141–142, 146, 152, 231
Mattea, Kathy, 110, 158
Matthews, Gordie, 29, 49, 68, 70–71,
  96, 121–123, 218
"Meat Stinks" PETA TV commercial,
  142–143, 145, 148–150
Melody Maker (London), 157
Melvoin, Wendy, 174
  k.d. lang, alleged relationship with,
    236
Meredith, Anne, 249
Messer, Don, 79
Miller, Roger, 95
Miller Sisters, 164
"Mind of Love" (lang/Mink), 188
Mink, Ben, 120, 125, 252
  on Dave Edmunds, 70
  k.d. lang, meeting in Japan, 68–69
  k.d. lang, relationship with, 236
  k.d. lang, song writing with, 121–
    123, 126, 161, 187–190
  on Nashville, 77–78
  recording *Ingénue,* 193–194
Minkowitz, Donna, 213
Minnelli, Liza, 113, 118
  and k.d. lang, 118, 183, 185
  k.d. lang, alleged relationship with,
    236, 239
"Miss Chatelaine" (lang), 107, 226
"Miss Chatelaine" (video), 230
Mistress Formika, 231
Mitchell, Joni, *xv,* 5, 11, 97, 118
Mitchell, Margaret, 227–228
Mixner, David, *xi*
Monroe, Bill, 104
Montana, Patsy, 163
Montana Slim. *See* Carter, Wilf
Montreal Film Festival, 182
Montreal Gazette, 3, 182
Moore, Demi, *Vanity Fair* cover, *xiv*
"Morningside" (CBC radio program),
  43
"Mother of Pearl" (lang/Wendy and
  Lisa), 174

Ms. magazine
  k.d. lang/Lesley Gore conversation,
    175, 177–178
MTV Ball (Clinton inauguration), *xi*
"MTV Unplugged," 225
MuchMusic (Canadian music televi-
  sion network), 43, 62
  k.d. lang interviews, 109–110, 117,
    139, 162, 233
Mulligan, Terry David, 191
  k.d. lang interview, 185, 188, 224
Murray, Anne, *xv,* 5, 34, 79, 104, 118,
  137
  k.d. lang, alleged relationship with,
    236, 239
Music Row (Nashville), 86, 93–94,
  125, 128–129, 159, 160
Musician magazine, 151
Musicland magazine
  Shadowland, review of, 102
Myles, Alannah, 45

Nashville, 77–79, 84–88
  Bluebird Cafe, 78, 115, 158
  Bradley's Barn, 94
  Country Music Hall of Fame, 86,
    127, 159
  Exit/In, 83–86
  Fan Fair, 103
  Grand Ole Opry, 78, 87–88, 162,
    164
  and k.d. lang, 157–159, 167–169
  Lawrence Brothers' Record Shop,
    110–111
  Music Row, 86, 93–94, 125, 128–
    129, 159, 160
  Opryland, 87
  Opryland Talent, 86
  prejudice against, 159–161
  provincialism of, 159–161
  Ryman Auditorium, 87
  Tootsie's Orchid Lounge, 82–83, 87
  See also country/western music

Nashville Banner, lang review, 84–85
Nashville Network, 88, 125
  and censorship, 151
  music videos on, 166
"Nashville Now," 86, 129
Nashville sound, 93–94, 96, 165, 166
Nashville String Machine, 96
National Association of Recording
  Merchandisers, 134
Navratilova, Martina, 217, 237, 243
  k.d. lang, alleged relationship with,
    236

Virgin Records, 52
Vogue magazine, 110–111

Wagoner, Porter, 113
Wanagas, Cheryl, 67
Wanagas, Larry "Lars," 247
  and *Angel With a Lariat,* 69
  Gzowski incident, 63–64
  and *Ingénue,* 190
  as k.d. lang's manager, 27–29, 40,
    41, 42, 46, 52, 57, 58, 74, 149,
    208
  Toronto appearance, 44
Warner Brothers, 52–53, 56, 57,
    72
  See also Sire Records
"Way I Walk, The" (Gordon), 30
"We Shall Be Free" (Brooks), 151
Webster, Ben, 95
Wells, Kitty, 58, 94, 98–100,
    104
Wenders, Wim, 174
Wendy and Lisa, 174
Western Development Museum (Sas-
    katoon, Saskatchewan), 50
western music. *See* country/western
    music
Western Report (Alberta), 146
"Western Stars" (Isaak), 95, 186
Weymouth, Tina, 91, 174
WFMS radio (Indianapolis), 133
When I Was A Boy (Siberry album),
    174
Willet, Slim, 95
Williams, Hank, Jr., 87, 149
Williamson, Chris, 200–201
Wimberly, Maggie Sue, 164
Winter Olympics (1988), 79–80
"WLS Barndance" (Chicago country
    music radio program), 79

WMZQ radio (Washington, D.C.),
    199–200
women and country/western music,
    127–130, 158, 162–165
  female artists, popularity of, 128
  "the Female Elvis," 164
  feminism, 110, 115–116
  sexuality and, 116, 131, 133–134,
    151–152, 184
  songwriters, 164
women and sexism, 199
women's movement and k.d. lang,
    175–176
women's music, 200–201
Wood, Gerry, 73
Wright, Holly, 27
"Write Me In Case of the Blues," 45
WSM radio (Nashville)
  "Grand Ole Opry" (country music
    program), 79
WSM-FM radio (Nashville)
  k.d. lang, playing, 133
WYNE radio (Appleton, Wisconsin),
    134
Wynette, Tammy, 82, 127, 163

Xavier, Sister, 4–5

Yarbrough, Jeff, 205, 207, 208–209,
    211, 212–215, 227
Yoakam, Dwight, 73, 89, 138, 166,
    174
"You Ain't Woman Enough to Take My
    Man," 104
"You Nearly Lose Your Mind" (Tubb),
    99
"Your Good Girl's Gonna Go Bad"
    (Wynette), 163

Zaica, Donna Alexander, 109
Zech, Rosel, 179, 236